DATE DUE

The Consumer Trap

THE HISTORY OF COMMUNICATION

Robert W. McChesney
and John C. Nerone, editors

*A list of books in the series appears at
the end of this book.*

The Consumer Trap

Big Business Marketing in American Life

MICHAEL DAWSON

University of Illinois Press

URBANA AND CHICAGO

Library of Congress Cataloging-in-Publication Data
Dawson, Michael, 1965–
The consumer trap : big business marketing in American life /
Michael Dawson.
p.   cm. — (The history of communication)
Includes bibliographical references and index.
ISBN 0-252-02809-0 (cloth : alk. paper)
1. Marketing—United States. 2. Marketing—United States—Costs.
I. Title. II. Series.
HF5415.1.D33   2003
380.1'0973—dc21   2002011038

For Marty, a train buff, my pride and joy,
and in memory of my aunt Lisa,
one of the 53,172 people who lost their lives
in American automobile "accidents" in 1980

Contents

Preface and Acknowledgments

The primary historical materials I quote in this book are housed at the Smithsonian Institution's Center for Advertising History and at the John W. Hartman Center for Sales, Advertising, and Marketing History at Duke University. Many of the printed reports I discovered and transcribed in the latter place had each of their pages stamped "Restricted: No Photocopying" in bold red ink. In my view, both the rarity of the semipublic Smithsonian and Hartman Center collections and those red "Restricted" stamps tell us something we very much need to know: Big businesses do *not* want us looking behind the scenes of their marketing operations.

In my humble opinion, this is one of the major reasons to look, and look carefully.

Over the decade it's taken me to produce this book, I have become a father, gotten divorced, finished my formal schooling, stopped and restarted a teaching career, moved several times, and stopped drinking alcohol. Through all the turmoil, I've managed to soak up an amazing quantity of mentoring, friendship, advice, and criticism, without which this book would not exist.

John Bellamy Foster gave me both the idea for this project and a huge share of the intellectual training from which it flows. It is no exaggeration to say that my effort in these pages is merely my attempt to elaborate on John's amazing knowledge and spirit. I hope my errors will not ruin any honor I manage to show him.

I also want to thank Howard Brick, Noam Chomsky, Samuel Coleman, John Lie, David Milton, Daniel Pope, and Marilyn Whalen, as well as three anonymous readers for the University of Illinois Press, all of whom read and critiqued full versions of the manuscript. Also, Mary Ager, Terri Barnes, Bryan

Dawson, Angie Jabine, Brian Klocke, Robert McChesney, Nancy Milton, Ingyu Oh, Sally Simpson, Paul Sweezy, and both my parents, Carolyn Cella and Larry Dawson, gave me much crucial moral, technical, and intellectual support. The directors and staff of the Center for Advertising History and Duke University's Hartman Center made my excavation of the primary historical evidence both possible and profoundly enjoyable. Crucial financial assistance came from the University of Oregon, the Hartman Center, and my beloved grandmother, Lena Atherton. Geof Garvey and Dick Martin of the University of Illinois Press taught me much and made this book better.

I offer special thanks to Susie Goodwin. Her tolerance for this project and her unwavering devotion to our son, Martin, have allowed me to finish this book.

Finally, I must mention Jennifer Sasser. Jenny provided copious editorial, intellectual, and logistical aid, without which I would undoubtedly have blown yet another deadline. My highest aspiration for this project is that it somehow helps people advance the politics of love, which Jenny so believes in and embodies. La lucha continua, J!

1. Thinking the Unthinkable

Big businesses in the United States now spend well over a *trillion* dollars a year on marketing.[1] This is double Americans' combined annual spending on all public and private education, from kindergartens through graduate schools.[2] It also works out to around four thousand dollars a year for each man, woman, and child in the country. Four thousand dollars, in turn, is *triple* the annual per capita Gross Domestic Product of the so-called low- and middle-income countries, where 85 percent of the world's people now live.[3]

Nonsense and niceties aside, big business marketing is class struggle from above. It exists to make commoners' off-the-job habits better serve corporate bottom lines, and, thereby, to further fatten the portfolios of the established ultra-rich families, who, in the words of the nation's leading business historian, "remain the primary beneficiaries" of large-scale private enterprise.[4] For our private jet set, big business marketing is a prudent investment in finessing underlings into profitable "free time" routines.

Meanwhile, for the vast majority of Americans who struggle to make ends meet, who only rarely sip from corporate profit streams, and who don't get to vote on major economic decisions, big business marketing imposes a heavy financial burden. Because corporations blend their marketing expenses, untaxed, into the prices of their products, buyers of Pepsis, Nikes, and Fords pay not just for the drinks, the shoes, and the cars, but for all the things Pepsico, Nike, and the Ford Motor Company do to lure and cajole them into purchases. And because, as a group, they buy most of the corporate products sold in the United States, working- and middle-class Americans also wind up paying for the lion's share of big business marketing.

For ordinary Americans, however, corporate marketing's burden is far more than merely financial. Over time, our increasingly marketing-saturated life spaces make us dumber, lazier, fatter, more selfish, less skillful, more adolescent, less politically potent, more wasteful, and less happy than we could and should be. The damage occurs on many levels. As corporate marketers press us to pack our activities with the maximum number of maximal products, they coax us into habits that clutter our homes, poison our bodies, undermine our independence, pollute our ecosphere, and waste our precious time and energy. As corporate marketers ratchet up the commercialism and commodity intensity of our personal lives, a vicious cycle of jobs, traffic jams, shopping, fast food, and television bleeds away quality time for family, friends, community, politics, and self. As corporate marketers invent and extend marketing "platforms," their sponsored programs and events crowd out noncommercial venues and pastimes. As this happens, sensationalism and titillation—the two great cultivators of receptive advertising audiences—corrupt our mental, emotional, and practical capabilities.

Of course, in some cases, big business marketing is directly homicidal. Pushing cigarettes and beer are obvious examples, but what about cars? Using modern marketing's standard tools—surveys, focus groups, databases, constant product changes, incessant advertising and promotion—as well as lavish public subsidy of the infrastructures their products require, the auto and oil corporations have sold Americans hundreds of millions of automobiles. Compared fairly with feasible transportation systems centering on trains, buses, and bicycles, our undebated autos-über-alles arrangement is as wasteful of our time, sanity, health, money, and natural resources as it is profitable to corporate barons. It is also massively deadly. Inevitably, despite air bags and other safety improvements, all our high-speed rolling around in independently steered metal boxes prematurely introduces tens of thousands of us to the Grim Reaper every year. In fact, car crashes have killed far more Americans *just since 1950* than have all our wars combined, from 1776 to the present.

Big business marketing is also pied-pipering the human race toward ecological disaster. How much longer can our societies and our planet withstand overpackaging, planned obsolescence, petrochemical artifice, and the promotion of ecologically wasteful products? All these toxic trends are part and parcel of corporate marketers' tireless efforts to sell us more, more ornate, and more "disposable" products. At some point in the very near future, such expanding efforts will almost certainly become environmentally intolerable, if they have not already.

Finally, there is the ugly irony that, despite all our piety about family values and putting children first, kids in the United States are already paying dearly for their growing immersion in corporate marketing. As the new millennium unfolds, the profusion of shootings and killings in commercial media have already begun to inspire real juvenile shooting sprees. Meanwhile, big businesses continue to spend billions to paint soda pop and junk food as fun and hip, in total disregard of the U.S. surgeon general's 1998 listing of childhood obesity—a contradiction in terms until the most recent decades of human history—as an epidemic in America.[5] Likewise, corporate entertainment and toys continue to render traditional kids' games and other "self-organized children's amusements," which were usually both financially inexpensive and physically active, "an endangered species."[6] As this happens, students reading below already watered-down grade levels masterfully debate the minutiae of the latest corporate combat toy or smart-ass cartoon character, while parents and teachers must battle ever harder to block and counteract these terrible trends.

A Great Evasion

Despite all this, and despite widespread private disgust with commercialism, coherent public debate of big business marketing has yet to materialize in the United States. As corporate marketers have invaded every nook and cranny of our personal lives, and as our off-the-job habits have conformed with our business elite's interests to a degree that would make Joseph Stalin blush, the most basic facts and consequences of big business marketing have escaped rational analysis. In the mass media, newscasts regularly expose two-bit con artists, government pork-barrelers, and city workers sleeping on the job yet stay dutifully mum about the gargantuan marketing swindle by which their sponsors meddle in people's leisure time. In academia, scholars wage "culture wars" over the curious sociopolitical malaise of post–cold war America but give no coherent accounting of corporate marketing's massive impact on how ordinary Americans live.

Opinion leaders' great evasion of the topic of big business marketing and its costs has seven major causes.

Cause 1: Business

As Leslie Savan, one of the few clear-headed critics of commercialism, puts it, "Conveyors of commercial culture are free to question nearly all of modern life except their own life-support system." Afraid of costing their employers advertising dollars, media personalities diligently avoid exposing big business marketing to critical reporting. As Savan explains, this evasion "means that, unlike 'official' cultural products—films, TV shows, books, paintings, and so on—advertising finds few regular critics in the mainstream press."[7]

Even Savan neglects to add that corporate *marketing,* the larger managerial discipline of which *advertising* is but a part, finds still fewer critics.

Cause 2: Business Secrecy

Any corporation that shows the world its marketing plans undermines itself in two ways. First, competitors who know your marketing methods can more easily copy, counter, or improve upon them. Second, customers who see how you're pushing their buttons are likely to refuse to let you continue to do so and may even fight back. For these and other reasons, corporate marketers keep honest discussion of their strategies to themselves. As a result, it's hard for public-spirited pundits to get primary, behind-the-scenes information about big business marketing.

Cause 3: Linguistic Bias

Before the twentieth century, the word *consumption* meant tuberculosis, and *consumer* was a nonentry in the lexicon.[8] Now, parroting capitalists, even our purportedly left-wing pundits label us "consumers," treat all our off-the-job product-related activities as acts of "consumption," and tell us we live in a "consumer society" with a "consumer culture."

For all that, do we roll our cars off cliffs to see them explode? Do we scramble to pour our just-bought beverages out in the grocer's parking lot? Do we rush home to smash our appliances with sledgehammers, then burn the sledgehammers in our fireplaces, then allow fire to burn down our houses—all to maximize our destruction—our *consumption*—of goods?

Of course we don't. We gas and fix our cars, cap and refrigerate our un-drunk beverages, and care for our homes and appliances until upgrade becomes possible or further repair becomes irrational or impossible. In general, we work hard to maintain the products we acquire and use. Whenever possible, we strive to counteract product wear and tear, which is ordinarily an unintended, costly, and regretted consequence of our product usage, not its goal. Usefulness, pleasure, longevity, and cost minimization are our normal goals as product users. *Consumption,* the final using up of a product, is almost never our intention.

Of course, it makes sense for corporate moguls and executives to ignore all this. In big business planning, off-the-job human beings count only as mere money-spending garbage disposals, mere programmable units for buying and using up the firm's wares—i.e., as mere "consumers." For corporate capitalists and managers, the plain fact that product destruction is neither an aim of nor a benefit to us "consumers" is both a point to be suppressed (at least at the level of public discourse) and a business problem to be managerially overcome.

Meanwhile, ordinary citizens needing to comprehend big business marketing and its impact on their personal lives can ill afford to swallow corporate capitalists' "consumer" vocabulary. To do so is to let language mask our real intentions and interests as product users, and, thereby, to stymie clear thinking about the political economy of these vital realities.

Tellingly, big business marketers themselves know that the kind of lazy, sloppy "consumption" talk that is now the standard coin of the public realm is not conducive to making sense of product users' activities. In fact, as every busy corporate marketer knows, the stuff we've been trained to slur as consumption is actually an interlocking set of social processes (see figure 1).

From the perspective of ordinary individuals actually living the social processes in figure 1, the main motive for action is to acquire and use products for the sustenance and enjoyment of life. Whatever its importance to capitalists, to noncapitalists consumption ought to have no meaning beyond denoting "the using up or destruction of a good or service." For ordinary product users, it is merely an unfortunate costly by-product of living life. Consumption happens, but it is not coveted by so-called consumers.

To fathom how perverse it is for us and our advocates to ignore all this and accede to our rulers' consumer vocabulary, consider figure 2. Aside, perhaps, from an undertaker, no sane person would think of this process as "death"

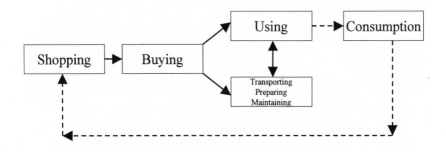

Solid Lines = Intended Actions

Dashed Lines = Unintended Outcomes

Figure 1. The Realities of Consumption

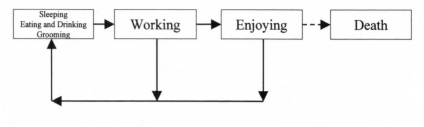

Solid Lines = Intended Actions

Dashed Lines = Unintended Outcomes

Figure 2. Life (or Is It Death?)

and call its participants "die-ers." So, why, then, do we talk about all the things we do to acquire and use goods and services as consumption? The only rational answer is that the consumer vocabulary is a particularly apt proof of an old sociological hypothesis: "The ideas of the ruling class are in every epoch the ruling ideas, i.e., the class that is the ruling *material* force of society is at the same time its ruling *intellectual* force."[9]

Ordinary people are product users who generally rue and work to minimize the consumption of goods and services. By desensitizing us to this massively crucial fact, the consumer talk that presently rules public discourse helps keep us from making good sense of our personal lives and the powers endeavoring to manipulate them.

Cause 4: Fear of "the Five-Letter Word"

In the post–cold war United States, there remains a very strong taboo against publicly discussing the social and economic costs of putting corporate investors first. This taboo has been especially effective in barring heretical questions about the evolution of personal life in America. As neo-McCarthyism and wall-to-wall Business Speak have made c-l-a-s-s "the unmentionable five-letter word" even in relation to labor and employment issues, the notion that class domination has anything at all to do with off-the-job experience has stayed almost unthinkable.[10]

As a result, even the best, most public-spirited commentators have simply never dared to explain big business marketing for what it patently is—a systematic effort by agents of the rich to use corporate resources and management to coerce the non-rich into off-the-job habits that make the rich richer.

Cause 5: "Free Market" Dogma

As the late Alex Carey documented, throughout the twentieth century corporate interests labored to teach Americans "to identify the free-enterprise system with every cherished value" and to vilify the very idea of public enterprise.[11] As part of this effort, our televisions and schoolbooks have long portrayed personal life in America as the kingdom of free choice, the best part of the best of all possible worlds, the new Garden of Eden. This quasi-official doctrine deflects attention from big business marketing by implying that, whatever its minor nuisances, corporate salesmanship is a necessary part of an economic system that is all for the best and, therefore, unworthy of democratic scrutiny.

It is important to note that this Panglossian attitude has been especially near and dear to the scholars, pundits, and media mouthpieces who have manufactured and distributed it. Indeed, most of our major opinion makers have accepted it on faith that, when it comes to procuring and using commodities, ordinary Americans get what they choose, rather than choosing among variants of what they are going to get. In mainstream politics, the big media, and leading think tanks and universities, capitalism means free markets, and free markets equal freedom of choice for product users—end of story, case closed. Among defenders of the status quo, not even the present trillion-plus-dollar-a-year reality of corporate marketing dents this doctrine.

Yet free market dogma cannot withstand serious contact with the core facts of big business marketing. If you bother to look at what corporate marketers actually do in their jobs, you find them talking of managing demand by concocting ways of shifting attention, pushing emotional buttons, spreading misinformation, and otherwise engineering prospective buyers' perceptions, choices, and actions. You also confirm, in spades, the truth of the advertising executive Gordon Webber's admission: "Oh sure, we're interested in the *people* who use the product, but only, to be candid about it, in relation to how we can influence them to buy it."[12]

As the renowned marketing scholar, teacher, and consultant Philip Kotler explains, this narrowness of concern is no aberration. "The marketing concept," Kotler admits, "overlooks the conflict between individual want satisfaction and long-run public interest." Hypothetically, marketers could ask themselves whether their creations are "really serving" their customers' "long-run interests." They could also ponder, Kotler acknowledges, "whether the marketing concept is any longer an appropriate organizational goal in an age of environmental deterioration, resource shortages, explosive population growth, . . . and neglected social services."[13] However, as this book or any other sustained look at actual practices proves, such concerns are less than peripheral in big business marketing. They are, as Kotler reports, sidestepped, and systematically so. Such is the iron requirement of the bottom line.

Sensing the wide gulf between free market doctrine and the cold truth about big business marketing, leading mainstream intellectuals of the cold war and post–cold war era have simply excused themselves from confronting all the troubling real-world evidence:

- In 1950 the publishing magnate Henry Luce introduced the twentieth anniversary edition of his property, *Fortune* magazine, by trying to rebut criticism of corporate capitalism's growing reliance on advertising. "American business is honest," wrote Luce. "The American Business Economy disperses and balances social power and therefore maintains a frame for political freedom." "The businessman makes money in America," Luce continued, "by serving his fellow man in ways his fellow man wants to be served." This, Luce insisted, is assured because corporate enterprise is "a built-in hostage to one kind of freedom—the consumer's freedom of choice."[14] Luce, of course, felt no need to bother with evidence of the actual relationships and comparative powers of big businesses and ordinary product users.

- In 1960 W. W. Rostow, soon to become an adviser to Presidents Kennedy and Johnson, published *The Stages of Economic Growth,* the book that launched modernization theory, still the leading mainstream theory of global capitalist development. There Rostow claimed that investment and production in America answer to "consumer sovereignty," are therefore "impossible to predict," and unfold as "a matter of economic choice or political priority rather than technological or institutional necessity."[15] Rostow, of course, backed these claims with absolutely no empirical evidence of either big business marketing practices or the workings of "consumer sovereignty."

- In 1973 the historian and future Librarian of Congress Daniel Boorstin won a Pulitzer Prize for a book in which he defined marketing as "a new science for sampling the suffrage of consumers." Early corporate "manufacturers and merchandisers," Boorstin held, were bent on "inventing ways for the consumer to vote his preferences." How, pray tell, did they do this? According to Boorstin, they *invented modern marketing,* which "democratized the market."[16] Boorstin's claims were, of course, utterly devoid of any factual illustrations of corporate marketers' behind-the-scenes motives and methods.

- In 1976 the Columbia University sociologist Daniel Bell, formerly a *Fortune* writer under Luce, completed the circle of conventional wisdom via the Big Brotherly device of simply defining away the connections between big business marketing and the upper class. In Bell's influential view, the core trend shaping personal life in twentieth century America was not the *expanding* power and reach of big business investors, but, rather, "the *abdication* of the corporate class."[17] According to Bell, what happened after the mid-twentieth century was a "radical disjunction between the social structure (the techno-economic order) and the culture."[18] Faced with ordinary people's swelling greed and hedonism, Bell contended, the corporate class chickened out and gave up trying to enforce capitalist discipline on their subordinates. Hence, for Bell, understanding late twentieth century American "cultural" (i.e., off-the-job) trends required an appreciation of "the weakness of American corporate capitalism in trying to deal with" the new, anticapitalist ways in which ordinary people were composing their personal lives.[19] Of course, Bell's Orwellian argument made no empirical reference to actual corporate marketing practices.

- In 1977 the Harvard professor Alfred D. Chandler published *The Visible Hand: The Managerial Revolution in American Big Business,* his Pulitzer Prize–winning history of the rise of corporate capitalism in America. There, Chandler showed that, contrary to prevailing ideology, major corporations use management's "visible hand" to plan and control a range of pricing, procurement, and labor processes where "the invisible hand of market forces" once held sway. On page one of *The Visible Hand,* Chandler, however, went out of his way to assure his readers that, despite his subsequent 608-page debunking of free market talk in other areas, he was not about to argue that corporate management's "visible hand" reaches buyers. After the "managerial revolution," Chandler comforted, "the market remained the generator of demand for goods and services."[20] Evidence for this contention? Chandler presented none.

- In 1989 a scholar writing under the pseudonym X caused a stir among intellectuals by publishing an essay that boldly enunciated the claim that the contemporary United States is indeed the best of all possible worlds, the highest embodiment of the happy, democratic "end of history." X turned out to be the think-tank writer and former State Department employee Francis Fukuyama, who, in 1992, expanded his famous essay into a book, *The End of History and the Last Man.* There, Fukuyama held that history's victorious "last man" is none other than the American product user, whom Fukuyama cast as the master and primary beneficiary of "a demand-driven price system" in a society without "fundamental internal contradictions," where economic development "tends to promote broad equality of condition" and maximizes freedom.[21] Fukuyama, of course, diligently avoided all facts about corporate marketing and its real-world relationship to supposedly bygone social contradictions.

Cause 6: Confused Critics

What mainstream pundits have suppressed, would-be radicals have simply missed. Flummoxed by the consumer vocabulary and often preferring theoretical gamesmanship to critique of real institutions, the political and intellectual left has produced very little useful criticism of big business marketing and its rising costs. To be sure, cold war and post–cold war radicals have belched out a steady stream of tracts on "consumption" and "consumer culture." With a few major exceptions, the results have been nearly as fact-free and intellectually paralyzing as mainstream free market incantations. Consider:

- In 1964 the radical scholar Herbert Marcuse published *One-Dimensional Man,* in which he argued that the economic institutions of the United States "bind the consumers more or less pleasantly to the producers, and, through the latter, to the whole."[22] This seminal, purportedly leftist, view interpreted big business marketing as a vehicle of mass consensus and class harmony, rather than of class coercion and conflict. Marcuse's diatribe against allegedly consensual trends, however, was a piece of wholly unsubstantiated speculation. High on Theory with a capital T and convinced he had correctly diagnosed the political apathy of the masses, Marcuse never seriously bothered with empirical evidence about either big business marketing or the quality of life of ordinary people.
- In 1976 Stuart Ewen published *Captains of Consciousness,* in which, following Marcuse, he portrayed corporate salesmanship as a distraction from class conflict. Ewen speculated that, in encouraging consumption, big business planners are primarily motivated by the desire to ladle out the fruits of industrialism in order to "produce pacific social relations" and crown themselves "captains of consciousness."[23] In Ewen's view, simple economic abundance caused this brainwashing project to reach fruition. Once it had abundance, Ewen held, America got its consumer culture, which has ever since kept class conflict off the nation's agenda. To substantiate this extension of Marcuse's argument, Ewen relied on a series of labored interpretations of a handful of early twentieth century advertising stories.
- In 1976 the postmodern theorist Jean Baudrillard argued that "consumers are mutually implicated, despite themselves, in a general system of exchange and in the production of coded values."[24] Of course, in holding everybody mutually responsible for commercialism and commodification, Baudrillard felt no need to use any actual empirical evidence to explain how the general system actually worked. After all, is the demand for evidence not a naive modernist ruse?
- In 1993 the cultural historian William Leach published *Land of Desire,* in which he defined the American economic order as consumer capitalism. In Leach's view, while capitalists have tweaked and promoted it, the main force governing "consumer capitalism" has been "the democratization of desire . . . alongside the cult of the new."[25] Like Ewen and virtually all other would-be critics, Leach presumed that diagnosing the psychic fever of con-

sumer culture is the main challenge for those concerned with the evolution of personal life in America. Also like Ewen and most other critics, Leach argued that consumer culture took root among the American masses once the U.S. economy could produce abundance, as if wealth itself, rather than specific class relationships, causes big business marketing. Also like Ewen, Leach based his theory of mass greed and delusion on overheated stretchings of a few random references to pre–World War II advertising and retailing.

- In 1997 the environmentalists John C. Ryan and Alan Thein Durning published *Stuff: The Secret Lives of Everyday Things.* Ryan and Durning used a fictitious character named Dana to guilt people into pursuing global ecological sustainability through lifestyle downshifting and voluntary simplicity.[26] At the beginning of *Stuff*, Ryan and Durning have Dana introduce himself or herself as a consumer, with no self-reflection about what a strange label that is for somebody just trying to live life. Dana then spends the rest of the book learning about the ecological damage inflicted by the manufacture and use of cars, clothing, food, and other products in what Ryan and Durning call "our economy." At book's end, Dana concludes that, given all this damage, "the time is right for confronting consumption." Of course, Ryan and Durning leave big business marketing out of Dana's tour of reality.

Cause 7: Ignorance of Thorstein Veblen

Though he died in 1929, Thorstein Veblen, whom C. Wright Mills aptly called "the best critic of America that America has produced," remains our greatest critic of big business marketing.[27]

This fact explains why the most helpful post-1945 criticisms of big business marketing were all penned by neo-Veblenians in the 1950s. Such works include Vance Packard's 1957 million-selling *Hidden Persuaders,* John Kenneth Galbraith's chapter "The Dependence Effect" in his 1958 book, *The Affluent Society,* and Paul A. Baran and Paul M. Sweezy's chapter "The Sales Effort" in their classic *Monopoly Capital: An Essay on the American Economic and Social Order.* Even counting these important writings, it remains true that nobody has yet bettered what Veblen said about corporate salesmanship in the first quarter of the twentieth century. In fact, appreciation of Veblen has unquestionably regressed since the heyday of Packard, Galbraith, Baran, and Sweezy.[28]

Eager to assimilate him as one of their own, latter-day consumer culture theorists, for example, virtually never look past their tremendously facile view of Veblen's first book, 1899's *Theory of the Leisure Class.*[29] In it, Veblen coined his famous and, given the linguistic biases I discuss above, rather unfortunate phrase "conspicuous consumption." Without acknowledging that the problem of conspicuous product display was but a minor part of Veblen's overall theory of corporate marketing and cultural development, today's would-be critics talk as if Veblen was history's first consumer culture theorist, as if Veblen would have concurred with their presumption that the challenge is to critique the delusions of the masses, rather than the surreptitious barbarity of the corporate capitalists. By so misrepresenting him, today's pseudo radicals have helped excise Veblen's powerful theory of big business salesmanship from contemporary consciousness.

The real core of Veblen's now-forgotten theory of corporate salesmanship was his view that big business marketing was neither more nor less than a new embodiment of class coercion. While other thinkers of his day were developing early versions of the end of history thesis, Veblen insisted that business society's new class of owners relied just as much on arbitrary carrots and sticks as did prior ruling elites. Then, as now, conventional thought rested on the claim that class coercion had ceased when the means of social dominance shifted, in Veblen's phrasing, "from a naively predatory scheme to a commercial one" based on "peaceable ownership."[30]

The truth, Veblen insisted, was that when businesslike capitalists displaced violent emperors and feudal lords, class coercion did not die but was reformulated and built into seemingly free, equal, and rational new relationships. Within such relationships, new styles of elite coercion served old ends, now hidden from view. "The institutional ground," Veblen wrote, had merely "shifted from free-swung predation to a *progressively more covert regime* of self-aggrandizement and differential gain."[31] Where sworded henchmen, fear-mongering clergy, and imperial magistrates once imposed wealth-extracting threats and enticements on commoners, Veblen argued that "the 'competitive system'" now "takes the place of the coercive methods previously employed."[32]

Thus refusing to let variation in the manner of coercion distract him from a continuing central theme, Veblen saw that corporate capitalism—"absentee ownership," in his terminology—is merely a new system of class domination. Look within its pseudo rationality, Veblen asserted, and you will still find potentates (absentee owners) and their henchmen (corporate managers) using their classic generic means—force and fraud—toward their classic ends—the extraction of a "surplus product of industry above the subsistence of the industrial community at large" to perpetuate the "class divergence of material interests, class prerogative and differential hardship."[33]

Veblen observed that the newly rationalized forms of salesmanship he was seeing in the 1920s were a crucial part of absentee owners' covert use of force and fraud to obtain surplus wealth for themselves. By employing growing staffs to study and redesign products' "line and color, shape and surface" and "the doctrinal matter that surrounds them," corporate capitalists were beginning to see how they could profitably intervene in prospective buyers' decisions. With some careful planning, corporate output itself could be made into a Trojan horse for elite behavioral manipulation. By making products and doctrinal matter secretly embody "merchandising *in absentia*," prospective customers' off-the-job experiences could be managed for gain.[34]

Having made this observation, Veblen pulled no punches in describing modern corporate salesmanship as a direct descendant of the classic force and fraud principles of class rule. Salemanship's "law of mind," Veblen asserted, "rests primarily on the principle of deception. It is an extension to other human beings of the method applied to the animal world by which the latter was subjected to man. The method is that of *the ambush and the snare.* Its ruling principle [is] cunning. Its object [is] *to deceive, circumvent, ensnare, and capture.*"[35] "The quantity-production of customers," Veblen observed, "is a craft which runs on applied psychology. The raw material . . . is human credulity, and the output aimed at is profitable fixed ideas. Current experience appears to show that among the human sensibilities upon which a sagacious salesmanship will spend its endeavors the most fruitful are Fear and Shame . . . [including] the fear of mortal disease and the fear of losing prestige."[36] Marketers, Veblen maintained, would operate via "what may be called creative psychiatry. Their day's work will necessarily run on the creative guidance of habit and bias, by recourse to shock effect, tropismatic reactions, animal orientation, forced movements, fixed ideas, verbal intoxication."[37]

Thanks to his deep knowledge of the political economy of absentee ownership, Veblen also correctly foresaw that corporate capitalist normalcy was going to fuel a continually expanding marketing race between its major firms, a race in which there would be "a continued increase of selling-costs and a continually more diligent application of salesmanship."[38] There were two sources of this coming race. First, because of their enormous capacities to use technology, scientific management, and sheer purchasing power to reduce their production costs, major firms would find themselves increasingly able to devote rising sums to their marketing operations. "Production-cost by modern industrial methods being less, the margin which can be taken up in sales-cost is more."[39] Meanwhile, as corporate staffs devised new and better methods of scaring and attracting people into profitable habits, Veblen predicted, business competition would ensure that "any device or expedient which approves itself as a practicable means of cutting into the market, on the part of any one of the competitive concerns, presently becomes a necessity to all the rest, on pain of extinction."[40]

"The net aggregate result" of rising marketing budgets and business competition, Veblen knew, would be "a competitive multiplication of the ways

and means of salesmanship at a competitively increasing net aggregate cost."
"The rising cost of salesmanship," Veblen predicted, would become "a rising overhead charge on the business . . . trending upwards . . . with a gradually accelerated rise."[41] As this trend continued, "the distinction between
workmanship and salesmanship" would be so "progressively blurred," that
"much of what appears on the books as production-cost" would "properly
be charged to the production of saleable appearances."[42]

Veblen knew the coming marketing race would also bring continuing *qualitative* refinement of its driving managerial discipline. By 1923 Veblen had already noted that "the fabrication of customers can now be carried on as a routine operation, quite in the spirit of the mechanical industries and with much
the same degree of assurance as regards the quality, rate and volume of the
output . . . under the surveillance of technically trained persons who might
fairly be called publicity engineers."[43] Moreover, as corporate revenues rose and
production costs fell, Veblen held, managers would see increased spending on
salesmanship as a "progressively more reasonable" proposition.[44] Greater funding would, in turn, allow publicity engineering, like the new methods of corporate labor process engineering, "to be effectually subdivided and appor-
tioned" among experts and to undergo "an extensive standardization and
specialization."[45]

Finally, Veblen's theory of corporate salesmanship as a device of class coercion included an indictment of its larger meanings and costs. Corporate
capitalism's normal operation, Veblen observed, "results [in] a division or
cleavage of the people who live under this system of industrial business,
whereby the business community . . . comes to stand over against the underlying population," who are "caught in the business system" and are "not
an executive factor," but merely "a body of ultimate consumers to be sup-
plied at discretion in the pursuit of commercial gains." Veblen saw that, for
the underlying population, corporate marketing imposed both financial and
existential costs.[46] "All the while," Veblen wrote, "the ever-increasing personnel and proficiency employed in salesmanship continues to turn additional
articles . . . into items of morally necessary use . . . the increasing expendi-
ture on sales-costs goes unremittingly to raise the price of living."[47] Likewise,
Veblen wondered whether corporate mechanical contrivances such as cars
"have not wasted more effort and substance than they have saved" and "are
to be credited with an appreciable net loss." Despite being "creditable technological achievements . . . of substantial service," as corporate commodities designed for maximizing sales rather than existential and ecological
efficiency, "their chief use," Veblen reminded his readers, "is in the service
of business, not of industry."[48]

Ending the Great Evasion

The Consumer Trap is my attempt to pick up where Veblen left off. Veblen, of course, was quite right: Big business marketing is an inherently expanding vehicle of class coercion. It is not, as even today's radicals treat it, part of some popular consensus signaling the end of history and the *decline* of class conflict. Hence, in these pages, I cast aside both mainstream free market dogma and pseudo radical consumer culture theories and instead get back to the Veblenian work of showing how big business marketing and its rising costs are part and parcel of corporate capitalism and the upper-class privileges it primarily serves.

The essence of my argument is that big business marketing is neither more nor less than a system for profitably crafting and applying stealthy little versions of the force and fraud that have always sustained class dominance. In ancient Rome, demagogues and patricians used centurions and bread and circuses to bring plebeians and slaves into line. In feudal times, landlords deployed sheriffs, knights, and priests to push and pull serfs into paying their tribute to nobility. Likewise, today, major investors reap their fortunes partly from the actions of the armies of market researchers, ad execs, product planners, and media creatives who, to the tune of a trillion-plus dollars a year in the United States alone, hone the commercial carrots and sticks that lure and cajole us into making increasingly commodified, profit-yielding, privilege-perpetuating product choices. In big business marketing, the force-and-fraud methods of bygone elites have transmogrified into the small-scale, surreptitious button pushings corporate planners call marketing stimuli.

In this process, most elite coercion has, of course, become subtler and less immediately dangerous to its victims. Nevertheless, neither the greedy and undemocratic point nor the social harm of the manipulation has changed: At the behest and to the primary benefit of our economic overlords, arbitrary threats and irrational enticements continue to flood our society and alter our behavior. As this happens, ordinary living comes at the price of unwittingly putting our masters' interests ahead of our own, to our own enormous cost.

If humane and democratic forces are to transcend this consumer trap, we must first understand why it exists and how it works. Let us turn now to these vital questions.

2. The Marketing Race

In the 1970s, to gather nominees for a series of commemorative U.S. postage stamps, Professors Daniel Wren and Robert Hay got 134 business historians to rank their top ten "outstanding individuals who had contributed the most to American business and management thought and practice in the past 200 years." Wren and Hay's "suggested candidates" list included the names Ford, Rockefeller, DuPont, Sears, Carnegie, and Westinghouse, as well as J. P. Morgan and J. C. Penney. The landslide winner of the poll, however, truly trounced his more famous compatriots. The experts' runaway #1 "business pioneer," who garnered more first-place tallies than the next nineteen vote-getters put together, was Frederick Winslow Taylor, "father of scientific management" (fig. 3).[1]

In 1911, having grown rich teaching early corporate-era bosses how to boost workers' on-the-job productivity, Taylor—who called human beings "the great raw material" and reminded critics that every business corporation "exists first, last, and all the time for the purpose of paying dividends to its owners"—published *The Principles of Scientific Management,* a pamphlet summarizing his life's work for those wanting to extend it.[2] In it, Taylor insisted scientific management—the study, analysis, and reconfiguration of profit-yielding human behaviors—was useful not just for controlling laborers, but could "be applied with equal force . . . to the management of the business of our tradesmen"—i.e., to corporate salesmanship. Taylor noted that, like employees' on-the-job tasks, "the motives which influence men" were amenable to "accurate study" and profitable managerial manipulation. The study of such "motives which influence," Taylor opined, "should receive special attention."[3]

Undoubtedly inspired by such suggestions, soon after their mentor's March

Figure 3. Frederick Winslow Taylor (courtesy of the Frederick Winslow Taylor Collection, Stevens Institute of Technology, Hoboken, N.J.)

1915 death, leading Taylor disciples began urging corporate planners to Taylorize their fledgling attempts to manage product users' activities. A prime example of such prodding came a week before Thanksgiving in 1922, at a New York City meeting of the Taylor Society for the Advancement of the Art and the Science of Management and of Administration, a group formed while Fred Taylor was still alive, with Fred Taylor's approval, and eventually absorbed by the American Society of Mechanical Engineers. In a speech to this executive gathering, Harlow S. Person, then the Taylor Society's managing director, argued that corporate capitalism itself was eventually "going to force" its leading firms into a new "inclusive system of management."[4] Person labeled the impending system "sales engineering" and predicted that once it took root corporate leaders would find themselves approaching the task of manipulating people's off-the-job perceptions and actions as rigorously and intentionally as they had already learned—thanks to Fred Taylor's teachings in workplace scientific management—to treat the task of engineering employees' on-the-job doings.

Corporations' need for sales engineering, Person argued, was a by-product of the upper-class privilege created and served by big business. Having reached maturity in its "appropriation of capital resources," Person observed, America's "industrial society . . . tends to become more stable and stratified." "On the one hand," there emerges a dominant "class of rentiers." "On the other hand" is "a larger class of laborers, clerks, sub-executives . . . and others, whose income is, on the whole, limited, and whose consumers' demand power tends to become correspondingly fixed."[5]

For rentiers and corporate planners, this stability and stratification embodied institutional success but also generated a core business problem: Entrenched socioeconomic inequality meant that the growth of purchasing power was, from the rentiers' perspective, "likely to remain so hesitant and uncertain as to be out of proportion to [rentiers'] capacity to produce." In fact, Person argued, the United States had already entered a lasting "period of maladjustment," in which rentiers' investment and production capacities had "overreached immediate demand," and were bound to continue to do so.[6]

Person reasoned that, given this maladjustment, corporations would have to be much more thorough in finding and motivating customers. In the coming sales engineering epoch, Person argued, success would flow to the firms that made themselves "more comprehensive, more skillful, . . . [and] more scientific" at understanding and managing the factors driving particular people to buy particular products. And doing that, in turn, would require major firms to get serious—Fred Taylor serious—about gathering "continuous and precise analysis of the market" to "provide data for masters plans" for new and improved sales campaigns "whose object is to convince."[7]

The overall result? Person saw that, as more and more corporations started using sales engineering to engender profitable reactions among product users, rivals would start fighting to replicate and advance one another's techniques. Thus, the future promised an "intense competition on the part of management to find the individual consumers and to sell them" and "a strife for the consumer's dollar," which, as it grew, would continually make past corporate salesmanship "seem but a child's game."[8]

* * *

Harlow Person was, of course, quite right. Big business sales engineering, long since better known as marketing, is, in fact, the use of Fred Taylor's core principles—disciplined study, analysis, and reconfiguration of human behavior—in the profit-seeking manipulation of people's leisure-time activities. Moreover, as Person also foresaw, corporate capitalism has fueled, does fuel, and, as long as we permit it to dominate our economic affairs, must fuel an expanding, increasingly sophisticated marketing race between its leading firms.

By showing how deeply it comports with the realities of corporate power and rentier primacy, this chapter advances Person's prescient and powerful class analysis of sales engineering. By chapter's end, you will see how big business normalcy generates both *the funds* and *the managerial motivation* behind the marketing race.

Corporate Power and the Growth of Marketing Budgets

How can big businesses afford to spend so much money on marketing? The answer emerges from a review of the basic institutional facts.

Big business corporations were invented for one reason and one reason only: to stabilize and boost their shareholders' capacity to make money. During and after the U.S. Civil War, capitalism was yielding thousands of unprecedented fortunes.[9] One leading historian estimates that the number of millionaires in the United States mushroomed from fewer than 20 in 1840 to more than 4,000 by 1892.[10] This two-hundred-fold increase is all the more amazing given the fact that from the Civil War to the 1890s price levels declined sharply. The intervening millionaire explosion was no mere paper phenomenon.

The size of the new fortunes soon clashed with prevailing business institutions. As the early Gilded Age rich got richer, their burgeoning bankrolls remained vulnerable to frequent price wars and chronic economic depression. In response to the high-stakes tumult, aspiring corporate players began, in the words of the economic historian Louis Galambos, to "look . . . for a solution that would protect their investments."[11] Nobody at the top doubted that the answer lay in the consolidation of new, gigantic business organizations.

In 1888 the New Jersey state legislature obliged would-be big business investors. Lobbied by a cunning young business lawyer named William Nelson Cromwell, New Jersey revised its statute books to allow corporations chartered there to own stock in other corporations, a privilege previously restricted to railroads and a few other "natural monopolies." Passage of the New Jersey Corporation Law of 1888, which Cromwell and his associates

drafted, soon sucked other states into a race to the bottom in the deregulation of corporate ownership.[12] Within a few years, other state legislatures,
similarly susceptible to private lobbying and similarly hoping to collect more
taxes and fees from new business behemoths, quickly copied, and then sur-
passed, New Jersey's deregulation of corporate combinations.

For our purposes, what matters about all this is the fact that, ever since their
late-nineteenth-century triumph, major corporations have enjoyed three
main business advantages, which, through their impact on big businesses'
gross profitability, have funded the rapid expansion of corporate marketing
budgets. These three advantages are

Advantage 1: Size

From the time of the 1888 New Jersey Corporation Law, relative handfuls of
very large businesses have increasingly dominated the U.S. economy. By the
first decade of the twentieth century, 300 corporations already controlled 40
percent of the country's manufacturing assets.[13] By the early 1990s—by which
time 51 of the world's 100 largest economic entities, including entire national economies, were business corporations—200 firms accounted for 42 percent of all value added in U.S. manufacturing.[14] Meanwhile, as the political
economist John Bellamy Foster explains, by the end of the twentieth century, because of steady corporate growth and successive merger waves, "few, if
any, of the giant firms [were] confined to a single industry." As a result, "the
entire system of industrial classification has lost much of its meaning," and
conventional statistics on concentration within single industries were, because of the size and reach of huge conglomerate corporations, "a poorer and
poorer . . . measure of [corporate] power."[15]

In business, size matters. Corporations big enough to control significant
shares of sales and profits in one or more industries enjoy tremendous
financial and organizational advantages over small businesses. As Boeing
Corporation chair Phil Condit explains, for the modern corporate manager, doing "what's best for the corporation" means helping it develop "the
flexibility to move capital and talent to the opportunities that maximize
shareholder value."

Bigness eases this endeavor in two ways. Financially, large revenue streams
mean big budgets, enormous purchasing power, and great bargaining lever-
age with providers of goods and services, not least with those who trade their
time and abilities for wages and salaries. Organizationally, bigness facilitates
development and application of specialized human and technological resources.

These monetary and bureaucratic advantages allow dominant corporations to keep turning themselves into new and improved capitalists. As Paul A. Baran and Paul M. Sweezy aptly put it, "the giant corporation of today is an engine for maximizing profits and accumulating capital to at least as great an extent as the individual enterprise of an earlier period." It "has a longer time horizon than the individual capitalist, and it is a more rational calculator."[16]

Advantage 2: Reduced Price Competition

Mainstream thinkers continue to treat corporate capitalism as if it were merely an extension of the small-business ideal proposed in Adam Smith's *Wealth of Nations*.[17] Modern industries, our leaders imply, remain full of aggressively price-slashing firms. Like the small proprietors of Smith's imagined system, modern corporate capitalists, we are told, are compelled by the market to pass the benefits of productivity improvements to customers via price cuts. Failure to do so, the story goes, would mean rival firms would soon copy your innovations and then lower *their* prices and run you out of business.

Actual history, however, shows that the aspiring corporate overlords of the late 1800s saw unrestrained price competition as one of the greatest threats to their mounting power and privilege.

Thomas Alva Edison, to cite one telling example, was blunt about this. In February 1892 Edison granted the *New York Times* an interview about the impending merger between his Edison General Electric Corporation—which had itself come into being in 1889, when the Edison Electric Light Company had taken quick advantage of the New Jersey Corporation Law of 1888 and, with J. P. Morgan backing, swallowed several smaller firms—and rival Thomson-Houston Electric. Edison favored the pending E.G.E./Thomson merger, he told the *Times,* because he wanted "to get as large dividends as possible from such stock as I hold." Price competition, Edison said, was interfering with that aim: "Recently, there has been sharp rivalry between the companies, and prices have been cut so that there is little profit in the manufacture of electrical equipment for anybody." "The consolidation" of Edison General Electric and Thomson-Houston, Edison continued, "gives the added advantage that a large concern has over a small one. . . . It will do away with a competition which has become so sharp that the product of the factories has been worth little more than ordinary hardware."[18]

Seven weeks after this interview, Edison General and Thomson-Houston, once again with J. P. Morgan financing, merged, forming General Electric, or G.E., still one of the world's largest business corporations.

Ever since Edison's day, big businesses have, in the classic phrasing of the conservative economist Joseph Schumpeter, continued to set their prices "in a way which should be called *corespective* rather than competitive." As Schumpeter observed, rather than trying to run one another under with price reductions, large corporations "refrain from certain aggressive devices" and "play for points on the frontiers."[19]

Conventional politics, punditry, and textbooks—where Schumpeter's observation is ignored and corporate capitalism is treated as if it belonged in Adam Smith's price-warring laissez-faire utopia—are thus wildly out of touch with the realities of modern corporate pricing. Indeed, if you bother to look at actual corporate pricing practices, the falsity of this portrayal is hard to miss. Contrary to prevailing assumptions, "the power pricer," explain two corporate consultants, "does not give up control of price to someone or something else; nor does he see it as less manageable than the other profit drivers." On the contrary. In setting its prices, the modern corporation "maps out the likely evolution of the industry," conducts "consumer analysis" to ascertain the maximum price the customer will pay, and only then "defines the price problem right—focusing on long-term profitability."[20]

In the real world, full-fledged price wars are now so anathema that, even in the most competitive industries, corporate wisdom is to try anything and everything before entering into even a single round of unrestrained price cutting. A team of *Harvard Business Review* authors, for example, recently listed some of the tactics major firms deploy when the norms of "corespect" and price leadership threaten to break down:

- "compet[ing] on quality instead of price"
- "alert[ing] customers to the risks and negative consequences of choosing a low-priced option"
- "reveal[ing] strategic intentions and capabilities [because] threat of a major price action might hold rivals' pricing moves in check"
- "seek[ing] support from interested third parties—governments, customers, and vendors . . . to help avert a price war"
- "using complex pricing actions [like] cutting prices [only] in certain channels"
- "introducing new products or flanking brands . . . [to] selectively target only those segments of the market that are under competitive threat"
- "engag[ing] in subtle forms of diplomacy . . . to discipline renegade companies that threaten industry profits"[21]

Such strategies are not just talk. Historical statistics show how profoundly the norm of corporate corespect has changed the drift of prices in the United

States. The basic story—as every modern citizen knows without thinking—is that corporate capitalism means price inflation.

Figure 4 depicts this sea change. Notice how, in the 1800s, price inflation was rare, occurring in only 21 of the 100 years. From 1900 through 1999, conversely, there were only 21 *non*inflationary years, 7 of which were Great Depression years. Since 1940, meanwhile, there have been only *two* years of noninflation—and *none* since 1955's 0.4 percent deflation.[22]

The story remains the same if you switch from counting individual years to tracking price levels over whole centuries. As the economic historian Robert E. Gallman explains, "there can be little doubt that American experience with the long-term drift of the price level was very different in the . . . nineteenth century from what it has been since. In the first period there was little trend (prices rose about 0.05 percent per year); in the second, the trend has been strongly upward, the index rising at a rate of about 3.4 percent per year." "In 1991," Gallman continues, "the price level was about 13.5 times as high as it had been on the eve of World War I."[23] By the year 2000, it had hit 17.8 times the same benchmark.[24]

Figure 4. Types of U.S. Consumer Price Index Changes

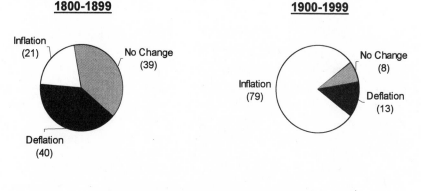

(x) = Number of years in period with change type

*Source:

Note: The number in parentheses is the number of years in the period with the associated economic conditition.

Sources: Rob Grunewald, "Consumer Price Index (Estimate) 1800–2000," On "Woodrow," World Wide Web site of the Federal Reserve Bank of Minneapolis, downloaded Apr. 12, 2001, from <http://www.minneapolisfed.org/economy/calc/hist1800.html>; U.S. Bureau of Labor Statistics, "Inflation Calculator," downloaded Mar. 22, 2001, from <http://www.stats.bls.gov>.

From a corporate capitalist's perspective, such steady, mild inflation is a very good thing. It means major firms can bank on being able to charge a bit more for next year's model than for this year's and on taking in a bit more revenue for the same output. And, of course, rising revenues are, other things being equal, certainly not unrelated to growth in managerial budgets and payments to shareholders. Generally speaking, as Thomas Alva Edison knew over a hundred years ago, a bit of inflation is excellent for corporate bottom lines.

Advantage 3: Systematic Management

The triumph of giant corporations as dominant vehicles of capitalist invest-ment also triggered a huge managerial revolution, which both made busi-ness management a distinct profession and astronomically expanded the amount of money and number of people engaged in it.[25] Because systemat-ic management has become so widespread and familiar, it is easy to forget that before corporate capitalism business bossing was done by individual proprietors with tiny or no staffs, on the basis of traditional arrangements, rules of thumb, and sheer guesswork. By contrast, within two decades of passage of the New Jersey Corporation Law of 1888, managerial accountants and mechanical engineers—new sorts of bureaucrats paid to work full-time refining the operations feeding corporate bottom lines—were numerous and specialized enough to have founded their own professional societies. Like-wise, business management, first taught as a serious academic discipline in 1881 at the University of Pennsylvania, was, by 1916, taught at 115 other col-leges and universities, including Harvard, Dartmouth, New York University, and the Universities of Chicago and California.[26]

To understand the rapid growth of business management under corporate capitalism, it helps to recall the phrase "spend a buck to make a buck." As gi-ant firms have grown in size, avoided full price competition, and taught them-selves to reorganize the human and mechanical processes feeding their coffers, they have become able to spend more and more money on new managerial endeavors. Whenever such new endeavors have promised not only to repay their own costs but to add significantly to the firm's bottom line, they have been undertaken.

Practicing corporate marketers describe spend-a-buck-to-make-a-buck as "a very basic thing" in their professional lives.[27] "[I]n the advertising business," reports the long-time ad agency executive A. G. Wade II, "you represent a company . . . and the amount of money you spend for advertising for that company has got to be in proportion to their profit structure. . . . When you spend a dollar for a client he has got to get two dollars or three dollars back."

"I'll spend as many dollars as I can," Wade reports being told by Charles Beardsley, a marketing manager at Miles Laboratories, maker of Alka-Seltzer, Bactine, and other proprietary medicines, "if I can get three back."[28]

One of the first to teach corporate owners the potential profitability of the spend-a-buck-to-make-a-buck principle was, of course, Frederick Winslow Taylor. In 1879, while studying mechanical engineering, Taylor became a gang boss in Philadelphia's Midvale Steel factory, where skilled workers forged raw steel into machine tools, train wheel tires, and U.S. Navy cannons. Taylor, whose upper-class background and bean-counting personality led him to see life through particularly capitalist eyes, soon chafed at the laxity of Midvale's other bosses. Taylor noticed that, while Midvale executives exhorted employees to finish jobs on time and at cost, they generally let workers themselves arrange the details of their work. This laissez-faire attitude to workers' on-the-job activities, Taylor insisted, constituted a major lapse in the modern manager's duty to ensure the maximum profitability of business processes. The only proper way to assure shareholders that workers' shop-floor doings were as productive and profitable as possible was, in Taylor's terms, to replace the traditional, personal, rule-of-thumb bossing style with a new scientific approach.

Under scientific management, managers would not only seize control of all decisions about how to configure workspaces, machines, and job tasks, but would make such decisions only after *studying* and *analyzing* every element of existing labor processes, with an eye to weeding out all unprofitable elements. To do this, Taylor and his disciples developed a host of new methods for conducting what they called time-and-motion studies. One such method was Frank Gilbreth and Lillian Gilbreth's attachment of lights to workers' bodies, so that their on-the-job movements could be analyzed with time-lapse "chronocyclograph" photography, then reconfigured for greater efficiency (see figures 5 and 6). Other Taylorian job-analysis techniques included stopwatch timing of tasks, detailed charting and modeling of workers' movements, maintenance of large databases of results from previous time-and-motion studies, and mathematical estimation of the productivity effects of possible alterations in existing job routines.

As Taylor proved in his three decades as a corporate consultant, his system very often worked. Incurring the expense of finding and eliminating even the tiniest inefficiencies, Taylor showed, frequently yielded tremendous dividends to corporate owners. By the time Taylor left Midvale in 1891, for example, its newly "Taylorized" workers were machining locomotive tires five times as fast as before the advent of scientific management.[29] Likewise, in the early 1890s, after Taylor studied and reorganized quality-inspection jobs at

Figures 5 and 6. Examples of Gilbreth's chronocyclograph photography (Smithsonian Institution, National Museum of American History)

the Simonds Rolling Machine Company of Fitchburg, Massachusetts, "thirty-five women were doing the work a hundred and twenty had done before."[30] A few years later came the example of Henry Noll, a laborer Taylor pseudonymized as Schmidt in his later speeches and writings. In 1899, after studying, analyzing, and reconfiguring Noll's way of unloading pig iron ingots from railcars at Pittsburgh's Bethlehem Steel factory, Taylor tripled the tonnage Noll could unload in a typical day. Generalizing what he learned, Taylor quickly downsized Bethlehem's railyard crew from 600 to 140 men without reducing the amount of work accomplished in the yard.[31]

Such profit-boosting results did not go unnoticed. In fact, by 1912, workplace scientific management was widespread enough to trigger congressional hearings into its social and economic impact. *Since* 1912, meanwhile, Taylorism has become so taken for granted in the design of corporate work processes that even expert commentators now often "no longer realize it's there."[32] Notwithstanding this blunder, corporate managers and consultants have spent almost a cen-

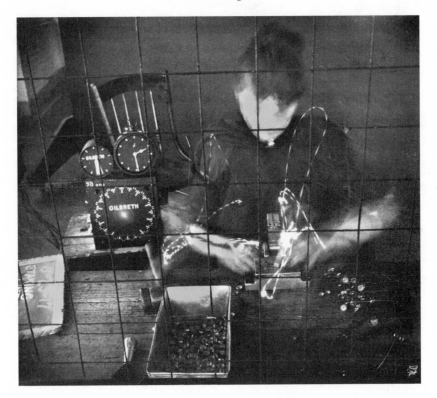

tury using new generations of computerized cameras, timers, models, and databases to refine and extend Taylor's project of studying, analyzing, and profitably reconfiguring employees' on-the-job activities. The overall effect of such industrial engineering, writes Peter F. Drucker, the world's leading management guru, "has been almost overwhelming."[33] Indeed, thanks largely to the continuing work of their workplace efficiency experts, big businesses have come to control a huge and growing majority of global sales and profits while employing only a small and shrinking minority of the world's workforce.

* * *

So how do these corporate advantages fuel a growing marketing race? The answer lies in their impact on major firms' gross profitability, or the gap between a corporate product's retail price and the costs of bringing it into physical existence and putting it on a store shelf. As they grow larger, become more sophisticated, avoid price competition, and elaborate workplace scientific management, major corporations get to gradually raise selling prices while continually lowering primary production costs per unit of output. In the words of the political economists Paul Baran and Paul Sweezy, "the monopolistic structure of markets enables [giant] corporations to appropriate the lion's share of the fruits of increasing productivity." Under corporate capitalism, Baran and Sweezy conclude, "declining costs imply continuously widening profit margins."[34]

If you doubt the reality of this trend, consider figure 7, which depicts U.S. corporations' profits, depreciation allowances, and net interest receipts as a percentage of U.S. gross domestic product from 1929 through 2001. Notice that, as the U.S. economy has grown, these three major sources of corporate spending power, the majority of which flows to the nation's several hundred biggest firms, have more than held their own as a percentage of the overall economic pie. The meaning of this is twofold. First, despite their incessant moaning, America's capitalists have never—not even for a single year, not even in the depths of the Great Depression—come close to reaping no surplus whatsoever on their investments. Second, consider what it means to say that somebody has at least held onto their relative slice of the pie in the growing U.S. economy. In inflation-adjusted terms, the U.S. economy was *eleven times* as big in 2000 as it was in 1929.[35] As that eleven-fold growth occurred, the monies available to big businesses for new investments, corporate mergers, and payments to shareholders and creditors grew by a similar factor.

Next, consider just how radically figure 7 *understates* the growth of big

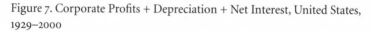

Figure 7. Corporate Profits + Depreciation + Net Interest, United States, 1929–2000

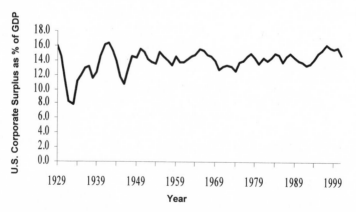

Source: U.S. Department of Commerce, Bureau of Economic Analysis, "National Income and Product Accounts Tables," Table 1.1 and Table 1.16, June 27, 2002 revision, downloaded July 22, 2002, from <http://www.bea.doc.gov/>.

businesses' gross profitability. The scale of the understatement dawns on you when you realize that the incomes depicted in figure 7 are sums that remain in corporate coffers *after payment of the expenses of marketing and all other forms of management*. In both national income accounting and U.S. tax law, these expenses, as well as corporate officer compensation, are, along with wages and raw materials costs, treated as part of the cost of goods sold and, thereby, do not get counted in the net surpluses shown above. This means that if, for instance, U.S. corporations spent $1.5 trillion on marketing in 2001, then U.S. corporations in 2001 had enough gross profitability to spend $1.5 trillion on marketing *and* to accumulate more than $1.3 trillion in profits, depreciation allowances, and net interest income, monies they used to pay dividends and make new profit-seeking investments.

Thus, when you understand the impact of corporate business advantages on gross profit margins, you begin to see how big businesses can afford to spend massive sums on marketing while still keeping shareholders happy: Big businesses use their growing primary profitability—the growing gap between their products' prices and their nonmanagerial costs of production—to finance the rapid growth in marketing expenditures that, in turn, boosts both sales and returns on investments.

Rentier Power and the Marketing Motive

Having the money is one thing. Why do big businesses actually decide to spend such astounding, rapidly growing sums on marketing? The answer is that the managerial decision to spend money on marketing is just what Harlow Person said it was—a rational, businesslike response to corporate capitalism's unequal distribution of ownership, wealth, and income.

Despite the ballyhoo over popular participation in stock markets, as of 1998, the wealthiest one-half of one percent of Americans still owned a third of all stocks and bonds.[36] This elite inspires the veteran political consultant and commentator Kevin Phillips's definition of the true American upper class as the richest 100,000 families. As Phillips explains, these top 100,000 households are rentier households, where the inhabitants "make their money out of investments" and stay fantastically wealthy, work or no work. Here, Phillips reminds us, circumstances are distinctly superior even to "the lower upper class or upper middle class or whatever you want to call it," where upscale professionals and small investors may earn $300,000 to $400,000 a year, yet still need to actually work.[37]

It doesn't take much calculating to begin to grasp what it means to have 1/200th of the household population taking in roughly a third of all dividend and interest payments to persons. We know, for example, that, in 2001, individual Americans received $416 billion in personal dividend income and $994 billion in personal interest income.[38] One-third of this $1.4 trillion in personal dividend and interest income equals $467 billion, or $880,000 for each of the roughly 530,000 households in the richest one-half of one percent of the 2001 U.S. population.[39]

One effect of so much money flowing to so few, already vastly rich, people has long been recognized by economists: A very large proportion of capitalists' incomes turns around and looks for new investment opportunities and further wealth gains. As the critic Doug Henwood puts it, "What portion of [rentiers'] booty that isn't spent on BMWs and Hamptons beachhouses goes back into the markets, to buy more stocks and bonds, and assert ever-more financial claims."[40] And remember: Such fresh investment-seeking sums from elite households merely add to the huge sums corporations themselves accumulate and keep, in the form of depreciation allowances and retained earnings, for the same purpose.

Meanwhile, just as Harlow Person predicted, as our vastly rich have gotten vastly richer, the vast majority of the U.S. population has remained all but excluded from access to substantial investment incomes. Indeed, Federal Reserve statistics show that, while the top one-half of one percent of U.S. households owned a third of stocks and bonds in 1998, the bottom 90 percent of the population owned but 18 percent of stocks and 14 percent of bonds, even counting all such assets owned through retirement plans.[41] The bottom 90–plus million U.S. households, in other words, control less than half as much private capital as the richest half million households.

Of course, there is also extreme polarity within the poorest 90 percent of American households. Consider, for instance, the Federal Reserve's latest statistics on the distribution of financial assets among the poorest three-quarters of American families. These data show that, in 1998, only 36 percent of the poorest three-quarters of U.S. families owned any interest in a retirement account; only 8 percent directly owned any mutual fund shares; a mere 6 percent directly owned any stocks; and less than 1 percent owned a corporate or government bond, other than savings bonds. Moreover, while, for the richest 10 percent of American families, the median value of all financial assets owned in 1998 was $456,800, the medians for the bottom three-quarters were paltry. For families in the richest of the bottom three quartiles (i.e., in the second-richest overall quartile), the median value of all financial assets owned in 1998 was $42,700, or just 9 percent of the top 10 percent's $456,800 median. In the middle of the bottom three quartiles, the same median was but $10,400, about 2 percent of the top 10 percent's median. Finally, among

Table 1. U.S. Net Financial Wealth, 1998

Family/household averages

Richest 1 percent	$10,044,000
Richest 10 percent	456,800
Second-richest 25 percent	42,700
Second-poorest 25 percent	10,400
Poorest 25 percent	1,100

Note: The figure for the richest 1 percent is a mean. All other figures are medians.

Sources: Edward N. Wolff, "Recent Trends in Wealth Ownership, 1983-1998," Working Paper No. 300, Jerome Levy Economics Institute of Bard College, downloaded July 24, 2002, from <http://www.levy.org/>; Arthur B. Kennickell, Martha Starr-McCluer, and Brian J. Surette, "Recent Changes in U.S. Family Finances: Results from the 1998 Survey of Consumer Finances," *Federal Reserve Bulletin,* Jan. 2000.

the poorest quarter of U.S. households, financial assets are but a rumor. More than one-fifth of the poorest 25 percent of Americans literally own no financial assets of any kind—not even a checking account, savings account, or life insurance policy. Among the other four-fifths of the bottom quartile, the median value of all financial assets owned in 1998 was a whopping $1,100, or *less than one-quarter of 1 percent* of the richest tenth's $465,800 median.[42]

Stark as they are, the above inequalities look narrow when we bring the true ruling class back into the picture. According to the economist Edward N. Wolff, as of 1998 the average household wealth among the richest 1 percent of Americans was more than $10 million.[43]

In the richer half of that top 1 percent, meanwhile, $10 million is chump change.

* * *

Their virtual exclusion from meaningful property income means that, just as Person prognosticated, the vast majority of Americans continue to live on their wages, salaries, and meager government stipends. Because of this, the relationship between popular incomes and big businesses is the opposite of the relationship between rentiers' incomes and big businesses. As the *New York Times* business-section columnist Floyd Norris puts it, corporate "successes, unfortunately, tend to reduce the income of consumers. And of course it is people—consumers—who are being laid off or, at best, not getting wage increases."[44] Generally speaking, when the corporate economy booms, corporations hire new workers while continuing to whittle their unit labor costs. The net result is usually a moderate increase in corporate employment and income for the majority, while rentiers' fortunes grow explosively. Conversely, in periods of stagnation or recession, big businesses redouble their labor-cost-cutting efforts while rentiers continue to reap rising property incomes.

For these reasons, statistics show, for example, that the average weekly earnings of U.S. nonsupervisory production workers did not grow at all in real (inflation-adjusted) terms from 1960 to 1990.[45] Even in the boom years of the 1950s and 1960s, which leading intellectuals have long treated as proof of the declining importance of class polarization in America, statistics suggest that working-class Americans' real income gains—certainly wondrous compared with later decades' losses—barely outpaced, in percentage terms, simultaneous increases in upper-class wealth. The economist David M. Gordon, for instance, estimates that the real, spendable, after-tax wages of productive, nonsupervisory U.S. workers grew by about 65 percent between 1948 and 1972.[46] Over the same period, however, the real value of Americans' personal interest and dividend income—then as now, income forms monopolized by the very rich—grew by about 60 percent.[47] Making the very safe assumption that very rich Americans received far more income from their stocks and bonds in 1948 than did workers from their pay packets, it is also safe to say that the very rich made far, far greater absolute per capita income gains in the purported heyday of "class convergence" than did ordinary Americans.

Hence, just as Harlow Person predicted, for corporate managers, big businesses' success at keeping investors happy and limiting labor expenses has kept the masses' incomes "correspondingly fixed" and, thereby, generated a chronic anemia in the growth of demand for products. For corporate overseers, capital has generally been readily available, but new buyers for what might be produced are hard to count on. In the words of the economist John Kenneth Galbraith, throughout the years of "high production and generous profits" since World War II, the relative weakness of popular spending power has remained "a ghost" that "haunts the boardrooms."[48]

The corporate marketers you will encounter in this book speak of this ghost's lingering presence behind their professional endeavors. Campbell soup marketers worry about flattening demand for soup. An advertising executive describes how his client, the Pepsi-Cola Corporation, was moved in the 1950s to expand its marketing operation because "They had hit a ceiling in their market." Head marketing managers fret over the difficulty of finding enough buyers. The CEO of Procter and Gamble explains that corporate packaged goods marketers nurtured excessive hopes for their Third World expansion plans because "We all needed growth."[49]

This ubiquitous worry of marketers gives the lie to business propagandists' claim that the main problem in economic life remains on the supply side, in a shortage of money and machines to increase production. "Production capacity is outpacing demand," the marketing guru Regis McKenna flatly states in a 2002 book. Despite all the public relations talk about supply-side concerns in recent years, corporate capitalism's basic, logical trend continues unabated. "Over the past twenty years or so," McKenna reports, "production systems have undergone vast improvements, to such an extent that almost every manufacturing-based industry can outproduce their market demand."[50]

Under heavy institutional pressure to do something to help their firms combat their susceptibility to anemic income growth among product users, corporate planners eventually did just what Harlow S. Person, in the fall of 1923, predicted they would: In the early and mid-1950s, a large number of big businesses entered into what has since become known in business circles as *the marketing revolution.*

The Marketing Revolution

In college marketing textbooks, the period before the 1950s is described as the era of the sales approach. The definition of the sales approach, marketing educators say, was a fixation on how to go about selling off the products the corporation was producing.

With the coming of the marketing revolution, the sales approach gave way to the marketing approach. As classically described by Robert J. Keith, this new approach struck corporate executives as a revolution in science comparable, for their purposes, to Copernicus's revolutionary idea. According to Keith, a Pillsbury Baking Company executive in the 1950s, as they were swept into this revolution, corporate planners came to see that it was not the product, but "the consumer, the man or woman who buys the product," that was "at the absolute dead center of the business universe." Struck with this insight, Pillsbury and other leading firms realized that they "needed . . . to build into our company a new management function which would direct and control all other corporate functions. . . . This function was marketing." Under its direction, Pillsbury and others would no longer treat themselves as a goods-purveyor to whom product users came for their own inscrutable reasons but would, instead, actively seek to find out and managerially manipulate "the needs and desires, both actual and potential, of our customers."[51]

The essence of the marketing revolution was the full and final managerial realization that "(a) demand is not an uncontrollable, incorrigible force, and (b) demand can be governed to a large degree by the marketer."[52] As Wroe

Alderson, the first great modern marketing scholar, explained in 1958, the realities of corporate capitalism "obliged . . . the marketing man" to disregard traditional capitalist dogma about the pristine independence of product users' decisions, to take "a closer look at the nature of" prospective buyers, and "to come to grips with the organized behavior system." The challenge and method of the new discipline of marketing, Alderson wrote, was to "borrow from the social sciences" in order to solve the managerial "problems of inducing consumers to accept innovations or the further proliferation of products to be included in the household assortment."[53]

Pushed to find new investment outlets, endowed with both swelling gross profit margins and new research and communications technologies, and struggling to keep up with rival firms, most big businesses had, by the 1960s, created marketing departments and moved to make the marketing approach their central organizing principle. In the process, most big businesses turned themselves into organizations whose central means to institutional success is conscious, Taylorian *engineering of the objects and environments that condition ordinary people's product-related activities.* "The large firm's constant purpose," observed one marketing revolution pioneer at the end of his career, "is to manufacture customers."[54]

And that is not all. Just as Harlow Person foresaw, ever since the triumph of its marketing revolution, corporate capitalist normalcy has generated a growing strife for the sales dollar, which not only continually makes its own past techniques "seem but a child's game" but also brings within its profit-seeking grasp a large and growing proportion of the infrastructures of personal life in America.

To see how this works, let us now examine the historical evolution of corporate marketing methods. Such is the subject of the next four chapters.

3. The Targeting Race

Big business marketing begins with marketing research, in which teams of corporate social science technicians try to do for marketing planners what corporate efficiency researchers do for corporate industrial engineers: study and analyze existing patterns of human activity in order to find ways to make them more profitable. Just as corporate industrial engineers design new, more profitable work environments and rules by first studying and analyzing, à la Fred Taylor, how employees enact existing ones, so big business marketers learn how best to push prospective buyers' buttons by first turning themselves into experts on the nature of prospective buyers' existing off-the-job habits.

Within marketing research, reality dictates that the first task is choosing the proper audience. While corporate factory managers know who their workers are and that, barring a strike, they will be bossable, circumstances force corporate marketers to make educated guesses about which people to bother trying to manipulate. Tellingly, in marketing circles, the individuals chosen to receive marketing messages are called "targets." The art and science of choosing targets is called "targeting."

This chapter explains targeting's logic and outlines how corporate targeting operations have, in response to the imperatives of the big business marketing race, continually grown larger and more sophisticated.

The Need to Weed

As of the year 2001, there were roughly 285 million residents of the United States. Because of its wealth, size, imperial history, and comparative domestic liberality, there was, as advertised, wide cultural diversity among these 285 million people. Because of capitalism, there was, as we saw in the last chapter, also very extreme wealth and income stratification within the 2001 U.S. population, as there was around the world. The lyrics of the Housemartins, a British pop-music group, certainly applied to turn-of-the-millennium America: "Paupers will be paupers, bankers will be bankers; Some own pennies in a jar, some own oil tankers."[1]

For corporate marketers, charged with the task of shaping their firms' output to alter prospective customers' off-the-job behaviors, ethnic diversity and economic inequality present a major dilemma: "Who are the folks who should buy our products?" How do we identify the "people we want to direct our marketing efforts toward?"[2] Which individuals might have "the potential interest, purchasing power, and willingness to spend the money to buy a product or service" we might produce?[3] To spend the firm's marketing dollars attempting to manipulate either the unmanipulable or the merely pointlessly—that is, unprofitably—manipulable would be to waste dollars and reduce the firm's profits. Because of this fact, "the targeting decision is one of the first issues a marketing manager considers."[4]

One primary cause of targeting unworthiness is poverty. *The Portable MBA in Marketing* puts the point bluntly: "People without money or some other means of making exchanges are not part of a market" and are, therefore, to be weeded from the list of prospective targets.[5] The reason for this exclusion is the corporate purpose itself—"the relentless pursuit of the consumer's cash" on behalf of investors.[6] Big business marketing, cautions Philip Kotler, is not about meeting needs, but about "meeting needs profitably."[7] The United States is home to millions—and the world, to billions—of poor people who intensely need a range of basic products but who lack the cash or credit to purchase them. To most corporate marketers, such people are irrelevancies to be avoided.

Targeting also helps big businesses avoid wasting marketing dollars on those whose circumstances or incompatible cultures make them too unlikely to respond correctly to marketing manipulation. It would usually be highly unprofitable, for instance, for corporations to market bacon to Orthodox Jews or baby formula to elderly people. For such reasons, corporations devote some of their marketing budgets to acquiring the sociological knowledge required to steer their campaigns away from unfavorable audiences and toward targets whose established habits and situations make them more susceptible to coercion.

The need to avoid wasting marketing dollars on the excessively poor and the excessively culturally hostile presses big business marketers to gather *demographic* and *psychographic* information. Demography—information on population and its distribution into economic, social, geographic, cultural, racial, sexual, age, and other groups—tells corporate planners how many individuals with certain traits are to be found in certain locales. Psychography—information on the preferences, awarenesses, reactions, interests, emotions, prejudices, and other mental tendencies prevailing among various demographic groups—tells marketers which groups already possess psychic habits that seem either more or less vulnerable to profitable manipulation. Marketers well know the value of such information. As R. Gordon McGovern, the former president of the Campbell Soup Company (now a subsidiary of the tobacco-derived conglomerate Philip Morris Companies), puts it, "the more you can target [marketing] to people who are much more prone to take the message in the form that you deliver it, then you're much more efficient."[8]

In practice, the work of gathering the demography and psychography that inform targeting decisions is done by the marketing research staffs of both corporations and the consulting firms and advertising agencies they hire. There, the first step in the work of targeting is "naming the market." This is the process of listing the demographic and psychographic groups in which "the firm has some chance of" doing "what it wants to do."[9] (What every big business "wants to do" is, of course, to "meet needs profitably," to "convert society's needs into opportunities for profitable business," to "match [such] opportunities to the firm's resources."[10]) As *The Portable MBA in Marketing* puts it, "Before marketers can do anything about understanding and predicting consumer behavior, they need to be able to *describe* the market."[11]

Corporate targeting researchers also conduct "environment scanning." This involves studying how prospective marketing campaigns might be aided or hindered by forces such as competing businesses, government policies, or social trends. "Within the rapidly changing global picture," warns Philip Kotler, "the firm must monitor six major forces: demographic, economic, natural, technological, political-legal, and social-cultural. . . . Marketers must pay attention to their causal interactions, because these set the stage for new opportunities as well as threats. . . . These forces represent 'noncontrollables,' which the company must monitor and respond to."[12] Of course, as we will see in chapter 7, big businesses do exert significant direct influence over such things as the political-legal milieux in which they operate, but Kotler still has a point: Because prospective targets live in complex environments that are significantly beyond the control of any particular corporation, it pays individual corporations to spend some time contemplating the wider nature of those environments before plunging into the rest of the marketing process.

The Evolution of Targeting

Over time, rising corporate marketing budgets and the competitive logic of big business marketing have led major corporations to expand and refine their targeting research abilities. While it always costs money to gather demography and psychography on people, ever since they entered the marketing race, big business planners have been convinced that it pays to spend enough on these things not only to help build the predictive models they need to profitably alter existing product-related behaviors, but to be better at this than rivals firms. Sayings like "If you don't know who your customers are, your competitors probably will" have long been commonplace in corporate boardrooms.[13] Hence, as popular spending power has lagged behind investors' wealth and big business marketing budgets and capabilities have grown, so has corporate targeting.

The Rise of Market Segmentation

In their review of the history of the field, the University of Michigan marketing professors Thomas C. Kinnear and James R. Taylor write that the "development of marketing research" has generally "paralleled the rise of the marketing concept." Like Pillsbury's Robert Keith, Kinnear and Taylor find that the key shift to a conscious focus on managing "consumer behavior" came sometime after "the late 1940s." Before that, targeting existed but was kept relatively small and crude by early management fixations on production and distribution rather than prospective buyers.[14] Not yet sharply focused on managing product users rather than products, pre–World War II corporate planners had not yet fully fathomed their need for targeting data.

World War II itself also briefly delayed the beginning of the marketing revolution. During the war, for the only time in the twentieth century, the United States economy provided "work for nearly everyone who wanted it, and for some who did not know they wanted it until they were magnetically attracted by high wartime wages." This, along with "favorable government policies[,] led predictably to a more equitable distribution of a much greater national income" than had prevailed before 1941.[15] Meanwhile, the material demands of the war, which diverted metals, fuels, and other basic substances into military production, also made it difficult for ordinary people to spend money on new cars, houses, and appliances. As a result, ordinary people *saved* their money at unprecedented rates. By 1944 Americans had amassed personal savings equal to about one-fifth of a booming U.S. gross domestic product.[16]

This unusual bolus of pent-up, relatively widely distributed purchasing power probably explains why the corporate marketing revolution was not launched until the 1950s. In the first few postwar years, ordinary people's rush to buy the products they had foregone during the war alleviated some of corporate capitalism's usual pressure on corporate planners. Avenues to increasing sales and profits were temporarily abundant and obvious.

This would explain why, despite the new supply of social-scientific researchers, data, and research methods the war had called forth, big businesses retained a rather leisurely attitude to "naming the market" until the mid-1950s. Early postwar business literature, for example, still lacked specialized words for targeting and its tasks. Likewise, as late as 1952, the authors of a now-classic early marketing textbook confined their instructions on this topic to explaining how to estimate *overall* population size, geographic distribution, and mobility. The same text reported that corporate staffs at this stage could "give only a general picture" of buyer demography and "how income is spent," but the complaint was hardly intense.[17]

In short, in the few exceptional years immediately after 1945, corporate targeting methods remained relatively undeveloped. As late as 1950, *Business Week* magazine contentedly reported on the issue of the U.S. Census Bureau's first postwar "Census of Business," which merely counted business establishments and roughly enumerated sales of broad categories of goods and services by locality: "You'll get detailed figures on how many concerns are doing how much business in what lines in what counties, cities, and states."[18] Less than a decade later, such rudimentary data would have generated alarm, not endorsements.

Because of corporate capitalism's powerful tendency to overaccumulate wealth and income for the rich, the conditions that allowed business to enter the 1950s with only rough targeting data would shortly be overturned. Targeting was about to make its first great leap forward. By the mid-1950s, business had once and for all renounced a monolithic approach to making markets.

In late 1956 *Business Week* reported with worry that a major new problem had emerged at one the country's largest corporations. For roughly ten years after 1945, the Ford Motor Company's Mercury Division had found success in targeting its output of one expensive, one medium-priced, and three low-priced car models at a relatively homogeneous market. By 1956, however, it found itself in dire straits:

> The auto industry's mass selling technique is a wondrous system. . . . Other consumer industries often look on the system as a model on which they, too,

should pattern their methods. But these days, the men in the auto factories have growing doubts about the efficacy of the system they've developed. . . . [Ford faces] the task of resolving one of the industry's most perplexing problems, one that has particular pertinence at Mercury—It is: Who are the buyers? It has become a problem because the auto market has changed. . . . A precisely defined market is gone, and even a supersalesman can't find it.[19]

Ford, in the response that rapidly became typical in the corporate world after the mid-1950s, stepped up its targeting efforts:

In essence, the job of [Ford's top marketing executive] George Coats' department is to broaden and deepen the X-ray study, nationally, regionally, locally, by income and other groupings, to nail down (1) the potential for any medium-priced car, and (2) the potential for Mercury. Broadly speaking, Mercury Sales Manager Charles E. Bowie tells dealers how to find customers; but Bob Chalmers, through Coats, tells Bowie where to instruct the dealers to look. . . . The upper and lower fringes of the medium-price class . . . are attractive [to Ford]. The difficulty is that no one is sure where those fringes begin or end. That's what Coats' General Marketing Dept. has to find out and exploit. "You can't approach this question on a brute strength basis," Coats says. "You have to change your methods with the times."[20]

Indeed, both times and methods had changed for marketers. Customers "got lost," and targeting them now demanded a more active approach. The title of *Business Week*'s report reflected Ford's new attitude: "Science Can Find Their Market."

The main force undermining the mass market was the rapid erosion of the special economic effects of World War II. By 1947 the huge reserve of personal savings was virtually spent, dropping in two years from $37 billion to only $5 billion.[21] Broad sectors of the population rapidly spent savings acquiring houses, cars, and appliances. Meanwhile, because of the cessation of wartime production planning and the consequent return of the normal polarizing tendencies of the big business economy, wage earners' battle to keep their incomes rising in step with productivity and profitability quickly became an uphill one again after 1945. Despite the fact that, by the standards of later years, the first decade after 1945 was an era of booming economic growth, there were already serious, year-long recessions in 1948 and 1954. Despite major federal spending on suburban infrastructure and the Korean War, unemployment rates in the decade ranged from, at best, twice the wartime lows of the early 1940s up to about five times these levels.

As a result, by the mid-1950s the problem of stagnant markets was once again unmistakable. In a book on the 1950s U.S. economy, the economist

Harold G. Vatter observed that the postwar "consumer durable boom came to an end in 1955 for automobiles and in 1956 for other durables. In both real and money terms personal consumption expenditures on durables fell in 1956 compared with the previous year, a drop for which automobiles and parts were chiefly responsible. This should not becloud the fact that the stagnation in *all* consumer durable demand had already set in, however."[22] Indeed, with the waning of World War II's economic effects and the return of the usual corporate capitalist restrictions on the incomes of working-class product users, the possibility of easily finding buyers by addressing business actions to a monolithic mass market was gone.

As this reality sank in, corporate leaders realized they needed new methods of targeting consumers more precisely, as Ford's George Coats suggested. Only with more and better knowledge of the ripest prospects could corporate investments be further expanded.

The first systematic description of the newly emergent methods of targeting appeared in 1956, in the American Marketing Association's *Journal of Marketing*. In an article titled "Product Differentiation and Market Segmentation As Alternative Marketing Strategies," Wendell R. Smith took note of the fact that businesses were finding fault with their "generalized programs of product differentiation." Such decrepit marketing schemes relied solely on "control over the demand for a product by advertising or promoting differences between a product and the products of competing sellers."[23] In response to the renewed difficulty of selling, Smith posed the question of how a superior response might be forged from "major marketing strategy alternatives that are available to planners and merchandisers of products in an environment of imperfect competition."[24]

Smith explained that what he termed the "heterogeneity" of power within markets—in other words, the dominance of large, oligopolistic corporations—tended to restrict popular purchasing power while also creating a glut of sales promotions. As these problems grew, marketers' existing efforts increasingly tended to "overgeneralize both markets and marketing efforts."[25] By continuing to assume that a homogeneous "mass" of buyers was the appropriate target at which to aim their output, businesses were failing to match their actions to the possibilities of more efficiently altering the configuration of effective demand. By trying simply to force buyers to "*converge* upon the product or product line being promoted," marketers missed out on the possibility that profit could be better maximized by "marketing programs designed for *particular market segments.*"[26]

Smith's point was that those firms that continued to rely on across-the-board marketing rooted in vague notions of the mass market would lose out to those that rooted their marketing practices in detailed social scientific description of the distribution of buying power and demographic traits among various segments of the population. Reminding business managers that in the prevailing climate of monopolistic business competition "rational selection of strategies is a requirement" and that a "premium [is] placed . . . upon products that are presold by their producers," Smith concluded that a strategy of market segmentation research should precede and supplement managers' product differentiation efforts. "Market segmentation," Smith explained, "consists of viewing a heterogeneous market (one characterized by divergent demand) as a number of smaller homogeneous markets. . . . *Segmentation* is based upon developments on the demand side of the market and represents a rational and more precise adjustment of product and marketing effort. . . . Successful application of the strategy of market segmentation tends to produce depth of market position in the segments that are effectively defined and penetrated."[27]

Smith argued that, by treating groups of consumers as "segments" or "wedge-shaped pieces" of a whole market cake and acknowledging that each piece was composed of individuals with unique levels of buying power, lifestyle habits, and demographic qualities, firms could create marketing strategies that would allow them to cobble together the most profitable "marketing mix" of commodities and symbolic communications. "The challenge to planning," Smith reiterated, "arises from the importance of determining, preferably in advance, the level or degree of segmentation that can be exploited with profit."[28]

Given the reemergence of the problem of stagnant growth in purchasing power, once the idea that Smith was proposing started to circulate in corporate circles, marketing planners wasted little time in rapidly deploying new segmentation research methods. In-house corporate marketing departments, advertising agencies, and specialized targeting research firms all rapidly began to explore and develop new strategies of describing and analyzing consumer demography and lifestyle. Many major corporations formalized and greatly increased their targeting research efforts. In the process, they invented and refined a range of new survey and interview techniques and sought to increase their abilities to obtain and use public and private sources of psychographic and demographic data.

The ensuing drive to feed and rationalize corporate targeting operations received crucial subsidies from major universities, capitalist "charities" such as the Rockefeller Foundation, and the U.S. government. Paul F. Lazarsfeld, for example, is widely credited with inventing the modern "focus group" technique of probing human motivations, with several improvements in the craft of surveying, and also with refining the statistical analysis of demographic and sociological data. It was Rockefeller grants that permitted Lazarsfeld to migrate from Austria to the United States in 1933 and to then found early marketing research think tanks at Princeton and Columbia universities. During World War II, Lazarsfeld was one of the many social scientists employed by the U.S. War Department to continue his work on new research methods.[29] After the war, Lazarsfeld and thousands of other newly trained market-research experts not only flooded back into a booming academia but were often ready, willing, and able to work as consultants to corporate marketers eager to rationalize their targeting and motivation research operations.

The irresistible attraction of the segmentation approach to targeting stemmed from market segmentation's inherent ability to boost the efficiency of the entire marketing operation by employing science to describe prospective targets more precisely than ever. As the marketing analyst Allan J. Magrath later explained, the "superior customer knowledge" that is achieved by "segmenting customers more cleverly than competitors and using segmentation knowledge . . . has tremendous productivity benefits" for marketers. "Money is saved because the selection of prospects ensures that only good sales candidates are targeted. Once potential buyers have been targeted, a variety of research techniques . . . can help the company understand how its promotions directly affect sales response."[30]

Big business learned this point quickly. Indeed, by 1962 *Glamour* magazine was able to pitch itself to potential advertising space buyers by showing in a report titled "Glamour in Fact" how it could describe the demographic and lifestyle characteristics of its targeted segment of "a select audience of young women [age] 18 through 35." *Glamour* could richly describe its readers in terms of education, age distribution, household size, marital status, occupation, income (the median *Glamour* reader belonged to a household where income was "56% higher than U.S. families"). It could also show prospective advertising space buyers statistics on its readers' usage and brand loyalty levels for more than 50 different types of goods and services.[31]

In fact, *Glamour,* by 1962, was already consciously operating as a targeting service for other businesses. It planned its editorial policy and "journalistic" content as devices for delivering the most desirable targets to its advertisers. In this, *Glamour* typified the functioning of other mass media and foreshadowed the future extension of marketing priorities into virtually the entire range of U.S. media outlets.

Over time, market segmentation grew more sophisticated. In a 1971 marketing study, Campbell Soup Company classified its prime targets into three segments: "the houseproud cooking enthusiast," "the untidy wife," and "the middle of the roader." Each segment was described in terms of its lifestyle characteristics, its socioeconomic and demographic characteristics, and its flavor preference; that is, each segment was judged by the classic segmentation dimensions of demography, lifestyle, and product usage.[32]

Toward the "One to One" Era

The success of market segmentation made corporations voraciously hungry for demographic information. For a time, segmentation's success also made its practitioners overconfident. Wendell Smith was among those who thought early market segmentation constituted the final frontier of targeting. "It is fortunate," wrote Smith in his 1956 article, "that available techniques of marketing research make unplanned market exploration largely unnecessary."[33]

Of course, given the realities of corporate capitalism, Smith's upbeat conclusion about the sufficiency of late 1950s targeting techniques was as naive as it was wrong. By the early 1970s, economic stagnation deepened once again in the United States, this time taking its most virulent form since the 1930s. Amid "stagflation" and the always-growing marketing race, Smith's early market segmentation methods were becoming less and less adequate to the task of locating prospective new customers. Just as in the 1950s, once again, "consumer researchers were frustrated by the ungluing of the mass market . . . [and by the fact that] standard demographic surveys that classify consumers by age, sex, and income had lost their edge."[34]

In such conditions, another quantum leap in targeting methods was required. In what can only be described as a true "scientific revolution," the means of leaping soon appeared.

In 1971 a young Harvard student named Jonathan Robbin had set out to apply to marketing research what he had learned about computer modeling of human behavior. Robbin had gotten his start in this area by programming computers to predict urban rioting in the 1960s. Noticing that marketing had come to depend upon a process of targeting individuals by "clustering" them along several relevant dimensions, and realizing that this endeavor had, up to the 1970s, underutilized both existing computer technologies and the wealth of already available public demography, Robbin founded the Claritas Corporation. (Fittingly, *claritas* is the Latin word for "clarity.") Its purpose and aim was to turn a profit transcending the limitations of conventional market segmentation. Robbin's results were shortly to prove that existing targeting methods were only in their infancy.

Prior to the 1970s, one of the tools marketers used for targeting market segments was to "cluster" groups of prospective targets by plotting two or more demographic or financial traits along the axes of a Cartesian graph. By placing dots where, for example, the age and income traits of a set of potential buyers intersected, then using either mathematical or "eyeball" calculations to draw boundaries around the areas where these dots clustered on the graph, marketing researchers could get a deeper picture of how their potential targets might be best segmented according to more than one dimension of lifestyle and demographic attributes.

Robbin saw that this research method held special promise as a means of describing how specific groups thought, felt, and acted. His strategy was to take existing targeting data from business firms—survey results, customer response information, and so on—and mathematically mesh them with publicly generated demographic information available from both the Census Bureau and the U.S. Postal Service, both vast sources of data that Robbin knew marketers tended to underutilize. The outcome was a new approach to targeting that turned upon what Robbin called "geodemographics." Its development is described by the journalist Michael J. Weiss, who reports that his extended research trip around the country confirmed the realism and descriptive power of Robbin's system:

> [Robbin] began with the 1930s theories of University of Chicago sociologists who described city neighborhoods as prime examples of "social clustering," where people tend to congregate among people like themselves. Then he programmed Claritas computers to analyze each zip code [a postal code containing groups of about 2,300 households] according to hundreds of characteristics in five groupings: social rank, mobility, ethnicity, family life cycle and housing style. From the morass of census results . . . Robbin identified thirty-four key factors that account, statistically speaking, for 87 percent of the variation among U.S. neighborhoods. Finally, he instructed a computer to rate each zip code on the thirty-four factors simultaneously in order to assign it to one of forty clusters. Why forty? In fact, Claritas analysts tested more than three dozen experimental models. . . . But the forty-cluster system proved the ideal compromise between manageability and discriminating power.[35]

The importance of Robbin's new approach to targeting is partly demonstrated by what Claritas has done with its own immediate results. Its targeting tools include a system of "ZQ"—"ZIP quality"—rating that neatly summarizes the geographical distribution of U.S. households based on a principle that one marketer paraphrased by Eric Clark describes as "something burglars have always known—that where people live is related to what they buy and own."[36] A few years after perfecting "ZQ," Claritas issued both an expanded classification system named "PRIZM—Potential Rating Index by Zip Markets—that further linked the ZQ clusters to dozens of media, product and opinion surveys," and the 3,000-page first edition of "REZIDE, the National ZIP Code Encyclopedia," which connected Robbin's targeting results to maps while also further improving the underlying statistical model by drawing on "a then little known cache of IRS information on income already tabulated by zip [code]."[37]

To grasp the marketing importance of this advance in targeting, consider how aptly Claritas's clusters describe the distribution and size of social classes in the United States: The ranked list shows a household population that readily falls into groups: a single top cluster ("Blue Blood Estates") with a median income far above the others, then clusters 2 through 8 ("Money & Brains" through "Young Suburbia"), and finally clusters 9 through 40 ("God's Country" through "Public Assistance"). Robbin's system thus tracks the all-important factor of social class hierarchy (which reveals basic levels of buying power) as well as the particular ways in which people tend to live near others who share both their lifestyle and their social class position.[38]

Despite the enormous practical impact of Robbin's new system—the Time-Life Corporation (now Time Warner/AOL), for instance, was one of Robbin's first clients, using his targeting index to hone its efforts to reach its relatively affluent readers more effectively with customized advertising—the story of the importance of computerized targeting is much bigger than the Claritas Corporation. Indeed, Robbin's main contribution was not so much his specific targeting studies, but his proof that it was possible and profitable to root corporate targeting in both the untapped knowledge reservoirs of public demographic information and the computer's capacity to store mountains of information and make rapid, complex scientific correlations that boggle the ordinary mind. Jonathan Robbin, in short, put targeting research on a new footing, further extending corporations' capacity to see and analyze the behaviors and behavior settings in which their targets live out their off-the-job lives.

As this computerized targeting juggernaut has grown, the possibility of "hypertargeting," or big businesses' ability to target not just groups, but *individuals,* has grown. By 1988 the Campbell Soup Company president, R. Gordon McGovern, for example, was able to report to a convention of corporate food processors that "the onset of computers has brought the lens focus from the mass market to the individual in a specific retail setting in a targeted market. Our means of reaching this individual consumer is fast changing to personalized approaches that break through the mass media tidal wave."[39] In a story titled "Marketing's 'Stepchild' Gets Respect," *Marketing News* reported on March 15, 1993, that major marketers were turning to close study of the methods of direct marketing (i.e., mailing-list marketing) to find

new ways to utilize the enormous computer databases on prospective customers. Time Warner, the article reported, by then had "52 million households in its data base."[40]

Feeding these huge marketing databases is a concomitant mushrooming
of available stockpiles of targeting information. Technology already exists
that can pinpoint the location of shoppers in supermarkets and flash advertising about nearby goods to them on screens attached to shopping carts.[41]
At the same time, businesses continue to proliferate "clever little intelligence
traps that trick us into shedding information" allowing them to connect
their marketing practices to the "real time" events of our individual lives,
such as the birth of a baby.[42] The A. C. Nielsen Company is developing a
"passive" television meter, able to sense and record when specific individuals are looking at a television set. A Polk Market Analysis Group advertisement in *American Demographics* magazine promises the following service
to retailers: "R. L. Polk & Co., will begin with a license plate survey of your
parking lot, matched against our national vehicle registration database, to
define the origin of your customers."[43] "Clickstream analytics" now permits
corporations to document virtually every choice and response of users of
the Internet and to connect that documentation with their demographic and
psychographic profiles.

The Future of Targeting

Jack Honomichl, a columnist for *Marketing News,* recounted in his publication's November 19, 1992, issue a story that conveys how marketers hope to
shape targeting's further development: "Barry Cook, senior vice president/chief
research officer of Nielsen Media Research . . . [described at a marketing con-
ference a] scenario for what he termed 'the utopia of media and marketing'
that could be available through 'hypertargeting.'" Here's how that went:

> After a hard day at work, where your income is tracked and fed into the hy-
> pertargeting data base, you drive home. The route you take, including the stores
> you pass, is captured from the homing signals of your car phone.
>
> Home at last, you have a great dinner, prepared with food that has been
> scanned at the checkout counter (along with the coupons your husband used
> when he bought them), and linked to your infoaccount because he charged the
> groceries on a credit card.
>
> Next, you settle down in front of the TV in the privacy of your living room.
> You just signed up for AT&TV; it's like having 10,000 channels and a Block-
> buster video store to choose from without your hand ever leaving the remote
> control. . . .

Your TV has everything you could possibly want to see, when you want to
see it, and it is absolutely free as long as you answer the simple questions at the
end of each commercial.

The commercials aren't that bad, actually. They are all pretty interesting
because they are selected especially for you. The hypertargeting data base takes
the information about how much money you have left, what you purchase, and
what you watch.[44]

"Cook's scenario continues to fascinate me," Honomichl concluded, "partly
because it's probably closer to the truth than I want to acknowledge. . . . This
scenario doesn't require new technologies. They exist now, although some may
be a bit expensive for large-scale application in the marketing/advertising research industry—so far."

A few years later, we now know that, in the United States, these corporate
targeter's fantasies are indeed quite close to our present reality. American
shoppers have been able to buy groceries with credit cards for several years
now. Computerized cable and satellite television capable of two-way communication have likewise become reality. According to the *New York Times,*
"many companies now use separate ads aimed at black viewers and at white
viewers; these companies include fast food chains, car manufacturers and
makers of athletic shoes."[45] The *New York Times* also reported several years
ago that "the unobtrusive cable [television] control box that sits atop many
television sets is about to become a battleground. . . . The ultimate prize:
control of the access to all the video entertainment and new types of electronic information that enter and leave the home."[46] Likewise, in early 1993,
Business Week magazine reported that, in a new development that makes the
simple performance of shopping activities themselves sources of detailed
targeting information, Advanced Promotion Technologies, Inc., has launched
a program called "Vision Value Network," which "offers credit or debit cards
that double as frequent-shopper cards" and simultaneously "provides manufacturers and retailers with demographic data to target specific buyers and
bring in repeat customers." The results of the system—"a 9% boost in market share for participating brands"—have already attracted large investments
from giant household goods marketer Procter & Gamble and from Von's, the
largest supermarket chain in southern California. Shoppers' potential doubts
and fears of the invasive nature of this system are compensated for by the fact
that each use of the Vision Value Network card yields "points" which accumulate and can be used to buy video cassette recorders and other items.[47]
"Reward cards," of course, have since exploded throughout the retail world.

Meanwhile, perfecting and integrating the elements for this next great leap forward in corporate reconnaissance has been a central corporate and governmental project since at least the early 1990s. The Clinton administration—which members of the business press described in 1993 as being gripped by "a devotion to the tools of market research" and by "a kind of market mysticism"—made the construction and commercialization of the "information superhighway," where corporate marketers can monitor "consumer behavior" and interests in fine detail, one of its chief domestic policy aims.[48] In a cover story in its April 12, 1993, edition, *Time* magazine reported

> During the 1992 presidential campaign, [President] Clinton and [Vice President] Gore made building a "data superhighway" a centerpiece of their program to revitalize the U.S. economy, comparing it with the government's role in creating the interstate highway system in the 1950s. The budget proposal the Administration submitted in February [1993] includes nearly $5 billion over the next four years to develop new software and equipment for the information highway. . . . "Make no mistake about it," says Vice President Al Gore, who was talking about information highways long before they were fashionable. "This is by all odds the most important and lucrative marketplace of the 21st century."[49]

Time observes that, as private industry moves to "lay claim to the pieces of the game," the resulting technology will facilitate a new age in marketing. The rapid exchange of "spending and demographic information" drawn from coalescing the high-tech corporate entertainment nexus will allow marketers to target individual homes with customized marketing blitzes. After considering the admittedly secondary possibilities of democratic and educational uses of such technology, *Time* concludes that "It's even easier to picture the information highway being exploited to make a lot of money."[50]

After taking stock of such emerging trends, the marketing guru Regis McKenna, a business consultant whose career has been built on supplying sound empirical business advice to corporations, concludes that the targeting methods of the past will soon

> seem like a rather obvious and primitive way to mold technology and marketing. The marketer [in the near future] will have available not only existing technologies but also their converging capabilities: personal computers, databases, CD-ROMs, graphic displays, multimedia, color terminals, computer-video technology, networking, a custom processor that can be built into anything anywhere to create intelligence on a countertop or a dashboard, scanners that read text, and networks that instantaneously create and distribute vast reaches of information. As design and manufacturing technologies advance into "real time" processes, marketing will move to eliminate the gap between production and consumption. . . .

The marketer will be able to look through windows on the workstation and manipulate data, simulate markets and products, bounce concepts off others in distant cities, write production orders for product designs and packaging concepts, and obtain costs, timetables, and distribution schedules. . . .

The marriage of technology and marketing should bring with it a renaissance of marketing R&D—a new capability to explore new ideas, to test them against the reactions of real customers in real time, and to advance to experience-based leaps of faith. It should be the vehicle for bringing the customer inside the company.[51]

No particular new targeting technology is yet a sure thing. Nevertheless, as the existence of clickstream analytics already shows, it is certain that corporate marketers will find a way to develop new and improved abilities to conduct time-and-motion studies of our off-the-job activities. Given the unrelenting pressure big businesses feel to refine and extend their marketing operations, the requisite technologies simply *will* get invented and pushed into our personal lives. As corporate capitalism expands elite wealth and restricts the growth of popular purchasing power, and as rival business giants continue to compete with one another by trying to outdo rivals at modern marketing, the clear tendency, over time, has been for more big firms to adopt advanced targeting research practices and for these practices to become steadily more refined. As long as big business dominates our economic affairs, corporate marketing planners will aggressively pursue greater knowledge of our demographic, financial, and behavioral patterns. Business as usual means there absolutely will be a widening "arms race" in targeting research.

The reality of this arms race logic was powerfully confirmed in a 1994 *Business Week* cover story on database marketing and the substantial sales benefits it often brings:

Companies are collecting mountains of information about you, crunching it to predict how likely you are to buy a product, and using that knowledge to craft a marketing message precisely calibrated to get you to do so.

First came the mass market, that vast, undifferentiated body of consumers who received identical, mass-produced products and messages. . . . Then came market segmentation, which divided still-anonymous consumers into smaller groups with common demographic or psychographic characteristics. Now, new generations of faster, more powerful computers are enabling marketers to zero in on ever-smaller niches of the population, ultimately aiming for the smallest consumer segment of all: the individual.

A growing number of marketers are investing millions of dollars to build databases that enable them to figure out who their customers are and what it takes to secure their loyalty. . . .

Database marketing is now moving into the marketing mainstream, as everyone from packaged-goods companies to auto makers comes to believe that in the fragmented, fiercely-competitive marketplace of the 1990s, nothing is more powerful than knowledge about customers' individual practices and preferences. . . .

According to Donnelly Marketing Inc.'s annual survey of promotional practices, 56% of manufacturers and retailers are currently building a database, an additional 10% plan to do so, and 85% believe they'll need database marketing to be competitive past the year 2000.[52]

By 2001, these forecasts had proved correct, and corporate databases had become so large that the field of computerized statistical "data mining" was, even in a moment of aggressive "downsizing," perhaps the hottest growth category in the job market for corporate consultants. "Data mining," reported one expert practitioner, "is evolving from a 'bleeding edge' application to a critical, everyday occurrence in many corporations. . . . As recently as five years ago, I spent more time speaking at conferences about the potential value of data mining than actually applying the technology for customers. Today, I'm seeing the data mining services that I used to deliver for only the largest banks in use across all industrial sectors."[53]

Meanwhile, Jonathan Robbin's Claritas Corporation had adopted a "62-cluster system" that it was able to correlate with the U.S. Postal Service's new nine-digit ZIP codes and more than 1,600 sources of demographic and psychographic data.[54] Symmetrical Research was advertising services such as its Advanced Analytic Solutions, which promised corporate clients "the power of one of the world's most advanced marketing data analytics teams, with proprietary tools enabling the statistical study of everything from small scale research studies to the 35 terabyte Mastercard dataset."[55] A terabyte, by the way, is one *trillion* units of computerized information.

Big Business Marketing, Targeting, and American Society

Having been systematized and expanded along with the rest of corporate marketing, corporate targeting operations are now more ubiquitous and sophisticated than anyone would have dared dream fifty years ago, at the dawn of the big business marketing revolution. In the earliest days of the marketing revolution, typical corporations relied rather passively on a few sorts of simple targeting information. By the turn of the millennium, many corporations' demographic databases rivaled the U.S. Census Bureau's in coverage, while greatly surpassing them in the richness and frequency of their detailed surveillance of American households and individuals.[56] By 2002 Claritas Corporation was openly remarking on the insufficiency of public census data for describing "your markets." Its response? Claritas UPDATE, its own private census of "demographic changes in every neighborhood in America."[57]

With their growing knowledge, corporate marketers gain more insights into how to alter the environmental, behavioral, demographic, and financial impediments that stand in the way of "inducing consumers to accept innovations or the further proliferation of products to be included in the household assortment."[58] As one marketing consultant puts it, "database marketing is a sort of collective memory."[59] It is also a powerful mechanical brain, which, when coupled with the various new eyes and ears that corporate marketers are also rapidly inventing and promulgating, brings the modern marketing corporation ever closer to being able to obtain the kind of close, detailed time-and-motion studies of their targets' personal lives that have allowed the scientific management of paid labor to achieve such astounding results.

Erik Larson aptly summarizes the ultimate meaning of this trend: "We are the most heavily probed, surveyed, and categorized society since the dawn of human history. The intensity of this assault has changed us, both as individuals and as a culture."[60]

4. The Motivation Research Race

Once corporate marketers know their targets, they turn their attention to "motivation research." How do our targets perceive and react to all the environmental factors that affect their decisions to buy and use our products? How are they likely to perceive and react to new factors we might introduce into their off-the-job milieux? How might we best push or pull them into acting as we want them to act—that is, into repeatedly buying and using up our products?

Such are the questions addressed via motivation research. This chapter explains the logic and historical expansion of this crucial branch of the big business marketing race.

The Logic of Motivation Research

In any given week in the United States, big businesses are busy asking and answering a blizzard of questions about their targets' off-the-job lives. How do people decide what condiments to use in cooking and serving meals? Would a proposed change in our product's packaging make it slightly more likely that supermarket shoppers will glance at it? What feelings do people have about soup? How many people watched the commercials during a particular television sitcom last night?

Like the targeting imperative, the need to answer such minute motivational questions arises from the fact that shopping, buying, and product-using activities take place outside the individual corporation's sphere of formal, contractual control. Because they can't openly boss their prospective customers, corporate planners know they must rely on stealth and superior knowledge to get prospective customers to do as the corporation wants. Effective marketing requires that product-related bossing—the marketing mission, that is—be effective enough to profitably alter product users' behavior yet also subtle enough to avoid recognition and resistance. Such effectiveness and subtlety demands very precise knowledge of prospective buyers' existing propensities and habits.

Okay, but what exactly is it that must be so effectively and subtly crafted? As Thorstein Veblen recognized three decades before the corporate marketing revolution reached fruition, the answer is, the same coercive stuff on which class domination has always rested—force and fraud, carrots and sticks. It is no oversimplification to say that big business marketing is the art and science of covertly crafting and deploying profit-boosting, behavior-altering threats and enticements. Everything marketers place before their targets is one or the other—or both—of these things.

This historical framework makes it easy to demystify big business motivation research. Motivation research is the process by which big businesses gather the social and psychological information they need to covertly design and deploy new and improved behavior-altering threats and enticements. In the trade, threats and enticements are called marketing stimuli.

* * *

Crafting effective marketing stimuli requires detailed knowledge of the minds of targets. Hence, the mental processes—styles of perception, learning, and decision making, for example—that govern people's shopping, buying, and product-using habits are to the big business marketer what the obedience and bodily motions of the factory worker are to the corporate industrial engineer. To the corporate marketer, the off-the-job lives of prospective targets are raw materials to be analyzed, dissected, and more profitably reassembled. "The work of marketing," the long-time advertising executive Marion Harper observed in his professional memoir, "is successful exactly to the degree it penetrates and organizes the milieu of the customer in ways favorable to the enterprise."[1]

What is interesting and important is that this managerial imperative forces corporate marketers, at least in their professional endeavors, to reject capitalism's traditional ideology of individualism. The classic marketing theorist Wroe Alderson enunciated this necessary rejection in 1958. "The general economist," Alderson wrote, "has his own justifications for regarding the exchange process as a smoothly functioning process" that unfolds from the isolated and primordial individual preferences of economics textbooks. "For the marketing man," Alderson continued, "this Olympian view is untenable. Marketing is concerned with those who are obliged to enter the market to solve their problems imperfect as the market may be. . . . To understand market behavior the marketing man takes a closer look at the nature of the participants. Thus he is obliged . . . to come to grips with the organized behavior system."[2]

Consequently, a sociological conception of individuals is a first principle of marketing practice. In practice, big business marketers concur with the German sociologist Norbert Elias, who argues that the human being is neither a primordially isolated autonomous unit of free will nor a totally determined automaton, but, rather, a specific agent within a particular "we-I balance." Just as there is no "we" without individual "I's," so it is, Elias observes, that "there is no I-identity without we-identity."[3] In short, individual human consciousness—including its unique processes of *choice* and *decision making*—is always a *process* that is at once willfully shaped by the person making the choices *and* heavily conditioned at several levels by shared group dynamics and experiences.

As Alderson knew, knowledge of this fact constitutes the crux of all of marketers' activities—and indeed makes marketing itself possible. If human beings really were either primordially autonomous and isolated decision makers that expressed wholly independent demands, or robots that expressed preprogrammed routines, there would obviously be no point in anyone's trying to influence people's off-the-job motivations and actions. Despite much propaganda to the contrary, however, reality is kind to marketers—individuals exist within a balance that includes a rich mixture of both autonomous individual conviction and strong outside social and psychological influences. Marketers, in short, have room for maneuver.

This room for maneuver is enhanced by the fact that people are not just social, but also deeply emotional. "What makes us human," explains the sociologist Douglas Massey, "is the *addition* of a rational mind to a preexisting emotional base" within our brains. While, as Massey reports, academic social scientists have underemphasized this reality and "unwisely elevated the rational over the emotional in attempting to understand and explain human behavior," big business marketers are not so foolish.[4] They devote a large percentage of their motivational research to discovering ways to use emotional cues to short-circuit our rationality and manipulate our emotionality.

To capitalize on the teachability and emotionality of prospective buyers, marketers have mobilized increasingly sophisticated marketing research operations. As we saw in chapter 3, this process begins with targeting, the effort to discover which households, groups, and—recently—individuals, fit the demographic and financial profiles most likely to make them pliable subjects for marketing management. Yet the need to "penetrate and organize the milieu of the customer" also compels marketers to address a consequent question: What are the *motivations* that might drive people to shop, buy, and use particular commodities? In other words, once businesses can be reasonably sure that they have weeded out those too destitute or too culturally unlikely to be profitably influenced, modern marketing boils down to a struggle to influence targeted *potential* buyers to become *actual* buyers. Hence, marketing becomes a struggle to scientifically manage—that is, to study, analyze, and profitably reorganize in favor of a particular firm—the psychological determinants of targets' product-related behavior.

For an authoritative description of the basics of motivation research, we can turn to Philip Kotler. Trained at the University of Chicago and the Massachusetts Institute of Technology, Kotler is the S. C. Johnson and Son Distinguished Professor of International Marketing chair at Northwestern University's Kellogg Graduate School of Management. A distinguished, award-winning marketing scholar and researcher, as well as a major corporate marketing consultant, Kotler's is perhaps the most respected name in contemporary marketing. (Kotler's instructional videotape "Philip Kotler on Marketing," in which Kotler presents "case studies and panel discussions with front-line marketing executives" sold for $995 per copy in 1993.) Kotler's introductory marketing textbook, *Principles of Marketing* (now in its ninth edition), cowritten with Gary Armstrong, a graduate of the Kellogg School, aims at "showing the major decisions that marketing managers face."[5]

Kotler and Armstrong begin with the institutional triumph of marketing after 1945: "During the early 1950s the supply of goods began to grow faster than the demand. Most markets became buyers' markets, and marketing became identified with sellers trying to find buyers."[6] In response to this crisis, corporations adopted "marketing management," a fundamental process of "the analysis, planning, implementation, and control of programs designed to create, build, and maintain beneficial exchanges with target buyers for the purpose of achieving organizational objectives."[7]

This new form of management, Kotler and Armstrong report, requires the resolution of a series of management dilemmas rooted in the core problem of "obtaining a desired object from someone by offering something in return."[8] Because firms normally find that the growth in the supply of product users able to "offer something in return" (money) to be anemic or worse, marketers come under an intense institutional need to create markets for their firms by manipulating the *motivations* of prospective buyers for the firm's output. Creating, building, and maintaining the will to buy among targeted groups of individuals thus becomes the central object of management. "Simply put, marketing management is demand management."[9]

Demand management, in turn, requires the firm to take "an *outside-in* perspective" in which the raw material is none other than the fabric of the human psyche itself.

When marketers approach this peculiar raw material, they find that it is not fixed forever in hermetically sealed autonomous individuals or brainless robots but is located in and around individuals who have real needs and wants and are open to a variety of environmental influences:

> The most basic concept underlying marketing is that of human needs. A *human need* is a state of felt deprivation. Humans have many complex needs. They include basic *physical* needs for food, clothing, warmth, and safety; *social* needs for belonging and affection; and *individual* needs for knowledge and self-expression. . . . A second basic concept in marketing is that of *human wants*— the form taken by human needs as they are shaped by culture and individual personality. A hungry person in Bali may want mangoes, suckling pig, and beans. A hungry person in the United States may want a hamburger, french fries, and a Coke. Wants are described in terms of objects that will satisfy needs. . . . When backed by buying power, wants become *demands.*[10]

To create demand, marketers must figure out a way to get their messages through a series of mental filters in prospective product users' minds. As Kotler and Armstrong explain, these filters are embedded in two concentric layers of dynamic forces.

First, there is the inner layer—the mind itself. Here, marketers are well aware that, far from being simple rational calculators or automatons, real people are complex decision makers. First, "decision making varies with the type of buying decision. There are great differences between buying toothpaste, a tennis racket, an expensive camera, and a new car. The more complex decisions are likely to involve more buying participants and more buyer deliberation."[11] Also, several mental conversions must occur (or be bypassed) in the would-be purchaser's mind before a sale ensues: The proffered product must favorably elicit awareness, interest, problem recognition, information search, evaluation of alternatives, a purchase decision, and proper postpurchase behavior.[12]

The mind, however, is only the first layer of raw material in demand management. As Kotler and Armstrong explain, "Consumer purchases are strongly influenced by cultural, social, personal, and psychological characteristics." Such factors "exert the broadest and deepest influence" on behavior. "*Culture* is the most basic cause of a person's wants and behavior. Growing up in a society, a child learns basic values, perceptions, wants, and behaviors from the family and other institutions. . . . Each culture contains smaller *subcultures,* or groups of people with shared value systems based on common life experiences and situations. . . . *Social classes* are relatively stable and ordered divisions in a society whose members share similar values, interests, and behaviors."[13] By describing and analyzing how such social patterns and relationships affect populations of targets, Kotler and Armstrong report, marketers enable themselves to better see the behavioral influence their marketing stimuli might exert.

* * *

As Kotler and Armstrong explain, "companies and academics have heavily researched the relationship between marketing stimuli and consumer response. Their starting point is the stimulus-response model of buyer behavior."[14] As those who are familiar with psychology will immediately recognize, this starting point is basically the same as that of the behaviorists Ivan Pavlov and B. F. Skinner. Both Pavlov and Skinner were pioneers in behaviorist theory and research, a way of viewing human motivation from the perspective of an engineer out to change the dynamics of a system of behavior. Behaviorism focuses not on the deep-seated meanings of actions and relationships for individuals, but simply on the question of what environmental stimuli produce and reinforce desirable or undesirable actions and responses. Behaviorists see the human psyche as a mechanism that learns to respond to a range of stimuli and reinforcers by their association with rewards and punishments. What counts in applied behaviorism is to design, configure, and communicate environmental stimuli that get people to respond the "right" way.

The relationship between formal behaviorism and marketing has been a close one. Early behaviorist scholars such as John Broadus Watson, who went to work for an advertising agency in the 1920s, were explicitly concerned with helping to solve the "consumer" problems that the rise of corporate capitalism so greatly intensified.[15] "The consumer is to the manufacturer, the department stores and the advertising agencies," Watson remarked in the 1920s, "what the green frog is to the physiologist."[16] More generally, while marketers' attachment to a fundamentally behaviorist professional worldview is rarely elaborated into formal theory, it is real and powerfully rooted in institutional imperatives. Indeed, it is no exaggeration to say that modern corporate marketing has been a huge, expanding project of applied behavioral research, by far the largest in human history.[17]

From the marketing perspective, the power of behaviorism, whether stated or unstated, lies in its demonstration that carefully planned manipulation of the stimuli impinging on subjects' consciousness—even by parties that lack total control over all aspects of the individual's existence—can produce extremely strong and efficient mental associations that induce desired actions. Behaviorist researchers have shown that dogs can be conditioned to salivate at the ringing of bells simply by the way they are fed, and chickens can be made to "teach themselves" how to gain access to food simply by manipulating the design of their cages. Likewise, big business marketers know, people's off-the-job behaviors can be modified by strategically manipulating their learning processes.

Like classic behaviorist experiments, corporate marketers also depend on keeping targets, in the words of the marketing psychiatrist Tom Snyder, "under the surface of awareness as much as possible."[18] Snyder is the head of Emotion Mining Company of Wellesley, Massachusetts, a firm that has performed motivational research for several major corporations, including Campbell's Soup. As Snyder explains, marketing success requires careful control of the operating depth of marketing stimuli in the consumer's mind: Explaining that the mind is like a lake, with consciousness at the surface, preconsciousness or subconscious in the depths of water, and a bottom that is the Freudian unconscious, Snyder observes that because buying responses tend to be inhibited by calculations and ego defenses when apprehended in full consciousness, marketers must operate at the level "where the trout swim."[19]

It should come as no surprise, then, to find that marketers—who by self-definition are engaged in demand management—relate to prospective buyers' motivations as pragmatic behaviorists. Indeed, Kotler and Armstrong explain modern corporate marketers' standard approach to buyer motivations in precisely these terms: For the marketer, "marketing stimuli consist of the four P's—product, price, place, and promotion. Other stimuli include major forces and events in the buyer's environment. . . . All these stimuli enter the buyer's black box, where they are turned into a set of observable buyer responses—product choice, brand choice, dealer choice, purchase timing, and purchase amount. The marketer wants to understand how the stimuli are changed into responses inside the consumer's black box."[20]

Of course, as every big business marketer knows, more sophisticated knowledge of buyer motives allows firms to more effectively configure stimuli before they "enter the consumer's 'black box' and produce certain responses."[21] Superior motivation research facilitates superior knowledge of the mental links between distinctive behavioral routines, which makes for more effective marketing and higher sales volume and better rates of return on investment.

Thus, the foundation of marketers' relation to their targets is, from a psychological perspective, thoroughly interventionist. At the Campbell Soup

Company, for instance, a top marketing executive described his "problem" as the effort "to trigger soup usage and accelerate . . . consumption." A little further investigation reveals that Campbell marketers describe efforts to re-inforce soup's "really mythical position in the culture"; to "reinforce love and relationships and mother-love with kids"; to integrate Campbell's soup at a strategic point of life so as to take advantage of the premium on time saving created by the overwork required of most consumer households to combat eroding wage rates and the rising cost of living; to find latent feelings about Campbell's and "bring them back to the surface"; to design line extensions for men around "macho, macho, macho" campaigns of persuasion designed "to convince women [who still do the lion's share of grocery shopping] that guys who worked their butts off would love to sit down to this soup"; and generally to increase the likelihood that their targets would be "triggered to buy."[22] And the examples from the Campbell case are wholly typical. Whether it is Pepsi-Cola's effort to train Americans to view their soda pop as the reflec-tion of the twenty-three-year-old image or Miles Laboratories' struggle to sell Alka-Seltzer tablets by making people "think they're sick or uncomfort-able," the illustrations are endless.[23]

Thorstein Veblen's "force and fraud" theory of marketing's content is, in other words, powerfully accurate. Corporate motivation researchers are pro-fessionally engaged in the art and science of planting subtle psychological carrots and sticks in popular behavior settings, for profit. The little psycho-logical threats, lies, flatteries, and promises marketers build into their mar-keting mixes are usually neither more nor less complicated than that. Mar-keting scholarship and research is full of such pieces of work as these: "The Role of Sexually-Oriented Stimuli in Advertising: Theory and Literature Review" and "The Processing of Marketing Threat Stimuli: A Comprehen-sive Framework."[24] The main arguments of these studies are, respectively, that sexual arousal conveyed through the "marketing mix" increases attention by evoking "an unexpected or surprise stimulus" that causes the individual to associate "an affective evaluation" with "the product being advertised"; and that built-in "threat appeals can be very effective" at creating "compliance" with suggested actions.[25]

* * *

Before we turn our attention to the historical development of the moti-vation research practices that undergird marketing's behavior modification campaigns, however, it is important to jump slightly ahead of ourselves on one point: It is crucial to note that marketers' real-world professional atti-tude to human motivations does *not* mean that marketing is a monolithic, conspiratorial system of ideological indoctrination. Quite to the contrary, as I have said before, marketers intervene in personal life *on behalf of competing business firms in order to motivate individuals to spend more money and use more of their own firms' commodities. Big businesses are not out to commit brainwashing for its own sake.* Moreover, political ideologies, while not separate from this process, are distinctly peripheral to it. In fact, from my own experiences and my detailed research into dozens of actual marketing campaigns (and my more casual encounters with thousands of others), I believe that marketers usually rely on one or more of four basic tactics:

Psychological Tactics

Psychological approaches seek to promote products by associating them with the satisfaction or release of strong emotions such as jealousy, envy, vanity, and fear. Another common tactic is smarmy emotional inflation, where the "good feelings" associated with a product are blown out of proportion in order to increase buying. Repetition of a marketer's planned stimulus-response associations, as in classical conditioning, is a crucial device in the psychological approach. Also, cuteness and mesmerizing catchiness play important associative roles in this marketing style.

As Thorstein Veblen argued, threats play a major part in big business marketers' psychological ploys. Sometimes the threats are direct, as when Michelin pictures a baby sitting in its tires or Florida orange growers make a television ad in which a toddler chugs a jug of orange juice after hearing a radio report about the possible health benefits of vitamin C. "Buy our tires or you'll kill your child in a flaming car wreck," Michelin gently implies. "Drink lots of orange juice or you'll get cancer and orphan your child," the orange ranchers threaten ever so lightly.

Often, the veiled coercion is also indirect, as when marketers deploy what they call "aspirational" images and messages. Perfect families, spotless houses, gleaming expensive cars, astoundingly beautiful models, tight butts, and six-pack abdomens—all typical in marketing, all nearly or literally impossible in the real world—but also all things we ordinary schmoes openly or secretly aspire to be, have, or look like, as marketers know. "Buy our product and you'll be a little closer to your dreams" is their aspirational promise. "Without our product, you'll never fulfill your dreams and be admired" is their aspirational threat. "In the factory we make cosmetics," quipped Charles Revson, the founder of Revlon, Inc. "In the store we sell dreams."[26]

Age aspirations are especially effective threat vehicles. Pepsi marketers, as we have seen, track and exploit the fact that kids want to be young grownups

and grownups yearn to be back "in their early twenties."[27] Products market-
ed to elderly people invariably use middle-aged or very young-looking seniors
in their advertising and on their packages. Products sold to preteen and early-
teen children deploy images and attitudes of mid to late teenagers.

One particularly telling illustration of the logic of aspirational manipulation is Marlboro cigarettes. In 1952 the Philip Morris (PM) corporation created its own internal marketing department. Among its first projects was boosting
PM's Marlboro cigarette brand. In "one of the largest research projects" of the
time, including 10,000 in-home interviews, PM motivation researchers began
searching for better ways of selling Marlboros, which then accounted for less
than 1 percent of all cigarette sales. Their studies soon revealed that, because
of its filtered tip, men perceived Marlboros as "effeminate or sissyish, and for
women." What PM needed was a way to transcend this perception with "a
macho campaign." Its answer came when its marketers realized that "people
liked seeing cowboys." "The cowboy," recounted John Benson, a Leo Burnett
ad executive who worked on Marlboro, "represents the last free American. A
lot of people are envious of him."[28]

"Psychologically," reports George Weissman, the former CEO of PM, "Marlboro did this: It came on the scene with the environmentalists, and it said open
spaces, green terrain, the natural, primitive life. It came on the scene when you
had the rebellion of the sixties, seventies, and even extending into now, against
the computerized world, and said, 'Hey, I'm a smoker, and I'm out there, and
I don't have to punch a time-clock, and I'm not following a computer.'"[29]

Philip Morris's Marlboro Man and Marlboro Country campaigns have
been among the most successful in modern marketing history. As other critics
have noted, it is hard to overstate the irony of the fact that these campaigns
operate via the ultimate American symbol of independence yet serve to draw
PM's targets into a web of carefully managed nicotine addiction. "Arbeit
macht frei" said the doorway to Dachau. "Marlboro makes you free" say our
billboards, magazines, t-shirts, race cars, and store aisles.

Information Control Tactics

Marketers often attempt to induce particular behaviors by strategic deployment of information. By saying that their cars are safe, foods are healthy, soaps
are new and improved, diet counseling services are easy, and so forth, marketers aim to control the terms of debate and the limits to knowledge. Much
of this control comes from the studied language of advertising, packaging,
and brand-naming, all of which is designed to induce buying by cleverly re-
stricting knowledge of a product's real qualities, context, and alternatives. The

marketing importance of controlling information is interestingly documented by the motivational strategy behind advertising for the proprietary medicine Alka-Seltzer. While all the major marketing executives in charge of
Alka-Seltzer are keenly aware that buyers often use the aspirin and sodium
bicarbonate tablets to relieve hangovers, Miles Laboratories' marketing executives take care in framing the product's perception without reference to
hangovers. Since users are reluctant to admit that they use it for hangovers,
Miles executives refer indirectly to the symptomology of hangovers: headache, upset stomach, or the blahs.

Existential Tactics

Marketers opportunistically use their firms' resources to shape the structures
and flows of individuals' everyday existence, knowing that if they can make
their wares unavoidable, then prospective buyers are likely to give in to their
suggestions. When cars are the only viable form of transportation and last
only seven or eight years, then buying a car (albeit not any specific brand) is
unavoidable. Likewise, when a fast-food or grocery chain has locations all
over a town, it is likely that sheer convenience will trigger many sales. When
advertising messages penetrate every nook and cranny of daily life, absorption of their conditioning becomes more likely.

An especially clear verbalization of the marketing importance of exploiting individuals' simple existential dilemmas was given by McGovern, the
president of Campbell Soup, who wrote in a 1982 trade magazine article, "One
thing remains solid: There are 220 million Americans who must eat daily to
survive and to enjoy life. The market is there for those who want it and make
the necessary adjustments."[30]

Promotional Tactics

Almost always in conjunction with other types of motivational strategy,
marketers often endeavor to provoke curiosity in potential buyers by making their products seem like important news. Loud, flashy, or curious messages are designed to attract attention. Temporary price reductions, comparative price claims, and coupons and discounts are also examples of
promotional strategies. Newness and temporary price discounts are key elements in promotional approaches. Even strategies as seemingly simple as
price discounts are the subject of motivation research. An example is the
article "Consumer Perceptions of Promotional Activity" from the American Marketing Association's *Journal of Marketing*. Its authors tested "the association between a household's characteristics and its perception of deal

[i.e., discount] activities"—perceptions such as awareness and ignorance of prices—with the objective of "improving models of consumer response to promotions" so that marketers "could take [consumer] reactions into account in designing promotions for different brands."[31]

The Evolution of Motivation Research

Corporate marketers' interventionist attitude to individuals' off-the-job motivations is neither an accident nor a matter of evil intention. Motivation research, like big business marketing as a whole, has been driven by the basic logic of corporate capitalism. As one marketing scholar explains,

> The increasing complexity of the environment, including the growth in competition . . . has led more and more firms to emphasize marketing strategy. This, in turn, creates a greater need for information provided by marketing research. More money will be spent for marketing research and managers will pay more attention to the value of the information provided. Researchers will work more closely with higher-level managers in the formulation of strategy and will be expected to make substantial contributions to the process by which strategy evolves.[32]

As the corporate marketing race has advanced, marketers have continually made their motivation research both more scientific and more comprehensive in reach.

The Origins of Modern Motivation Research

In the period before the triumph of the marketing revolution, techniques of motivation research moved from infancy to adolescence. By 1912 the marketing pioneer Arch Shaw was able to articulate a clear vision of the emerging drive toward consolidation: "Only in more recent years, when the development of production (potentially outstripping the available market) has shifted the emphasis to distribution, has the businessman . . . become a pioneer of the frontier of human wants. Today the progressive businessman is searching out the unconscious needs of the consumer, is producing goods to gratify them, is bringing to the attention of the consumer the existence of such goods, and in response to the demand so aroused, is transporting the goods to the consumer."[33] This statement was more of a prescient call to action than a description of mature marketing practices, in that neither the sophistication of actual motivation research practices nor the extent and degree of their institutionalization was very great before the 1950s.

While the years before World War II did see the rise of the first motivation research and the first commercial use of opinion polling by figures such as Elmo Roper and George Gallup, the scope of motivation research was narrow. Rebecca Piirto reports figures that reveal the meagerness of the pre-1945 motivational research effort: "between 1900 and 1930, there were fewer than half a dozen practicing commercial psychologists," while "by the late 1930s, at least six college textbooks on market research techniques had been published."[34] The number of firms with formal market research departments was also small. The American Marketing Association's 1973 issue of its pentennial *Survey of Marketing Research* found that of the 936 firms that then reported having marketing research departments, 21 reported that their departments had been formed before 1932, another 30 between 1933 and 1942, and the rest after 1943.[35] Overall, the marketing professor Harper Boyd reports, "While the late 1920s and the decade of the 1930s saw improvements in research techniques, the amount of research activity was still relatively small. Annual expenditures for marketing research by businesses did not exceed several million dollars."[36]

Evidence shows that the quality of motivation research was as comparatively low before 1945, as well. Boyd concludes that motivation research techniques were relatively "crude and unimaginative," since "behavioral scientists had done little research on data collection methods."[37] Piirto concurs: "Before World War II, market research was involved mainly in volumetric measurement, using techniques derived from survey research and economic analysis. . . . Accuracy of the sampling was paramount, and little attention was attached to psychological considerations."[38]

Yet there was progress. By 1940 Douglas McGregor published an essay in the *Harvard Business Review* that voiced a growing dissatisfaction with the ad hoc, arbitrary "list-making" that most often passed for motivation research at the time. McGregor sharply criticized the tendency of marketers to accept slapdash research on prospective buyers' motives: "Our major aim is to be able to predict how human beings will behave, and through our skill in prediction to control behavior. . . . [Yet] with few exceptions one finds the literature of market research to be devoid of direct attacks on problems in this area. In spite of much evidence to the contrary, the conviction seems almost universal that motives are such intangible things that one cannot hope to deal with them 'objectively.'"[39] Concerned to debunk the notion "that accurate prediction was possible in terms of a simple list of motives," McGregor called for shifting motivation research from "abstract logical generalization to the level of concrete empirical research."[40]

The Initial Triumph of Modern Motivation Research

As the corporate marketing revolution took hold after World War II, a rapid proliferation of marketing research commenced among corporations. Just as it did with the other components of the marketing process, this revolution brought motivation research into line with the nascent scientific management of off-the-job behavior settings. As Boyd notes, "it was not until the late 1940s and 1950s that marketing research emerged as a critical instrument in the operation of most business organizations." At this time, marketing research's "growing popularity coincided with the increased adoption of the marketing concept which . . . argued that the critical job of management is to anticipate the needs and wants of selected markets and satisfy them better than competitors."[41]

Between 1947 and 1969, expenditures on marketing research rose from an estimated $50 million to nearly $600 million.[42] By 1973 the American Marketing Association found that of 1,322 companies it surveyed, 68 percent conducted their own research into market characteristics. By 1978, 92 percent of 798 responding firms were doing "determination of market characteristics" research.[43] From 1945 until 1968, after only moderate expansion during the 1930s, the growth rate of marketing research departments was 7 percent annually; from 1968 to 1973, it was 16 percent annually.[44] As of 1983, although relatively few small firms had formal research departments, "almost all firms with sales in excess of $500 million" did.[45]

The spread of formalized *motivation research* was an inseparable part of this general rise of marketing research after 1945. By 1988, in each of seven categories of buying behavior research, well over half of 587 businesses reporting to the American Marketing Association said their marketing research departments conducted studies. The incidence rate for each research category was (1) brand preference, 54 percent; (2) brand attitudes, 53 percent; (3) product satisfaction, 68 percent; (4) purchase behavior, 61 percent; (5) purchase intentions, 60 percent; (6) brand awareness, 59 percent; and (7) segmentation studies, 60 percent. Also, these overall incidence rates jumped significantly when the survey was narrowed to exclude industrial products manufacturers, who mainly specialize in selling capital equipment to other businesses. For instance, among all reporting consumer products manufacturers, the incidence rate of the seven types of motivation research was, respectively, 80, 81, 77, 80, 78, 78, and 70 percent.[46] Moreover, the occurrence of formal marketing research departments increased with firm size. The survey found that 97 percent of consumer goods businesses with yearly sales in excess of $500 million had marketing research departments.

By the 1980s virtually all large firms were doing formal in-house motivation research.[47]

This quantitative explosion of formal motivation research was accompanied by a steady rationalization of its qualitative basis. "Our problem," remarked the renowned marketer Steuart Henderson Britt in a speech at the 1949 convention of the American Marketing Association, "is that we have available all kinds of facts and figures about *markets,* but that we sometimes forget that these markets, after all, are made up of *human beings.*

> The one eventual aim of advertisers and salesmen must be to see that consumers develop an *intensified desire to buy.* But, in stimulating consumer buying, have the best approaches always been used? . . . I think you will agree that no *list* or classification of motives . . . is sufficient to answer questions of this kind. . . . Man is more than an animal or a *physiological* being. . . . He belongs to all sorts of clubs, and institutions, and organizations . . . and every one of these and other social institutions has an "emotional pull" for him.[48]

For Britt, the problem was the stubborn fixation on product attributes that made "three out of four of the advertisements for each type of product read almost alike." The solution, Britt held, was to take into account "the tremendous importance of *unconscious* motivation" by pursuing "the *clinical* approach to interviewing."[49]

Just such a turn to psychology came to define the first wave in the integration of motivation research. Until the 1960s, motivation research in the generic sense tended to come under the influence of a specifically psychoanalytic approach to studying consumer wants and needs. As Piirto reports, this approach "became so popular among U.S. market researchers that by 1954, half of the 64 members of the Jury of Marketing Opinion of the trade journal *Printer's Ink* said they had successfully used motivation research."[50]

The method of psychoanalytic motivation research was pioneered by figures such as Ernest Dichter, an Austrian psychologist who fled to the United States in 1938 and soon began to apply psychology to marketing problems. A new way of organizing research emerged:

> The motivationist movement relied on projective techniques borrowed from clinical psychology that were designed to get subjects to talk about and reveal their unconscious motivations. One popular technique was the in-depth interview in which the subject responds at length to a series of general questions designed to make "yes" or "no" responses impossible. Designed to keep respondents under the surface of their awareness, these techniques are projective because they allow respondents to project their own feelings on neutral stimuli.[51]

By studying how individuals tended to project values and beliefs onto neutral objects, marketers could learn which marketing conditioning strategies were most likely to yield increases in sales.

Business employed the results of such big-M, big-R Motivation Research in a variety of ways. To name one example: When food corporations found in the mid-1950s that they were having difficulty marketing instant coffee (which was invented for combat soldiers' convenience during World War II) because people saw the product as implying laziness on the part of the preparer, they found themselves at a loss to explain their failure to boost sales by advertising the apparently obvious convenience of instant coffee. In response to the crisis, the Nestlé Corporation, maker of the Nescafé brand of instant coffee, commissioned a psychoanalytic motivation research study. The consequent depth interviews showed that, if people were exposed to image cues of real, unprocessed coffee beans, they would be far more willing to equate instant coffee with regular coffee. Because of the study's findings, Nestlé shifted its marketing strategy to emphasize the social acceptability of serving Nescafé, which, Nestlé explained, was after all made from rich, brown, *real* coffee beans. Meanwhile, Ernest Dichter was counseling the Pan American Coffee Bureau that it could overcome regular coffee's dull, commonplace, utilitarian image by portraying it as a sophisticated drink enjoyed in romantic places like Vienna. As a result of such motivation research projects, instant coffee became a market success and the general image of coffee was decisively shifted.[52] Indeed, the successful piggybacking of instant and regular coffee still thrives. In 1992 and 1993 a soap-opera-esque series of advertisements for Nestlé's Taster's Choice instant coffee brand featured a young, attractive couple courting over the product in upscale apartments. The emotive ads produced a 10 percent increase in U.S. sales of Taster's Choice and a 40 percent hike in England.[53]

In another case, Miles Laboratories used psychoanalytic motivation research in the 1950s to discover that there was more to the buying motivations of heavy users of Alka-Seltzer than their apparent desire to cure headaches. As Miles found in 1950, when it commissioned Social Research, Incorporated, to conduct in-depth interviews with 278 people, there were two distinct personality types who tended to be receptive to using Alka-Seltzer. One type appeared in passive, fearful people "who are dependent and need protection" and tended to follow rituals. The other type appeared in rugged, nonintrospective individualists who "are aggressive, reality bound, unimaginative people who are deeply concerned about *overpowering* their world and controlling it."[54] The former group tended to worry about preventing major internal disease, while the latter merely wanted to tame headaches. On this basis, SRI researchers recommended that "headache and stomach appeals might be more effective if separated."[55] Years later, Treva Van Solingen, a long-time head of Miles's marketing research department, professed great satisfaction about the usefulness of such studies. Remarking on her firm's use of classic motivation research in the 1950s, much of it conducted by Ernest Dichter, Van Solingen recalled: "Well, I thought it was terrific, you know, and it was what the company needed. . . . We needed a great deal of psychology and whatnot in selling medicine. We've got to make them sick. We have to tell them they're sick so they go ahead [and buy and use Alka-Seltzer]."[56]

Toward a Science of Consumer Behavior

It was logical that the first step in the development of modern motivation research took the form it did. The first step away from abstract guesswork based on arbitrarily deduced lists of motives demanded that marketers pay much more attention to the actual psyche of the targeted buyer. The power and importance of the psychoanalytic depth approach to gathering knowledge about targets remains tremendous up to the present day. As Rebecca Piirto observes,

> Motivational research is still alive and flourishing in the 1990s. The Freudian connotations have largely disappeared—researchers don't advise shaping gas pumps like breasts anymore—but many researchers report that their use of psychological research tools is up today from ten years ago. Major manufacturers and their market researchers are probing consumers' subconscious minds using everything from the one-on-one interviews and projective techniques once favored by Ernest Dichter to new high-tech tools that scientifically pinpoint consumers' emotional responses to brands and advertising."[57]

Nevertheless, by the late 1950s and early 1960s, marketers began to feel constrained by the one-dimensionality of the depth approach. Psychoanalysis, dwelling as it does on subconscious forces within individual minds, did not allow much room for a more panoramic view of human perception, learning, and decision making. Specifically, it did not facilitate motivation researchers' need to understand how societal forces impinged on targets' psyches. Hence, problems as wide-ranging as a lack of generalizability of psychoanalytic motivation research results, its relative inattention to social distinctions among its interviewees, and its pervasive tendency to lapse into contrived explanations of behavior—the 1950 SRI Alka-Seltzer study, for instance, tried to connect orality and anality with the buying motives of Alka-Seltzer users—became more obvious as corporate capitalism and business competition expanded. Depth interviews were strong at uncovering individual feelings but weak at systematically relating such feelings to the larger environment from which they mostly arose. As Piirto explains, by the late 1950s marketers were beginning to see that "finding out that a woman hated her father wasn't too helpful to a researcher trying to learn why she didn't buy Tide detergent."[58] Freudian psychology alone was too small a peg on which to hang marketers' widening knowledge demands.

Since the purpose of motivation research is to explain how people experience, operate in, learn from, and react to particular off-the-job behavior settings and marketing stimuli, it was only logical that motivation researchers would soon transcend the limits of their discipline and develop richer research procedures. By the 1960s, researchers began searching for fuller models of what corporate marketers began to call "consumer behavior."

The first step in this direction was to draw many formerly peripheral social sciences to the core of motivation research in order to broaden the agenda of its scientific questions. As one textbook explains, consumer behavior research was from its earliest roots "an interdisciplinary science" that "borrowed heavily from concepts developed in other scientific disciplines, such as psychology, sociology, social psychology, cultural anthropology, and economics."[59] Each of these disciplines made a special contribution to the widening effort to describe and comprehend the complex motivational dynamics affecting product users: psychology probed motives and learning processes, sociology laid bare group dynamics, social psychology charted the interface of individual and group, cultural anthropology facilitated the study of habits and patterns in everyday life, and economics touched on rational decision-making calculations.[60] Other important disciplines later brought into the motivation research fold were semantics, communications theory, and even philosophy.[61]

This new conception of the science of motivation research was accompanied by a profound methodological advance: the fusion of motivation research with market segmentation strategies in what came to be called psychographics. As Daniel Yankelovich pointed out in his 1964 *Harvard Business Review* clarion call to marketers, segmentation not only was useful for finding out which consumers had money but could be used to perform "nondemographic ways of segmenting markets."[62] By adapting the rapidly expanding analytical methods being developed in targeting research, motivation researchers could distinguish and document "important differences in buyer attitudes, motivations, values, usage patterns, aesthetic preferences, or degree of susceptibility."[63] By correlating such data with information about social position and general psychological profiles, marketers could develop a powerful new way of describing the empirical links between their targets' minds and specific behavior settings. Such methodology, Yankelovich concluded, could help ensure that marketers "never assume in advance that we know the best way of looking at a market."[64]

With this spread in the 1960s of a new breadth and sophistication on both the conceptual and methodological sides of motivation research, marketers were able to create within corporate walls increasingly nuanced and accurate models of the perceptual, learning, and decision-making processes of groups of targeted individuals. As Daniel Pope observed in his highly regarded history of modern advertising, from the 1960s on marketers have created increasingly refined focus techniques that have provided them with ever more fully fleshed portraits of how buying motives emerge from people's off-the-job experiences:

> Focus strategies, based on segmenting markets, targeting audiences, and positioning products, were behind many of the campaigns that typified the "new advertising" and the "creative revolution" of the 1960s. . . . [Such] segmentation campaigns are user-focused and concentrate on consumer benefits rather than product attributes. They show people with whom the target audience can identify, people who represent a credible source of authority for them or who express their latent desires and dreams. Marketers home in on consumers whose life-styles and personalities have been carefully profiled.[65]

As they have gathered better and broader psychographic knowledge about Americans—their color fetishes, their habits of television viewing, their brand preferences—and paired it with their increasing demographic knowledge, what had been in the 1950s only a keyhole view of people's off-the-job psychological processes has become a decreasingly blurry, increasingly lifelike three-dimensional image of shopping, buying, and commodity-using motivations. Moreover, the computer revolution has "rapidly increased the pace of methodological innovation," with the same powerful effects that we saw in chapter 3.[66] Indeed, as the Internet and other new media have been commercialized and disseminated, motivation researchers' tracking of individual minds has become even sharper, and the likelihood of further quantum leaps in two-way communication with households forebodes big businesses' eventual "real-time" monitoring of our off-the-job lives.

Consider, for instance, the Campbell Soup Company's progress. Drawing upon the fusion of empirical social science research and computerized control methods, Campbell has adopted an official policy of grounding all its marketing operations in a marketing research program that it calls the "Value of the Customer Process." As Piirto explains, this process "underscores the importance of core customers to the success of the business and recognizes the importance of finding out what makes them buy." Using databases, sales reports generated by supermarket scanners, and the Emotion Mining Company's "Emotional Sonar" system (a computer program that contains all the emotion words in the English language and gets focus panels of consumers to reveal their responses to marketing stimuli in a lifelike way), "Campbell segments households based on their degree of profitability and enthusiasm for the brand . . . [as] measured by tenacity and frequency of use. Once they rate panel participants on enthusiasm, they replicate the sample and get attitudinal and emotional data from them." The whole resulting program allows Campbell to go "one step beyond" its past ability to reconstruct accurate models of buyer motivations. The results, according to Campbell marketing executive Anthony Adams, have made the firm "close to ecstatic."[67]

Finally, while it remains to be seen how far marketers will ultimately get in their continuing efforts to abandon seat-of-the-pants approaches to describing and analyzing individual minds, consider what has already been achieved in this direction: Whereas instant coffee marketers were befuddled by the motivational causes of stagnant demand for their product in the early 1950s, by the late 1980s, another beverage marketer knew precisely where its problem lay. When Kraft–General Foods, a giant subsidiary of the mega-conglomerate Philip Morris Companies, found in 1987 that its primary targets, children four to nine years old, had come to prefer soda pop to its powdered Kool-Aid brand drink mix, it turned to its motivation research department to reverse the trend. Using a small part of its annual $1.7 billion marketing budget, it combined the information on 4 million working-class families stored in one of its computerized databases with motivation research into children's worldviews to create a marketing campaign that sharply boosted Kool-Aid sales. By 1990 children's previous 60-to-40 percent preference for Coca-Cola and Pepsi-Cola over Kool-Aid was exactly inverted—in favor of Kool-Aid. Sales boomed, and Kool-Aid claimed an 83 percent share of the powdered drink mix market.[68]

As such examples show, there has been steady pressure on marketers both to increase the sophistication of motivation research techniques and to widen and deepen their focus on specific groups, some of whom had previously been peripheral. Along with ethnic minorities, children are one such group. For example, the marketing professor James U. McNeal, the author of a book called *Children As Consumers,* in an article titled "Growing Up in the Market" in *American Demographics* enunciates the marketing motives behind this dual pressure: "The spending power of children is substantial . . . because children's income is almost all discretionary. They can spend it on just about anything they want, and they like to make their own decisions." Among trends documented by McNeal are a "remarkable growth" in childrens' "role in household decision-making," their preference for "fun" food, and their obsession with neon colors.[69] Given that the business race for profits is also now a marketing race in which large corporations endeavor to outpace their rivals in locating and stimulating new targets, this kind of expansion of the Consumer Trap is entirely logical.

By the turn of the new millennium, one could see the outlines of another new phase in the ongoing deepening and widening of motivation research. Their predecessors having passed from list making through the depth approach to social-scientific modeling of "consumer behavior," twenty-first century big business marketers were moving to draw the newest surveillance technologies into the science of CRM—customer relationship management.

The new and improved Taylorian nature of customer relationship management's methods was apparent in the example of the Brickstream Corporation, which offered big business retailers "discreet in-store video technology and patented 'image understanding' software to automate the collection of customer activity data in the store." Through its spy cameras and analytical software, Brickstream (note the intentional kinship to Internet-based clickstream analytics) offered to help its clients build "a complete understanding of your interactions with customers across all channels."

- "Where do customers go after stopping at a display?"
- "What path do customers take through the store?"
- "Do my in-store promotions attract customer attention?"
- "Are my self-service kiosks in the right location?"
- "What are the busiest sections of the store?"

Answering such time-and-motion questions about shoppers, Brickstream pointed out, required more vision and more understanding. "[E]xisting techniques for developing this understanding in [retail environments] aren't enough. Analyzing transaction data only provides limited insight into customer behavior. . . . Other traditional approaches—such as clipboard surveys, mystery shoppers, and focus groups—tend to be slow, expensive, and incomplete. You need hard facts that can show you the effectiveness of your relationship initiatives in brick-and-mortar channels, so you can make more informed decisions."[70]

Now, free time is not factory work. Yet as the advent of Brickstream and many other new motivation research techniques show, as corporate capitalism advances, there is less and less of a quality gap in big businesses' abilities to observe and analyze, à la Fred Taylor, subordinates' profit-producing "real-time" activities, on the job and off.

Big Business Marketing, Motivation Research, and American Society

The late, great sociologist C. Wright Mills once observed that power relations get worked out at points where people with institutionally generated interests meet and interact with one another. At such points, the conflicting purposes of individuals and institutions generate little everyday "crises" within which people strive to act out their intentions meet their goals as they relate to and influence each other. As they temporarily resolve these crises day in and day out, the resulting arrangement of verbal and physical surroundings forms the basis of "working vocabularies of motive" that "have careers that are woven through changing institutional fabrics." "Through such vocabularies," Mills concluded, "types of societal controls operate."[71]

The interaction of corporate marketers and their selected targets is a "crisis of motives" in precisely this sense. On one hand, people are moved to compose and conduct their personal lives and to decide whether to come to the point of purchase by their biological requirements and by their loyalties to, and memberships in, institutions such as households. Marketers, on the other hand, enter the nexus of off-the-job human motivation striving to support the inexorable profit making that drives their firms. Because marketers control goods and services and prospective buyers control the money that represents potential sales revenue, each party can perform his or her institutional role only by interacting with the other. Each makes choices, but these choices embrace and wrestle at a crisis point.

There is, however, a crucial difference in the institutions that bring ordinary product users and marketers together: ordinary product users' immediate decision-making environments are widely open to marketers' detailed influence, while marketers' institutional decisions are closed to everyone but authorized personnel. Hence, while decisions about shopping, buying, and using commodities remain a crisis for both product users and marketers, the former enter this crisis largely ignorant of the latter's motives and decisions and able—and perhaps to a diminishing degree—only to "take it or leave it." Marketers, however, come armed with formal, increasingly scientific analytical knowledge of their targets' motivations and with the consequent ability to intervene in planned and subtle ways in the environmental determinants of these motivations.

By the beginning of the twenty-first century, corporate consultants were even beginning to make a subindustry of "under-the-radar marketing," a motivation research specialty devoted to evading and exploiting the "marketing radar" by which many commercial-weary product users have learned to "immediately identify an incoming message as marketing" and ignore or dismiss it. "Pardon me, your strategy is showing," warn two under-the-radar specialists. To assist their clients in "finding the weak spot in those shields and getting through to the consumer's nerve center," the specialists recommend a host of new tactics, including maintenance of a room in their ad agency "that resembles a nine-year-old boy's bedroom" and to which they invite focus groups of children "to help our agency stay under kids' radar." Proper diligence in motivation research, they conclude, will provide "more ammunition with which to wage the costly battle to get under the radar." "One thing is for sure, advertising people are very resilient," they conclude. "Who knows more about 'new and improved' than we do? We're the ones who created marketing radar, and we're the ones who will figure out how to keep getting through it. Stay tuned."[72]

For commoners and their allies, all this is well worth tuning into. "This is the future—not a far-off future, but one that's just around the corner," writes journalist Simson Garfinkel. "The future we're rushing towards," Garfinkel notes, "isn't one where our every move is watched and recorded by some all-knowing Big Brother. It is instead a future of a hundred kid brothers that constantly watch and interrupt our daily lives. George Orwell thought that the Communist system represented the ultimate threat to individual liberty. Over the next 50 years, we will see new kinds of threats to privacy that don't find their roots in state totalitarianism, but in capitalism, the free market, advanced technology, and the unbridled exchange of electronic information."[73]

Garfinkel might have added that privacy is hardly the only thing corporate marketing puts at risk, and that, rather than Big Brother, our dominant institutions give us the now all-embracing ghost of Frederick Winslow Taylor, with its insatiable drive to make every particle of human activity feed the bottom line. As it works together with the targeting race, motivation research completes a process that is the direct counterpart of the time-and-motion studies that modern corporate production engineers have used to break human labor processes down into the smallest constituent parts and then reassemble them in fantastically more profitable—and, most often, deskilled, forms. As corporations adopt such marketing research practices as "Segment-of-One Marketing," in which they keep detailed, computerized, and cross-tabulated records of customer traits, preferences, and histories, and as they use their motivation research procedures to discover how colors stimulate children's senses, how teenagers view and interpret the world, how young adults form mental associations, how they can "build images" that get people to express their desire for helping with social causes by buying their commodities, and so on, they gain a powerful knowledge base from which to plan and implement campaigns of marketing mixes—commodities and sales communications—in ways that turn off-the-job behavior settings into showcases for behavior-modifying carrots and sticks.[74] In the process, the ground is scientifically prepared for the actual interventions into personal life that we examine in the next two chapters.

5. The Product Management Race

In the workplace, corporate industrial engineers and efficiency experts study employees' on-the-job practices in order to profitably redesign the machines, workspaces, and job instructions that shape those practices. Meanwhile, in corporate suites and laboratories, big business marketers use marketing research to redesign their firms' "marketing mixes"—the actual objects, images, and events that convey the carrots and sticks they hope will profitably alter targets' off-the-job behavior.

Nobody would be surprised to hear that advertising is a major element of most corporate marketing mixes. It may be surprising, though, to learn that corporate marketers conceive of goods and services themselves as vehicles for profitably manipulating our off-the-job behaviors. But it is true. Miles Laboratories, for example, defines its Alka-Seltzer products not just as aspirins, but as bundles of opportunities to create favorable perceptions and reactions among its prospective buyers. Likewise, Richard Courtice, a long-time marketer and product planner at Kraft Foods, reported that his job involved using "the product itself" as "support to get that product off the shelf, out of the grocery store."[1]

In big business marketing circles, the discipline of designing products as communications assets within the overall marketing effort is often called "product management." This chapter highlights product management's basic history and logic.

The Consolidation of Product Management

Well before the marketing revolution of the early 1950s, major corporations were using their new powers to proliferate unprecedented volumes of new products in new ways, but they did so without the benefit of mature marketing principles and operations. In 1912, for example, the Procter and Gamble (P&G) Company introduced its Crisco brand vegetable-oil shortening not as a way of managing end users' perceptions, but merely as "an attempt to generate a product that would assure P&G its supply of cottonseed oil."[2] While Crisco showed traits, in its packaging and brand name, that foreshadowed the future, P&G's concern with branding and selling it arose only *after* the fact of its design. In the history of modern marketing-driven product planning, its design was rooted in distinctly premarketing principles.[3]

The first major step toward consciously and rigorously making customer manipulation the main objective of corporate product design probably occurred in the 1920s, at the General Motors (GM) corporation. When Alfred P. Sloan became president of GM in 1923, he created a new formal relationship between marketing and engineering within the overall structure of management. Observing that GM existed "to make money, not just to make motor cars," Sloan reasoned that this overriding fact required the firm to abandon its inherited managerial habit of conceptualizing products mainly in terms of simple physical engineering standards. Sloan's idea was that the first principle of GM's product design processes should be marketability, and that physical engineering should serve this end. GM products were means of getting into prospective buyers' wallets, and their physical features should, Sloan insisted, do all they could to make that access easier.[4]

Hence, from the mid-1920s on, GM conceived of its products not simply as manifestations of automobile design, but as devices consciously arranged to attract prospective buyers' favorable perceptions and, of course, money spending. While Henry Ford had become famous for quipping that people could buy his cars in any color they preferred, as long as the color was black, GM aimed to use its products to engineer "consumer dissatisfaction with today's car."[5] The two main ways of doing so were the introduction of colorful paint jobs and "the innovation of the annual model change, which called for major styling revisions every three years, functional or not, with minor facelifts in between."[6] Behind these gimmicks was the first major case of a corporate managerial team trying to be systematic about using product attributes as ways to push buyers' buttons. In the process, GM's cars ceased to be merely cars and became aggregations of what would later be called marketing stimuli.

Corporate product management was also advanced by P&G in the 1930s. During this decade, P&G set out to introduce a new brand of soap called Camay, which it hoped would increase the large soap market share it already held with its Ivory soap brand. The firm's managers found, however, that, because they were still operating on the old, guesswork-based system of product management, their efforts were yielding less than stellar bottom-line results. To overcome this problem, P&G took a step that, for the first time, fully subordinated a corporate product management process to modern marketing administration: It created for each of its major product lines a "brand management team responsible for the marketing program and its coordination with sales and manufacturing."[7]

Despite the enormous—and underappreciated[8]—importance of these revolutionary developments in corporate product planning, most firms did not begin to coherently organize their product engineering processes according to marketing principles until after World War II. As *The Encyclopedia of Management* explains, both formal product management and its subordination to "the overall responsibility of Marketing Management" are "a post World War II phenomenon."[9] Indeed, even at GM, the triumph of marketing over engineering within management was somewhat shaky at the beginning: "Throughout the late 1920s," the corporate historian Arthur Kuhn reports, "Sloan's biggest managerial problems were to convince the Finance Committee to reinvest capital for GM's perpetual retooling and to cajole the divisional managements to change their products annually."[10]

In fact, most large firms seem to have followed the pattern described in the late 1950s by Robert J. Keith, the former president of the Pillsbury Corporation and classic recounter of the first days of the marketing revolution:

Our attention has shifted from problems of production to problems of marketing. . . . Here is the way the revolution came about at Pillsbury. The experience of this company has followed a typical pattern. . . . First came the era of manufacturing. . . . Our company philosophy in this era [c. 1869–1930] might have been stated this way: "We are professional flour millers. Blessed with a supply of the finest North American wheat, plenty of water power, and excellent milling machinery, we produce flour of the highest quality. Our basic function is to mill high-quality flour, and of course (and almost incidentally) we must hire salesmen to sell it."

In the 1930s Pillsbury moved into . . . the era of sales. . . . Pillsbury's thinking in this second era could be summed up like this: "We are a flour milling company, manufacturer of a number of products for the consumer market. We must have a first-rate sales organization which can dispose of all the products we can make at a favorable price. We must back up this sales force with consumer advertising and market intelligence. We want our salesmen and our dealers to have all the tools they need for moving the output of our plants to the consumer." Still not a marketing philosophy, but we were getting closer.

It was at the start of the present decade [the 1950s] that Pillsbury entered the marketing era. . . . With the new cake mixes, products of our research program, ringing up sales on the cash register, and with the realization that research and production could produce literally hundreds of new and different products, we faced for the first time the necessity for selecting the best new products. We needed a set of criteria for selecting the kind of products we would manufacture. We needed an organization to establish and maintain these criteria, and for attaining maximum sale of the products we did select. We needed, in fact, to build into our company a new management function which would direct and control all the other corporate functions from procurement to production to advertising to sales. This function was marketing.[11]

As they entered the marketing revolution of the time, other major corporations' replication of this "typical pattern" also reordered the relationships between their marketers, their product engineers, and their prospective customers. For example, in its 1952 annual report to stockholders, the General Electric Company (GE) trumpeted its adoption of the new, marketing-centered product management arrangement: "It introduces . . . marketing . . . at the beginning rather than at the end of the production cycle and integrates marketing into each phase of the business. Thus, marketing, through its studies and research, will establish for the engineer, the design and manufacturing person, what the customer wants in a given product, what price he is willing to pay, and where and when it will be wanted."[12]

As other major firms emerged from World War II and entered the marketing race, they took similar measures. "Once the new system proved its effectiveness," writes one marketing scholar, "it quickly spread to . . . consumer packaged-goods companies," and, shortly thereafter, to virtually all major "consumer, industrial, service, and high-technology companies."[13]

Products: "The Marketing Approach"

The supremacy of marketing over product design comes as bad news to some naïve engineers. Would-be corporate product designers, counsels one expert, "need to appreciate the aims and methods of marketing if they are to fully contribute to their companies' commercial success." Only by accepting this can they "understand otherwise inexplicable decisions . . . which limit their freedom of action. . . . All engineers need to understand that even in high technology companies, technological superiority is not sufficient by itself to guarantee success."[14] The hard reality is that, in the age of marketing, corporate product managers are not hired to build better mousetraps, but to provide "marketing design services"—that is, to build better peopletraps.[15]

* * *

Marketing professors break the same news to their beginning students. Fixation on product traits themselves, they point out, is old hat. In big business, the marketing approach rules. Products are viewed as means of behavioral control, not ends in themselves.[16]

In the millennium edition of *Marketing Management,* for example, Philip Kotler explains how the prospective new corporate product "moves to R&D or engineering to be developed into a physical product" only after "management is satisfied with [its] functional and psychological performance" as a bundle of marketing stimuli.[17] Prior to that, corporate planners engage in complex analyses of how a particular product idea might serve as a vehicle for "meeting needs profitably." In such analyses, marketers think about how the prospective basic product—the physical attributes to be produced and sold—might serve as tools for creating and managing "a set of attributes that buyers normally expect and agree to when they buy the product."[18] In making this assessment, big business marketers use focus groups, databases, test markets, and statistical models "to derive the consumer's utility function for each of the [possible product] attributes" under consideration.[19] For corporate managers, products can be judged well designed, Kotler states, only when their attributes and packaging promise to create sufficient "promotional value for producers."[20]

Some of the major strategies big businesses use to turn their knowledge of existing consumer behavior into "well-designed" product attributes follow.

Branding

Under the normal economic conditions of corporate capitalism, there are three great threats to the chances that any firm's products will successfully generate profits, two of which involve problems of user perception. First, there is the general problem of chronically stagnant demand. Nested within this larger problem lie the two problems of perception. On one hand, there is the possibility of people's *inattention* or *indifference* to a firm's products. If targeted customers are unaware of, dislike, or do not care about a commodity's existence, then sales and profits are impossible for its seller. Second, there is the possibility that prospective buyers will view the firm's products as qualitatively *indistinguishable* from competing products, that is, as standing in the relationship to other products that marketers call product parity. In that case, sales may occur, but they tend to become caught up in what Levitt calls "the purgatory of price competition alone."[21] When unchecked price competition prevails, as is the deepest fear of large corporations, commodities become embroiled in a downward spiral in which profits are undercut as prices drop.

These perceptual threats to business profits have presented marketers with intensely real challenges since before the triumph of the marketing revolution. Targeted individuals' inattention is always a threat to sellers and the risk of inattention is intensified by the incredible proliferation of commodities that has transpired as firms have waged expanding marketing battles. As more commercial goods and services flood the market, it follows that without more sophisticated marketing, the chances of any one item being perceived as useful tend to decrease.

Product parity is also a constant demon. Indeed, Tom Dillon, a long-time marketer on the Pepsi-Cola side of the famous "Coke versus Pepsi" marketing struggle, admitted in an interview that knowledge of the objective interchangeability of Coke and Pepsi always lay behind Pepsi marketers' activities: "In all honesty, most of the people we taste-tested these things on had a very difficult time discriminating one from the other. . . . It takes a large sample to find that edge. . . . And in fact, other than the image of Pepsi-Cola . . . it was really the equivalent to Coca-Cola. You were dealing here with a product parity situation. There was nothing to distinguish it in terms of its ingredients or stuff like that."[22] Likewise, Sheri Colonel, an advertising account manager who has handled the marketing of Cover Girl makeup for many years, admits in an interview that "There is definition between product lines—I could tell you what it is—but you'd be hard pressed to tell me what it is."[23]

This phenomenon is hardly confined to the soft drink or cosmetics industry. As Stuart Agres, the director of strategic planning at a major New York advertising agency, told the business journalist Eric Clark, "With rapid technological advances in manufacturing methods, a product doesn't hold its advantage for very long. Any product advantage can be ripped off very quickly. . . . The next manufacturer can not only duplicate those factors, but can make a feature of one upmanship."[24]

If you doubt the ubiquity of product parity, consider the evidence from just one batch of records from the files of a single advertising agency, which happen to be housed at one university library:

- "There are no unique Features that distinguish Champion from other spark plug brands," reads a July 1974 J. Walter Thompson "Account Summary" report to its client, the Champion Spark Plug Company—before recommending an advertising campaign designed for "gaining share of market by convincing mechanics and owners . . . Champion is top quality plug."[25]
- "Because of its "policy . . . to advertise and promote Shell's Premium Grade gasoline . . . there are many motorists using Premium Grade who do not need it," J. Walter Thompson happily reported to Shell Oil in September 1957.[26]
- "Under the new 1974 claim line ('Reynolds Wrap. The Best Wrap Around.'), the

creative execution is designed to position the advantages and benefits of Reynolds Wrap as being superior to other cheaper quality wraps," the Thompson agency reported in June 1974 to the Reynolds Metals Company corporation. Thanks to such efforts, "Reynolds Wrap's most unique feature is the brand's remarkable quality image with the consumer and the dominant share of the market it has been able to maintain over the years despite the fact that it is a 'parity product' . . . [the physical character of which] does not provide the product with an advertisable difference."[27]

- "The margin of difference [between film brands], virtually all offered at lower consumer prices, is slight and often unnoticed by the non-expert consumer," Thompson reported to Eastman Kodak in 1963.[28]
- "Virtually no smoker can tell his brand from others in a blind product test," it told the Liggett and Myers Tobacco corporation in 1969—in a presentation dedicated to planning new products.[29]

Thus it is no exaggeration to say that corporate product management is a battle to get targets to perceive firms' wares as useful, beneficial items while *studiously combatting the twin threats of inattention and the possibility that targets might perceive the parity of product quality within a product category.*

The conceptual foundation for marketers' war against the twin threats of consumer inattention and perceived product parity is aptly described by the marketing gurus Al Ries and Jack Trout in their 1981 book, *Positioning: The Battle for Your Mind.* In this marketing classic, Ries and Trout describe how, since marketing means making business-designed stimuli yield desired customer perceptions, marketing success means that "you have to sharpen your message to cut into the mind. . . . It's a selection project. You have to select the material that has the best chance of getting through."[30] The goal of this selection project, Ries and Trout underscored, is to calculate the best positioning of the firm's stimuli in relation to the targeted individual's mind. "Positioning starts with a product," they continue. "A piece of merchandise, a service, a company, an institution, or even a person. . . . Positioning is what you do to the mind of the prospect. That is, you position the product in the mind of the prospect."[31] This is accomplished by implementing in and around the product "changes done for the purpose of securing a worthwhile position in the prospect's mind."[32]

The general strategy that Ries and Trout call positioning was first enunciated by the General Foods Corporation (which later merged with Kraft Foods) in the 1950s.[33] From about that time, it has constituted the first layer of the foundation of product management. Ever since marketing's triumph over product planning, firms have universally struggled to combat their targets' inattention and the possibility that targets might judge their commodity to be qualitatively equivalent to competing products in the same category by designing product attributes so as to create a unique (or, in marketing lingo, "differentiated") position for them in consumers' minds.

In practice, marketers do this by creating and protecting *brands*.

In their modern form, brands are essentially managed personalities for products. As a leading expert on the subject explains,

> A brand is a distinguishing name and/or symbol (such as a logo, trademark, or package design) intended to identify the goods or services of either one seller or a group of sellers, and to differentiate those goods or services from those of competitors. . . . Although brands have long had a role in commerce, it was not until the twentieth century that branding and brand associations became so central to competitors. In fact, a distinguishing characteristic of modern marketing has been its focus upon the creation of differentiated brands. Market research has been used to help identify and develop bases of differentiation. Unique brand associations have been established using product attributes, names, packages, distribution strategies, and advertising. The idea has been to move beyond commodities to branded products—to reduce the primacy of price upon the purchase decision, and accentuate the bases of differentiation.[34]

Hence, product management becomes brand management, the point of which is to use product attributes to create in targets "a general liking or affect which is distinct from specific attributes that underlie it."[35] Success comes when such liking or affect becomes brand loyalty.

As Aaker notes, firms that maintain adequate brand loyalty among their targets enjoy six specific advantages in the race for profits:

> First, it [brand loyalty] can enhance programs to attract new customers or recapture old ones. A promotion, for example, which provides an incentive to try a new flavor or new use will be more effective if the brand is familiar, and if there is no need to combat a consumer skeptical of brand quality.
>
> Second, . . . the perceived quality, the associations, and the well-known name can provide reasons to buy and can affect use satisfaction. . . .
>
> Third, brand equity will usually allow higher [profit] margins by permitting both premium pricing and reduced reliance upon promotions. . . .
>
> Fourth, brand equity can provide a platform for growth via brand extensions. Ivory [soap] . . . has been extended into several cleaning products, creating business areas that would have been much more expensive to enter without the Ivory name.
>
> Fifth, brand equity can provide leverage in the distribution channel. . . . A strong brand will have an edge in gaining both shelf facings and cooperation in implementing marketing programs.
>
> Finally, brand-equity assets provide a competitive advantage that often pre-

sents a real barrier to competitors. . . . A strong perceived quality position, such as that of Acura, is a competitive advantage not easily overcome—convincing customers that another brand has achieved quality superior to the Acura (even if true) will be hard.[36]

For these and other reasons, corporate product managers define their duty as the careful development of product attributes that will make the best marketing stimuli. In their work, the physical properties of commodities become, in the words of journalist Naomi Klein, "filler for the real production: the brand."[37]

Planned Obsolescence

There are three standards of quality assessment that are relevant to the commodities that pervade American society: user-defined, science-defined, and marketing-defined. User-defined quality is the extent to which a given product approximates the ideal possible means of satisfying a human need. For instance, while it is always necessary to take into account the historical standards and contexts surrounding users, we can say that fresh organic fruits possess more user-based quality as foodstuffs than do pesticide- and fungicide-laden fruits and vegetables.

Science-defined quality is the extent to which a product embodies the highest possible technical standards laid open by science at a given point in time. If we judge, for example, writing instruments by today's technical standards, a ballpoint pen has more science-based quality than does a sharpened quill and a pot of ink.

Marketing-defined quality represents the extent to which a product strikes the optimal balance between a firm's need to (1) minimize its costs, (2) attract brand loyalty, and (3) fend off price competition. Although marketers would have us believe that the marketing-defined quality standard that governs their actions is always compatible with and reverent of user- and science-based quality, the truth is that both of the latter are secondary considerations within the big business product management process.

If we listen to the public statements of marketers, we might be tempted to overlook the real priorities of product management. Many corporations loudly proclaim their "commitment to quality"—the Ford Motor Company, for instance, has for years run marketing campaigns centering on the claim that at Ford "Quality Is Job 1." Likewise, slogans like "total quality management" and "zero manufacturing defects" have become commonplace in business literature. A little digging in marketing discussions of product quality, however, shows that *designing products with excessively high quality is in fact stu-*

diously avoided by marketing-era big business firms. As Kotler and Armstrong express this marketing rule, "we should not leap to the conclusion that the firm should design the highest quality product possible."[38] After all, too much user- or science-defined quality tends to cause two profit-dampening outcomes: Excessive quality both causes production costs to rise and extends the time that end users' needs are satisfied by the product, slashing into or—if quality levels were truly sky-high—killing repeat purchases.

In reality, corporate marketers *manage* commodities' quality based on their assessments of three factors: (1) users' perceptions of quality, (2) the degree of monopoly prevailing in a product category, and (3) the imperative to defend the commodification of human need satisfaction.

The first of these factors, what marketers call perceived quality, is fairly straightforward. As Aaker explains, modern product managers count on the fact that buyers' quality perceptions are "not necessarily based on a knowledge of detailed specifications"[39] and are usually shaped not by objective assessments of what it is technically possible to produce under given technological conditions, but are formed "relative to an intended purpose and a set of alternatives."[40]

Luckily for big business, because both these purposes and alternatives and users' perception of how to meet them are open to conditioning and control by marketers, there is wide leeway for engineering perceived quality via the marketing mix. While it is true that corporate products must ordinarily possess some degree of user- and/or science-defined quality—perceptions, after all, must normally have some basis in physical reality—it is equally true that modern big business product planners' first priority is the *perception* rather than the *reality* of product quality.

The second factor that determines the degree to which marketers consider user- and science-defined quality is the degree of monopoly in a given product category. In general, the greater the number of competitors' products and the smaller the relative market shares of each firm in the category, the greater will be the competition to win buyers via increased user- and science-defined quality levels. Thus, for instance, the notoriously abysmal quality record of the U.S. auto industry rose in the 1980s and 1990s, after globalization allowed six or eight corporations, rather than three or four, to hold significant market shares in selling cars to Americans.

A third factor that determines the level of quality built into products in the age of product management is business itself. If the Big Three auto firms *really* decided, for example, that they would use all their resources to provide Americans with the highest-quality transportation system possible, they would be forced to admit that this means a first-rate national railroad, extensive streetcar and subway lines, with a supplementary mixture of bicycles, buses, and safe, fuel-efficient, long-wearing basic cars and trucks. By making this entirely imaginary and unbusinesslike decision, they would obviously undermine their own existence as perpetual profit maximizers, since rapid car sales would wither away and perhaps die. Back in the real world of capitalist enterprise, because of their common interest in the profitable commodification of personal life, corporate marketers are extraordinarily careful about the directions in which, and the extent to which, they permit themselves to pursue objective quality standards.

In sum, the place of product quality management within product management is altogether different from what business publicity and the prevailing wisdom would have us believe. Rather than trying to put product users' interests first and then striving to make what users and objective scientists would define as the highest-quality, most practical, most beneficial, and most durable products, marketers manage all the facets of potential product quality in relation to what one marketing expert terms the minimum "threshold of [perceived] value" needed to win sales. This threshold is created not by product users' enforcement of absolute standards, but by user perceptions, market conditions, and competitors' offerings.[41] While there is obviously a wide variance in how such different firms' products embody the ideals of user-defined quality, there can be no doubt that the universal imperatives of profit making restrict and distort virtually all actually existing products' fulfillment of these ideals.

Marketing-defined quality management thus tends to generate a particular pattern of relatively high commodity quality in the narrowest sense and often egregiously low quality in the fullest sense, as entire categories of relatively well-made goods and services are called into existence that, from the product user's or scientist's perspective, are of dubious quality. As a result, U.S. travelers buy cars that, while certainly not near to embodying the objective ideals of possible scientific design, are nonetheless fairly functional and useful in the short run. Yet travelers also sit in traffic jams and experience death, disease, and injury in and through these products, all while marketers work to ensure that auto buyers lack the opportunity to weigh the merits of diverting the massive stream of auto-relating spending into public transport. Americans also buy and drink staggering amounts of soda pop that is tasty and refreshing. They also remain largely unaware that marketers are planning their childrens' early acquisition of the taste for soda pop, all the while knowing, in the words of long-time Pepsi-Cola marketing executive Tom Dillon, that "Children really don't give a damn about the quality of what they eat" and that pop sellers' business turns on cultivating the tastes of "the little rascal here who swigs the stuff—which he shouldn't."[42] People also buy and use proprietary medicines that are relatively safe, hygienic, and convenient. Many of these same products are also extremely expensive compared to simpler, less packaged versions of the same remedies and can only be defended under questioning as not evil. Indeed, although it fizzes when dropped into a glass of water, Alka-Seltzer, for instance, is little more than a simple compound of aspirin and sodium bicarbonate, two of the modern world's least expensive commodities.

Planned Physical Obsolescence

Product managers also engineer products to maximize the rate of repeat purchases. This involves either consciously arranging features of products so that their useful lives will be briefer than they could be or designing new "generations" of commodities with the intention of rendering still-functional old ones obsolete.

The first common strategy of planned physical obsolescence is the most straightforward variety of what Thorstein Veblen aptly called sabotage. Big business owners' pursuit of maximum profits, Veblen observed, rests on their strategic "evasion, secrecy, shortage, waste, and delay" in the use of industrial assets. Along with restriction of employment and output to what the market will bear, corporate capitalists, Veblen argued, instruct their product designers to stick to business and forget about certain unprofitable frontiers of technical possibility. The absentee owner's care, Veblen noted, "is to create needs to be satisfied at a price paid to himself. The engineer's care is to provide for these needs, so far as the business men in the background find their advantage in allowing it." Such advantage, Veblen saw, insisted on building "a temperate scarcity" into the physical life of corporate products.[43]

The most famous example of designing a commodity to wear out before it would have if resources had been used to prioritize longevity of wear is the automobile, which has carried trillions of dollars' worth of gadgetry and styling over the years but still usually wears out after 10 or fewer years. Indeed, in the age of the corporate marketing race, the creation of artificially short lifespans for commodities is part of the planning of even the most seemingly innocent and mundane items, as demonstrated by this story, recounted by John Bergin, a vice chair of the McCann-Erickson advertising agency:

> A guy from [hygiene and pharmaceutical conglomerate] Johnson and Johnson said to me . . . this wonderful line in regard to baby shampoo. He said to me: "You know, John, I've always wanted to find out the greatest hero of our com-

pany and track him down. . . . He's the guy that put the screw cap on the bottle of baby shampoo, because we know that if you use one of those little dispenser-type things [a lid with a small squeeze or spray hole], the perfect pool will come out. But if you use one of *these* [a screw cap], a) it'll fall, slip, and b) the whole thing will be on your hands. . . . We've sold billions of dollars worth of this stuff because of that cap."[44]

A second way corporate product managers engineer early physical obsolescence is "reformatting" the attributes of commodities to force people to purchase new means of satisfying existing needs and wants. A good illustration of this type of manipulation is evident in the history of the compact disc (CD). Allan Kozinn, a music critic at the *New York Times* began to wonder whether the sound clarity of the compact disc really was, as music industry public relations insisted, the justification for supplanting the long-playing (LP) vinyl record album. He reported:

> Recently, some of my doubts about the CD revolution were confirmed in an interview with Norio Ohga, the president of the Sony Corporation, and one of the fathers of the CD. . . . I asked him whether he missed anything about LPs. In his response, he did not dwell on the new format's sound quality or its convenience, but on Sony's need for something to sell. "At the time we developed the compact disk," Mr. Ohga said, "the LP market was saturated, and the cassette market was beginning to slow down. We knew that we needed a new carrier. [W]ithin five years, we had kicked the LP out of the industry."[45]

As LP records and their supporting paraphernalia disappeared from stores, people were forced by this product management decision to buy new equipment and recordings to hear their favorite songs, even though few if any were complaining about records before they "died."

Marketers also have other, more surreptitious ways of planning the physical obsolescence of commodities. One such means frequently occurs when a corporation promulgates two or more apparently unrelated products with uses that impinge upon one another as part of the same profit center. For example, Michelin is a large French corporation that makes and sells tires. It also makes and sells a set of famous Michelin travel guidebooks. While these two products seem unconnected, the genesis of the travel guides reveals that marketing-driven product management secretly links the two. Kotler and Armstrong report that "Some years ago, the Michelin Tire Company found a creative way to increase usage per occasion. It wanted French car owners to drive more miles per year, resulting in more tire replacement. Michelin began rating French restaurants on a three star system. It reported that many of the best restaurants were in the south of France, leading many Parisians to take weekend drives south. Michelin also published guidebooks with maps and sights along the way to further entice travel."[46]

Styling: Planned Aesthetic Obsolescence

Because people tend to assess objects according to the standards of beauty of their times, all material things inevitably possess potentially perceived aesthetic qualities. Enjoyment of these qualities is an important part of life in any society, and the character of aesthetic enjoyments is one important yardstick with which we can judge the overall quality of life made possible by a social order. By consciously controlling the style conveyed by the product attributes they treat as marketing stimuli, corporate marketers profitably exploit the fact that people have aesthetic reactions to objects.

Product managers use style to stimulate attention and condition targets to associate products with images that increase the likelihood of purchase. Evidence of the priority of this principle within product planning abounds. Automobile shapes, for instance, are frequently changed to maximize their perceived sportiness, family values, and so on—all in order to attract more sales. One observer of marketing aptly describes cars as "two-ton packaged goods, varying little beneath the skins of their increasingly outlandish styling."[47] The style conveyed by packaging, a product attribute discussed further below, is especially important in creating favorable associations and in attracting attention to a product. Campbell Soup marketing executives, for instance, have spent time developing a special shade of the color red "associated with the color of Campbell's Tomato Soup" that is used in Campbell labels and advertising.[48] By the 1990s, corporate marketers were regularly commissioning "studies of involuntary physical reactions—eye movement, neural activity, heart rate—[that] show that color is the element of a package that triggers the fastest and largest response."[49] Moreover, in the words of one historian of packaging, despite the seeming inanity of marketing strategies based on such minutiae and "despite increasing consumer sophistication . . . , defensiveness, and cynicism . . . about marketing tactics, . . . it still works."[50]

The second major use of styling principles in product management is for "obsolescing the perception" of an existing product.[51] Whole industries in fact operate largely on the primacy of stylistic obsolescence. Clothing designers and manufacturers rely on a carefully managed fashion cycle of revolving colors, cuts, patterns, logos, and hem lengths to boost their sales by outmoding last year's apparel. Likewise, the sports shoe and apparel manufacturer Nike designed a new generation of basketball sneakers in the mid-1980s that "had kids lining up at stores an hour before they opened" to replace their existing shoes. The secret to this revolutionary design? The basic color of Nike basketball shoes was changed from white to black.[52] Even among products commonly referred to as consumer durables—household items intended to last more than three years—marketing research reveals that planned style changes are significantly effective in making "the mean replacement time ... smaller (i.e., earlier) than the failure time of the product" by an average of three-quarters of a year.[53]

Packaging

In the age of marketing, product managers have treated packaging as an inherent part of the commodity, one that is as important as—and sometimes more important than—other product attributes. Kotler and Armstrong explain that under the constantly mounting pressures of corporate capitalism, "marketers have called packaging a fifth P, along with price, product, place, and promotion.

> Most marketers, however, treat packaging as an element of product strategy. Packaging includes the activities of designing and producing the container or wrapper for a product. The package may include the product's immediate container ... ; a secondary package that is thrown away when the product is about to be used ... ; and the shipping package necessary to store, identify, and ship the product. . . . Labeling is also part of packaging and consists of printed information appearing on or with the package. Traditionally, packaging decisions were based primarily on cost and production factors; the primary function of the package was to contain and protect the product. In recent times, however, numerous factors have made packaging an important marketing tool.[54]

Indeed, a large proportion of corporate product packaging exists only to serve marketing objectives. This becomes more obvious when we consider, for instance, what shoppers find on a trip to the grocery store. Rather than bins or shelves of minimally packaged items described by simple labels and signs such as "toothpaste" or "soda pop," there are rows of toothpastes and soda pops whose ornate packages compete to bond buyers' attention to brand names such as Coke, Pepsi, Crest, Colgate, and Aqua Fresh. With a few minor exceptions—for example, in the case of truly fragile or potentially dangerous products that require special protection and care—the elaborate packages that have become typical since World War II change neither the objective usefulness of the commodities they contain and advertise nor the basic objective parity of the objects behind their brand auras. Nonetheless, they are essential platforms for marketers' planned behavior-modification campaigns.

Consider familiar packages as big business brand managers do—as stimuli designed to raise your brand awareness and interest. We find that Campbell Soup marketers tend to refer to their soup products as a mere substrate to the brand's familiar red and white labels. Meanwhile, Pepsi-Cola marketers, like so many other corporate sellers, spend enormous energy adjusting the color, shape, and iconography of the packaging of their flagship product, knowing full well that "It is the visual that carries nine-tenths of what it is you're saying, particularly in a thing like this, where there is in fact not a concrete, functional message. . . . We're in effect creating a little day-dream, and the link to this is this bottle of Pepsi-Cola."[55]

Product Proliferation

If we view commodities as marketers do—as managed aggregations of product attributes that work either more or less effectively as behavior-shaping carrots and sticks—we can see why the growing number of corporate products is another major logical consequence of marketing-era product management. Generally speaking, the more product attributes marketers sell, the more perceived value they can engender, and the more sales and profit revenue they generate. Hence, it should come as no surprise that product managers never stop trying to promulgate new commodities and add new features to existing ones.

Managed product proliferation has been a conscious part of modern marketing since at least 1957, the year that the *Harvard Business Review* published the definitive article on the subject. Its authors observed that "It is a rare company that can escape the impact of today's rapidly shifting markets and expanding technology. Existing products can be expected, in the course of time, either to be pre-empted by new and improved products or to degenerate into profitless price competition. Only through continually bringing forth new products can most manufacturing companies sustain their long-run growth and profitability."[56]

The first form that product proliferation assumes is what we might call the "new and improved" phenomenon, whereby firms churn out "line extensions" to get customers to use existing brands in new ways. Campbell Soup marketers, for instance, are constantly tinkering with packaging and other product traits in order to get people to buy and use up more Campbell's soup. Different can sizes (large "for the whole family," small for the growing number of single adults), package forms (plastic microwave dishes for children), and product formulations ("drinkable soups" for those interested in between-meal snacks) are all developed to increase the number and kinds of situations in which targets will meet their food needs by purchasing Campbell products.[57] In 1992 *Business Week* magazine reported that Campbell's product managers were at work developing products that could be eaten with one hand, so as to extend Campbell's reach into the automobiles of morning commuters too busy to eat breakfast at home. As the firm's former CEO explains, such planned extension of Campbell's products into more and more areas of targets' lives is a consciously planned response to "stagnant demand" for standard forms of canned soup.[58]

A second means by which product managers increase profits via product proliferation is the creation of completely new products and brands. By judiciously measuring the contours of how people buy and use products in existing markets, firms are often able to find a way to increase their market share by introducing a new product that complements their existing brands. By "filling out the line" of products offered by their firms, marketers aim to absorb more of the potential buying power associated with particular off-the-job habits. Offering full product lines assures firms that they are able to reach all classes of potential buyers of products. The automobile corporations, by following Alfred Sloan's dictum of proliferating car models "for every purse,"[59] are masters at managing this aspect of product planning, as are most large firms.

One interesting example of big business efforts to commodify previously uncommodified behaviors was the Noxzema Chemical Company's creation of Cover Girl makeup in the late 1950s. Noxzema's marketing staff had been telling upper management "We need products to advertise, and you don't have any for us. Now, what you've got to do to help your company grow is to get some new products." Noxzema marketers eventually came up with a plan to add the medication from Noxzema skin cream to the new Cover Girl product, in part to justify anti-acne claims designed to lure teenage girls into becoming buyers and users of makeup. In the late 1950s, teenage girls did not generally wear makeup.[60]

Full product lines also often serve to ensure that consumers use a large number of products to accomplish tasks that once required few or none. Hence, Peter Troup, the senior vice president for domestic marketing at Noxell, the P&G subsidiary formerly known as Noxzema, which now markets more than 600 items in its Cover Girl line of makeup, observes with obvious marketing pride that "today's consumer—she may use up to 11 products to get the natural look."[61]

A third product proliferation strategy involves adding functionless features to justify increased prices. One example of this type of product engineering occurred at the athletic shoemaker Nike. In the mid-1980s, Nike found that one of its main advertising slogans—the word *air,* which was intended to imply pillowlike comfort while running—was confusing to its targets, who didn't understand exactly what Nike meant to imply. In response, Nike product planners changed the design of Nike shoes by adding a new feature, the genesis of which is candidly described by the Nike marketer and product designer Peter Moore:

> There was a shoe that they [Nike research and development experimenters] had that they had cut a hole in . . . and you could see the [air] bag. Well, I thought that was an ingenious bit. I didn't give a damn if the thing worked or didn't work, I mean if the hole did something or didn't do something. But it was a great way of finally showing somebody what this thing "Air" was. Because people didn't understand—we did all the diagrams and everything else you wanted—but they didn't get it. They didn't really know what it was. But this thing . . . was a visual thing. . . . It wasn't pure. It didn't really do anything. There was really not much of a benefit to it.[62]

Despite the fact that it was functionally meaningless, Nike's vice president soon decided to "relaunch" Nike as "a technical company who does 'Air.'"[63] The business beauty of this "great bit" was that it allowed Nike to sell more profitable features to its targets by increasing their *perceptions* of Nike shoes' usefulness. Nike sales boomed throughout the late 1980s and 1990s.

A fourth product proliferation strategy involves building work that used to be done by commodity users into their firms' products in order to justify higher prices. Campbell, for instance, was in the early 1990s consciously planning to have its canned soups replace homemade soup cooking in Argentina and Poland. Lee Andrews, the new product manager of Campbell's Polish operations, explained to *Business Week* the difficulties of his firm's campaign to "replace mom."[64] According to a leading food historian, this sort of product proliferation strategy has dominated food product management since 1947, when firms first began to market what they called the built-in service of processed foods.[65] And, of course, the food industry is merely one example among many industries that thrive on commodifying people's off-the-job routines.

The Social Meaning of Product Management

Mainstream thought, which equates capitalism with consumer sovereignty and treats sales as a mere sequel and servant to product design, has things exactly backward. In the real world of corporate capitalism, material engineering is the mere sequel and servant to big business marketers' behavioral engineering projects. Rather than giving their engineers, designers, and scientists the freedom to explore the full range of possibilities for using science and technology to meet user-defined quality standards, marketers keep designers and scientists tightly leashed to the imperatives of their campaigns of profit-seeking demand management. Instead of making user-defined quality the basis for their plans, marketers gear product quality to their profit goals, which depend on threatening, enticing, and cajoling people to accept more commodified ways of living. "Research," in a famous quip by GM president Charles F. Kettering, "is an organized method of trying to find out what you are going to do after you can no longer do what you are doing. It may also be said to be the method of keeping a customer reasonably dissatisfied with what he has. That means constant improvement and change so that the customer will be stimulated to desire the new product enough to buy it to replace the one he has."[66]

While I discuss the enormous social and ecological consequences of corporate product management more fully in the final two chapters, it is important to note how profoundly institutional reality contradicts the ruling dogma that big businesses are diligent appliers of objective engineering science. In reality behavioral manipulation is the ruling principle in precisely the area that is supposed to justify big business's dominance over society.

In sum, products themselves—the very stuff of our vaunted American "abundance"—have, in the age of big business marketing, become sly reworkings of Dr. Pavlov's bell. Their wrappers, boxes, and attributes are, from their designers' perspective, mere carrots and sticks, albeit ones consciously and scientifically designed. They come into existence not to meet our needs in the best possible ways, but to get us to continue swallowing the power, privilege, and depredations of our overclass.

6. The Sales Communications Race

In the corporate workplace, telling employees what to do is the simplest part of scientifically managing their labor. "Use this machine in this way, or you're fired" covers most of what bosses need their work crews to understand. Scientifically managing people's off-the-job behaviors, however, requires much more elaborate and subtle methods of entering and instructing targeted brains. For big business marketing campaigns to be successful, prospective buyers must be made aware of the existence of the products to be sold and also persuaded to buy and use them, with luck repeatedly. In corporate circles, the art and science of using sounds and images to attract and "convert" prospective customers' minds is called sales communications. This chapter highlights the logic and expansion of this, the most famous of marketing's subdisciplines.

The Logic of Sales Communications

Making sense of the sales communications race is potentially fun, easy, and democratically productive.

Corporate sales communications, the most readily visible part of the marketing process, have only two functions, (1) to attract the attention of targets, and (2) by strategically focusing targets' attention on selected marketing stimuli, to reshape targets' attitudes, feelings, knowledge, decisions, and habits with respect to the proffered product. In marketing slang, attracting targets' attention is "delivering eyeballs." To deliver eyeballs *and* create profitable changes in targets' product-related perceptions and behaviors is to fulfill sales communication's professional tasks.

Although there is much academic hoopla about the importance of decoding the political ideology of advertisements, the truth is that most advertising and other kinds of sales communications are, as their best critics have realized, 99.9 percent simple behavioral coercion. "Force and fraud" was Thorstein Veblen's excellent diagnosis of the methods of both class-struggle-from-above and its corporate marketing branch. Force and fraud, in the form of psychological tropes, verbal intoxication, mental agenda shifts, subtle threats, false promises, and simple misinformation, was Veblen's diagnosis of how corporate advertising functions. "When trying to understand what an ad's really up to," writes the outstanding, level-headed modern ad critic Leslie Savan, "following the flattery is as useful as following the money. You'll find the ad's target market by asking who in any 30-second drama is being praised for qualities they probably don't possess."[1]

As Veblen and Savan suggest, properly decoding sales messages means correctly seeing what the message sender is trying to do to you. This is usually not about discovering hidden political messages but about recognizing and analyzing the devices by which the seller is trying to make you believe a false promise, surreptitiously threaten you, or simply change the mental context in which you see their product.

Because they have theorized themselves right past these simple but powerful points, even well-meaning advertising critics have had a disturbing tendency to botch their explanations of sales communications. The resulting critical void helps explain why, as the journalist and advertising historian Eric Clark has noted, despite their deepening annoyance with runaway commercialism, ordinary Americans remain underinformed about the basic logic of sales communications. "By the time he or she leaves High School, the typical American has seen over a quarter of a million TV commercials," Clark observes. Nevertheless, the process of advertising remains curiously opaque, perhaps even *increasingly* opaque. As corporate sales communication "has become more insidious, more persuasive, more a part of our everyday life, so it has become largely invisible. Its images are taken for granted. Advertisements have achieved a natural quality."[2]

Much of the blame for this passivity belongs on the doorsteps of academia, where advertising is frequently drenched in the latest theoretical fashion in hopes of unlocking its supposedly inscrutable ideological secrets. Theorist after theorist wades into advertising, ready to prove that it is political code designed to brainwash people into accepting their roles in industrialism, sexism, consumerism, and so on. Given their preference for theory-proving over realistic interpretation of known facts, however, such explanations always fail to convince. As a leading advertising historian puts it, the trouble with academic consumer culture stories is that, despite their heated "deconstruction" of sales imagery, their authors usually "read into advertisements more than meets the unaided eye" and "press too hard on the rather flimsy and evanescent material they are scrutinizing. Too often, they divorce advertisements from the business conditions and marketing strategies behind them."[3]

* * *

To help readers transcend the limitations of existing advertising criticism, I offer this brief review of its five main myths:

Myth 1: Advertising Equals Marketing

Would-be analysts and critics tend to equate advertising with marketing and assume that, by talking about the former, they have exhausted the task of explaining the latter. As readers of this book are by now aware, such an assumption is a very grave mistake. Advertising is but one part of modern marketing. To treat the two as equivalents is to radically understate the scale, scope, and power of big business marketing.

Myth 2: Advertising Is a Deep Ideological Force

Many—probably most—critics of corporate product advertising treat it as though its immediate aim were politics and its immediate power profound.

Critics such as Stuart Ewen have premised their analysis of corporate advertising on the proposition that corporate advertisers' main motive is "combatting bolshevism and 'class' politics in general."[4] Ewen's, though, is simply a false interpretation of the motives behind advertising. While most owners and managers of big businesses are undoubtedly opposed to the growth of coherent class struggle from below and often take or condone strong action to prevent and combat it, while ads do generally reinforce market values and can and perhaps should be read politically, and while advertising and marketing certainly have tremendous political side effects and implications, the truth remains that the vast majority of corporate advertisements are neither intentionally motivated by politics nor dedicated to directly political ends. In fact, corporate advertisers usually studiously *avoid* including political elements in their sales communications: A rejected Pepsi campaign "was open to possible interpretation as having a political significance at the time. Obviously, what you *don't* need to do is get a corporation in a place where its advertising may be made to appear to be for the benefit of some political purpose. It's a stupid thing to do. You just get yourself in trouble. You're practically bound to annoy half the people, one way or the other."[5]

A kindred misinterpretation is the common critical assumption that advertising is somehow magical, mystical, and profound in its effect on the human mind. One recent book by a major social historian of advertising, for instance, characterizes advertising as a carrier of "transcendent meaning," a "lyric of plenty," a "notion of magical self-transformation," "a magical aura," and a "dominant discourse."[6] The problem with such readings is that, whatever literary value they may impart to professorial tomes, they badly misinterpret the actual mechanisms of advertising, which are simpler in intent and shallower in effect than many critics imagine them to be.

Indeed, judging from what actual practitioners say, the basic principles of advertising are quite straightforward. Max Sutherland, an Australian marketing professor, psychologist, and director of MarketMind Technologies, explains:

> Why is it so difficult to introspect on advertising and how it influences us? Because we look for major effects, that's why! . . . We look for a major effect rather than more subtle minor effects. . . . These minor effects are not obvious but they are more characteristic of the way advertising works. . . .
>
> It is like a 'beam balance' [teeter-totter] situation in which each brand weighs the same. With one brand on each side, the beam is balanced. However, it takes only a feather added to one side of the balance to tip it in favour of the brand on that side. . . . When we look for advertising effects we are looking for feathers rather than heavy weights.[7]

Sutherland goes on to explain that advertisements are often designed to do nothing deeper than simply change "the order of alternatives" within the mind, to tweak targets' mental reactions and agendas.[8] In trying to engender what they call "top-of-mind awareness," marketers certainly rely on many important, meaningful, and complex forms of psychological manipulation, but the point is that the needed effects of such manipulation are not ordinarily as soul-penetrating as advertising scholars like to imagine. Often, sheer repetition of a message is enough to alter targets' behavior. As the Campbell Soup Company president, R. Gordon McGovern, observed "Simplicity and repetitiveness, of course, is coming on. If you look at television, we slam you over and over and over again and hope that some of it sticks."[9]

Even the *threats* marketers promulgate are quite flimsy, aiming to implant gentle little quasi-conscious reactions, not to transform an entire personality. Consider the advertising campaign of the Association of Playing Card Manufacturers from the early 1960s. Worried over stagnant demand for their product, corporate card makers hired the J. Walter Thompson agency to help them boost sales by "encouraging [people] to replace their old cards more frequently." The plan JWT developed was to run advertisements designed to "'shame people' into buying and having new cards on hand so that when company comes, they would no more have dirty, tattered, dog-eared cards than they would have filthy hand towels in the bathroom." Quite aware of the silliness of this trope, JWT reported to its client that the campaign would require "the whole problem of developing social pressure around the concept of dirty cards" to be "treated lightly."[10] This was not psychotherapy, in other words. It was selling.

This is not to deny that advertising has important psychological impacts or agendas. On the contrary, one of the most important traits of corporate advertising is its endemic antirealism. As Ed Vorkapich, a cinematographer's son who filmed Pepsi commercials for two decades, explains, advertising's guiding ethos, which he believes has now pervaded all forms of commercial photography, is deeply hostile to rational description and honest context. The advertising power of film, Vorkapich says, lies the fact that "it's a visual medium, not a literal one. It's a way to create an emotional response with visual language . . . on the screen. It's not what people are saying on the screen, it's what's happening."[11] The Campbell Soup marketer Joseph A. Prior, like other advertising managers, concurs with this view, explaining that advertisers tend to have a strong preference for television because they can control and "deliver more impressions via television . . . than in print."[12] Indeed, while he worked for Pepsi, Vorkapich's talents went into traveling the country shooting 25,000 feet of film of sun-drenched beach activities in a way that made the sports look "more beautiful than just the sport," that diligently avoided "tragic existence," that conveyed an idealized image of "feeling free," and that skillfully deployed "Freudian symbolism."[13] Vorkapich's scenes provided much of the imagery for Pepsi-Cola ads of the 1960s and 1970s.

So deep is advertising's antirealism that even when advertisers talk about using "realistic" imagery, they are almost always referring to *conjuring the impression* of realism rather than telling the truth. Hence, when Cover Girl makeup found that a combination of widespread feminist sympathies and hardened economic times meant that "perfection was no longer in," they very carefully altered the "perfect woman" tone of prior Cover Girl campaigns:

> The fact that she [the Cover Girl model] is not full-eyed looking at you, the fact that she has hairs flying, the fact that she has a chain that you can't see what's on the other end of—this is all by design, OK? We took her out of the frame as opposed to the way that you've always seen. . . . We made her a lot more friendly, a lot more approachable. Women [in focus groups] looked at this picture and said "She's so real." . . . *This [however] is still Jennifer: aspirational, Cover Girl*

model, on a set, voyeurism—all the buttons, but this lady's in control, she's running that set.[14]

Comparing any corporate advertisement to, say, a classified ad in one's local newspaper helps reveal how small a role pure description and objective information play in big business advertising. Even thinking about the themes of ad campaigns is revealing in this respect: As we've seen in this book, Pepsi's core advertising theme is youth imagery, Cover Girl's is whiteness, cleanliness, and youth, Nike's is superstardom and the appeal to nonfunctional "air," Alka-Seltzer's is relief of nondescript illness, *Glamour* magazine's is eponymous, and Campbell Soup's is warm feelings. Kraft Foods, perhaps, could be said to have something at least remotely resembling a realistic central theme—convenience—yet Kraft invariably presents even this theme in an idealized, syrupy, and target-flattering manner.[15] In addition, marketing researchers themselves have documented their own antirealism: one study in the American Marketing Association's *Journal of Marketing,* for instance, documented that by the 1970s, fewer than half of all U.S. television ads contained even *one* of fourteen possible sorts of informational cues about the product being depicted, and that only about half of magazine advertisements contained more than one such cue, while 99 percent of television ads conveyed fewer than three.[16]

This, of course, is not the place for a full discussion of the important subject of advertising's basic logic, but I would propose that the best way to understand advertising is to recall that marketing is a set of methods for turning elements of popular off-the-job behavior settings into effective behavior-modifying carrots and sticks. The best way to summarize how advertising works is to say that it is a set of managerial principles and methods for inserting symbolic threats, commands, promises, and enticements into such settings, with the intent, not of forever brainwashing the population, but of profitably altering mundane, often individually trivial, mental agendas.

Myth 3: Advertising Does Not Work

The mistake of treating marketing as a political or ideological brainwasher has an obverse, which is the claim that, because it typically makes some reference to established habits and attitudes, advertising is simply "a mirror" that has little independent effect on the people who perceive, learn from, and respond to it.[17] In his book *Advertising, the Uneasy Persuasion: Its Dubious Impact on American Society,* the sociologist Michael Schudson, with the academic radicals' labored interpretations in mind, argues that advertising is a relatively trivial influence on modern American life. In Schudson's view, because "people attend to messages they already agree with, perceive primarily those parts of complex or ambiguous messages that fit their preconceived ideas, and rely on trusted friends and relatives to develop opinions about the world," corporate advertising gets off as a minor force in the preexisting "consumer culture" Schudson believes the United States has always had.[18] Schudson portrays advertising (and, by extension, marketing) as, at bottom, merely "a signal system within the business world" which, although it has its marginal effects, does not cause "consumers to change their minds or to think a certain way about a product."[19]

While Schudson rightly takes advertising critics to task for their phantasmagoric, sophomoric pseudo-critiques of advertising, and while he recognizes that advertising is part of the larger institution of corporate marketing—which he treats as a mere ideology—his overall argument is misleading. Marketing studies have repeatedly shown that advertising often affects people's purchase, selection, and usage of commodities.[20] Indeed, if advertising did *not* produce important alterations in the movement of human minds and bodies—and this is not to deny that individual advertising campaigns often fail—why in the world would corporations pour so many hundreds of billions of dollars into it? Would shareholders and prospective corporate raiders not pounce upon and eliminate advertising, if it were not effective at boosting profits? Of course, they would.

Schudson also bypasses the question of how much of what people already know—how much of the knowledge and attitudes of the trusted friends and relatives to which Schudson appeals for his theory of wider, cultural knowledge—has been governed, constrained, or specifically formulated by corporate sales communications. When we know, for example, that "in four distinct instances over the past 100 years, innovative and directed tobacco marketing campaigns were associated with marked surges in primary demand from adolescents only in the target group"[21] and that the flow of massive cigarette advertising revenues into magazines that accompanied the ban of cigarette ads from American television led to a precipitous drop in the rate at which commercial magazines ran realistic and critical stories and features about smoking, it is dubious indeed for Schudson to conclude, on the basis of highly abstract social history, that "major consumer changes are rarely wrought by advertising. Advertising followed rather than led the spread of cigarette usage, and it was the convenience and democracy of the cigarette, coupled with specific, new opportunities for its use, that brought the cigarette into American life."[22]

It is important to note another major logical slip in Schudson's "dubious persuasion" argument: Schudson talks about what "brought the cigarette into American life," but this is not at all the same thing as asking what independent catalyzing effect advertising has had in this process. It is a truism to say that wider social, historical, and cultural trends always play an important role in facilitating the rise and spread of lifestyle trends. Indeed, if people did not possess lips, lungs, bloodstreams, and brains capable of deriving pleasure sensations from nicotine fixes, surely nobody would smoke tobacco leaves. Corporate advertising and marketing are not God. "We know only half our advertising works," goes a common corporate quip. "The trouble is, we don't know which half."

The point—which Schudson, in his scramble to lay it all at the doorstep of consumer culture, bypasses—is, as Max Sutherland puts it: What force tips the balance-beam in one direction or another? If this force is advertising, then advertising, however small its immediate impact on the mind might be, *deserves the lion's share of the blame for the spread of the costly habits it promotes.*

Myth 4: American Television Is Bigger Than Advertising

Because they are blind to the corporate management behind it all, Americans tend to think of advertising as a subordinate part of television. Indeed, the maintenance of such a perception is integral to the continued success of the only true function of the thoroughly commercial U.S. television system—namely, the hooking and conditioning of viewers of advertisements.

In reality, television in America has always been permitted to operate as a subsidiary institution of modern corporate marketing. Marketers pay for the lion's share of the U.S. television system, which is devoted almost entirely to transmitting sales communications. Under such arrangements, as every television veteran knows, the programs are mere lead-ins to the advertisements, which are the raison d'être for the whole institution. Likewise, properly understood—that is, seen from the perspective of the marketing-funded architects of commercial television—the advertisements are there to force viewers to do *unintended shopping.*

Hence, American television, from the perspective of the corporate marketers who sponsor it, is merely another sales communication channel: The shows are hooks leading to the ads, which are vehicles of the flattery, threats, cajoling, and misinformation that serve as hooks for and teachers of profit-yielding behaviors. In the words of Ed Papazian, an advertising executive and consultant, "Commercial television is an enterprise ruled by business managers, whose primary responsibility is to their stockholders, not their viewers."[23] In the age of marketing, during which public broadcasting has remained puny, timid, and commercially beholden, American television has been neither more nor less than a machine for conveying marketing-designed sales communications.

Myth 5: Advertising Equals Sales Communications

Contrary to prevailing ways of thinking, advertising, while certainly the most familiar and intrusive of the functions of modern marketing and sales communications, is not the only means of corporate sales communication. Neither is it the part of corporate sales communications that absorbs the most money. And so, let us clear up this confusion by briefly examining the major varieties of sales communication campaigns that supplement and support modern advertising.

SALES PROMOTION   One gap in the possible range of selling activities left by advertising is the potential for distributing sales messages through special gimmickry outside mass media—coupons, rebates, sports and "event" sponsorships, "scratch and win" games, and so on. Marketers' term for such sales tactics is *sales promotion*. Kotler and Armstrong explain the typical rationale behind sales promotion: "Whereas advertising offers reasons to buy a product or service, sales promotion offers reasons to buy *now*."[24] Put differently, sales promotion functions like the catalyst in a chemical reaction: It is a special substance introduced to trigger a successful mixing of the main agent (the product stimuli and their general packaging in advertising imagery) with the reagent of the prospective buyer's perception.

The marketing consultants Kevin J. Clancy and Robert S. Shulman report that, in the early 1990s, major corporations were spending three times as much on product promotions as they were on advertising—at a time when U.S. advertising spending was approaching the $150 billion annual rate, and that in 1992 marketers distributed 310 billion coupons in the United States.[25]

PERSONAL SELLING   In addition to advertising and sales promotion, both of which address targets through nonhuman media, modern corporate sales communications includes what marketers call personal selling. This is the practice of employing people to make an "oral presentation in a conversation with one or more prospective purchasers for the purpose of making sales."[26] Because of the continuing need for the subtlety and sophistication brought to sales by human-to-human contact—a need that is especially great when "the unit of sale is large enough to support the cost of the contact[,] when the product is rather complex, . . . and when the product benefits have to be carefully matched to consumer's desires"[27]—this oldest form of capitalist selling not only still survives, but booms.

RETAILING   Selling products obviously requires not only the physical existence of products and the communication of sales messages, but a method of actually making them physically available for purchase. In the age of marketing, this has been defined as the problem of managing distribution channels, which marketers view as sets "of interdependent organizations involved in the process of making a product or service available for use or consumption by the consumer or industrial user."[28] In simplest terms, "a distribution channel moves goods from producers to consumers. It overcomes the major time, place, and possession gaps that separate goods and services from those who would use them."[29]

The aim of major corporations has always been to impose order and discipline on their particular distribution channels in no small part to maximize their effectiveness as venues for deploying sales messages. While intense interfirm conflict within distribution channels continues to shape decisions in this area—giant corporate manufacturers routinely squabble with giant corporate retailers over how to design and maintain distribution networks—the central story of retailing since the marketing revolution has been its increasing subordination to and integration with the overall marketing process.

One of the main by-products of this integration has been the post–World War II explosion of chain stores. As business journalist Stan Luxenberg reminds us, the postwar consolidation of marketing provided the institutional model that created "the crucial advantage of the chains":

> In the 1950s the franchise companies began their explosive growth by introducing corporate methods of finance and marketing to traditional small businesses. While once restaurants and barbershops were individual operations financed by the saving of one family, the chain builders discovered that they could raise huge sums by licensing outlets to owner-operators. Pooling funds from hundreds of small investors and borrowing from large institutions, franchise entrepreneurs could build big, eye-catching outlets. They could display standardized products in attractive surroundings. Compared to the gleaming chain stores, local businesses would seem shoddy and outdated. Unlike most local businesses, the chains could advertise heavily in the newspapers and on television. They could market hamburgers and motel rooms.[30]

As big businesses have taken over the bulk of the U.S. product-distribution infrastructure, they have increasingly made retail space itself a vehicle for promulgating sales communications. Corporate managers now look at retail outlets not simply as places to expose their wares to prospective customers, but as places that can be arranged as a further layer of marketing stimuli, as spatial and experiential propagandizers for brand names and corporate claims about their "distinctive ways of operating."[31] As the overall capacity and precision of their marketing programs have grown and as concentration of control over distribution channels has increased—Pepsico, for instance, by the 1980s owned the Pizza Hut and Taco Bell restaurant chains, each of which was previously a giant chain in its own right—the ability of corporate marketers to extend and refine the network of sales outlets has grown in roughly equal proportion.

As a result, big business marketers look at retail and other architectural spaces as "'packaged environments' that must embody a planned atmosphere that suits the target market and draws consumers toward purchase."[32] In effect, retail space thus takes on the same relationship to management as the factory floor: Both are manipulable and precisely controllable behavior settings.

DIRECT MARKETING   Direct marketing is "junk mail," "spam," and "telemarketing." It is growing at an astronomical rate. Clancy and Shulman report that "since 1980, for example, we've seen a compounded annual growth rate of approximately 16 percent in . . . the number of catalogs mailed to U.S. households."[33]

Such explosive growth stems from both the proliferation of sales communication outlets and the time squeeze engendered by the ongoing radical commodification of personal life. As Clancy and Shulman explain, "Americans today are pressed for time, are searching everywhere for convenience, and consequently are not cruising the malls the way they did a decade ago. They're shopping from catalogs that come in the mail, and responding to telemarketers on cable television. And they're buying everything from everywhere."[34]

PUBLIC RELATIONS   Finally, corporate sales communications includes public relations, which marketers define as the practice of "building good relations with the company's various publics by obtaining favorable publicity, building up a good 'corporate image,' and handling or heading off unfavorable rumors, stories, and events."[35] In its marketing role, public relations involves the use of communication tools such as press releases, product "news" announcements, lobbying and counseling activities, and strategic information dissemination to groom the general climate of public knowledge and opinion and to create goodwill for the more direct operations of demand management.

The Evolution of Sales Communications

Sales communication's development under modern corporate marketing has followed the same pattern as targeting, motivation research, and product management. The big business marketing race has caused major corporations continually to seek to create for themselves more efficient and effective sales communications operations than their business rivals possess. As corporate capitalism has continued to make it hard for corporate investors to find new investment outlets, and as marketing budgets have risen, sales communication, like the other subcomponents of the modern marketing process, has tended to grow larger in scale and more coherent in organization.

* * *

Up to the beginning of the twentieth century, tactics of what marketers now call sales communication remained comparatively very simple. When businesses were still relatively small and not highly rationalized, and when the commodification of off-the-job life was just getting off the ground[36]— business owners possessed neither the means nor the motivation to create highly developed sales efforts. Traveling sales agents jawboned storekeepers, who jawboned their own customers. Both performed, from rules of thumb, any coaxing that might be required to get shops and end-users to try manufacturers' new products.

In addition, from about the middle of the eighteenth century, sales agents were supplemented (mainly in the United States, England, and a few areas of Europe) by the bare rudiments of a system of printed mass-media persuasion that came to be known as advertising. Although Samuel Johnson, the great English scholar, opined in 1758 that "The trade of advertising is now so near to perfection that it is not easy to propose any improvement,"[37] judged by modern marketing standards advertising before the twentieth century was unsophisticated in design and execution, not very highly managed, and comparatively meager in its penetration of and impact on daily life.

This began to change with the rise of corporate capitalism. By creating an endemic tendency for the growth of popular purchasing power to lag behind the expansion of wealthy shareholders' investment-and-production capacity, the rise of the modern corporation almost immediately increased the need for more and better ads.

Consequently, many new, expanded selling methods soon emerged. This explosion was most evident in the emergence of modern, closely studied advertising planning. As Stephen Fox explains in his authoritative history advertising in the United States transcended its "prehistory" only at the end of the nineteenth century: "In the first decade of the twentieth century, the advertising agency evolved into something close to its present form. The innovations of the late 1800s pointed the business toward an emphasis on the ad itself instead of the selection of media or the size of the advertiser's budget."[38] Driving this transformation was the fact that, as more coherent sales communication became a commonplace necessity of business, advertising for the first time became comprehensively planned.

As ad planning took hold, a parallel deepening and widening in other dimensions of sales occurred. The number of sales clerks employed to help and cajole shoppers grew. Department stores greatly increased sales pressure through more convenience and more alluring displays. Firms began to engage in rudimentary forms of public relations.[39]

Despite the importance of this boom in selling activity during the early twentieth century, sales communications did not achieve full maturity until after the corporate marketing revolution. Only then were they first widely integrated within the overall structure of large corporations' marketing operations, and, thereby, fully and truly designed in accordance with the central business purpose of scientifically managing "consumer behavior."

The history of advertising proves this point. Before the maturation of marketing, advertising was very important to large corporations. Before modern marketing systems became supreme within most big firms' management regimes, however, most aspects of advertising were performed on the basis of indirect analysis and a patchwork of intuition, common sense, and guesswork. For instance, before targeting and motivation research became widespread central aspects of business planning, corporate advertising planners had only comparatively crude, generalized notions of who their customers were and how they perceived, thought, and acted. Likewise, without a conception of product management that consciously treated product attributes as part of a general campaign of stimulus manipulation, advertising was a much more after-the-fact affair than it would be when marketers could coordinate the whole marketing operation conjointly. Lacking a basis in these marketing disciplines, firms created advertising that was unclearly related to its intended purpose, which was to use mass communications to change the mental patterns of those who were likely buyers of particular products. Despite the leap forward from the precorporate age, early big business advertising was based in what the journalist Naomi Klein rightly describes as "rigid, pseudoscientific formulas."[40]

Marketers and advertising historians widely concur that, before about 1950, advertising campaigns were product-centered and pitched "reason-why" buying arguments to largely undifferentiated audiences. Since the marketing revolution, meanwhile, the trend has been user-centered messages intended to persuade precisely targeted audiences through themes of "self-fulfillment, escape, and private fantasy."[41] The product-centered strategy of advertising creation relied mainly on the deployment of advertising personnel to study the *product* and think of ways to promote it to prospective buyers. User-centered advertising planning involves analysis of *prospective audience members.*

As we would expect from knowledge of the marketing revolution, the transition between these two approaches to advertising management came in the 1950s, when advertising underwent what Fox calls its "second boom." This boom centered on a consolidation of advertising agencies that was driven by "the demand for more services. . . . In the years after the war, clients began to expect—in some cases were induced to expect—more service from an agency than simply the preparation of ads."[42] The new sort of demand was defined by the fact that the corporate clients of advertising agencies were widely transforming advertising into a subordinate part of their overall marketing operations. As a result, they demanded that agencies start "hiring more people in such fields as market research, merchandising, and publicity"—in other words, precisely in the areas that corresponded to the major functions in the marketing process.[43]

Evidence of the immersion of advertising within the structure of marketing after World War II appears frequently in the reminiscences of marketing executives. For instance, a long-time Kraft Foods corporation product manager, Jim Blocki, describes the place of advertising in his firm's transition to the marketing regime: "In 1956, the marketing concept evolved with Kraft and there was a marketing manager designated, under whom came a national advertising manager, a product manager, and a national sales manager."[44] Recall, as well, that Miles Laboratories moved decisively away from a haphazard sales approach to marketing by forming a marketing research department in 1946, at the same time that its top executives recognized that "when you get into advertising . . . you can't make off-hand decisions. You have to be steamed up [fully powered] with the background."[45]

In subordinating advertising to marketing, firms were simply responding to the new pressures arising from the marketing revolution's Taylorization of sales efforts. These pressures stemmed from the fact that, as Harlow Person foresaw and we have repeatedly seen, once marketing began to replace rule-of-thumb selling, firms who continued to plan any aspect of their selling operations via premarketing methods fell behind in the sales race. And, as J. P. Jannuzzo, the director of advertising and sales promotion at the ITT corporation, explains, when *advertising* is not rooted in marketing, "there is no optimum target market. Distribution plans are fuzzy, priorities are absent, and no thought is given to positioning or market segmentation. Under those circumstances, if you cannot fill in the gaps in the marketing plan yourself, you are defeated before you start."[46]

* * *

As the marketing scholars David A. Aaker and John G. Myers explain, the modern advertising planner is charged with the articulation and development of effective advertising plans that are "a part of the total marketing program" and therefore "must take into account the rest of the marketing program with which the advertising plan must be integrated." "Such an observation may seem trivial," Aaker and Myers note, "but there are many contexts in which this simple fact is forgotten. The result can be a marketing program in which the component parts work at cross-purposes instead of in a coordinated, synergistic manner."[47]

Modern advertising managers set advertising goals and budgets, plan advertising copy (the ads themselves), and select media to place the copy in. In so doing, they use a wide array of services and resources, including crucial institutions outside the direct ownership sphere of their firms. Most important among these facilitating institutions are advertising agencies, research providers, and available forms of communications media.

By the early 1980s, there were more than 8,000 advertising agencies operating in the United States, ranging from giant full-service agencies prepared to aid clients in developing all aspects of their marketing operations to small creative boutiques specializing in consulting on small aspects of the overall advertising process. Virtually all large corporations in the United States employ at least one advertising agency to supplement their internal marketing operations. As Keith L. Reinhard, the chair and CEO of the Needham Harper Worldwide advertising agency, explains, one reason that firms hire ad agencies is the relative distance of agencies from the internal culture of the corporation:

> Marketers—like the parents of prodigal children—are only human in viewing their products and services through rose-colored glasses. They have invested so much of their time, their money, and themselves in bringing to market that which they hope to sell that they are more or less blind to the possible drawbacks that exist in the products or in the market they are intended to capture. Agency people are the counterparts to a client's marketers, and they are able

to view the market itself and the products or services a client wishes to introduce in the context of other . . . marketing conquests in other worlds, so to
speak. They can spot a product's defects much more quickly than the client,
and they can assess the need for that product as a consumer would regard it.
Therefore, they provide an *objectivity* a good client finds well worth paying for.[48]

As the advertising apparatus continued to expand along with the marketing operations of firms—by the early 1980s, for instance, there were also more
than 500 specialized advertising research firms in the United States[49]—big
business gained increasingly sophisticated means and methods of relating
sales messages to targets. As Eric Clark observes: "In pursuit of why and how
people are prompted to buy, millions of consumers are constantly watched,
quizzed, divided and examined in almost every conceivable group and sub-
group. Their circumstances, beliefs, habits, and behaviour are continuously
measured and pored over. Trends are continually charted and analysed to help
determine which products are likely to become ripe for selling. . . . *The bat-
talion of researchers that provide the backup for the admakers is vast and constantly growing.*"[50]

As a result, although sophistication of design does not itself guarantee that
a particular advertising message will achieve its aim, there is little doubt that
the sophistication of advertising planning has steadily increased. As the advertising structure grows and becomes more refined, advertisers are able to
tap into expanding targeting and motivation research processes and adjust
their communication stimuli more finely and rapidly. "For the client," observes the advertising executive David Cowan, the connection between advertising and a constantly expanding marketing structure generally "means
more effective advertising, advertising that's more grounded in reality, advertising that's more scientific. . . . It's less risky."

For instance, Cover Girl makeup advertisers are able to draw upon increasingly sophisticated research techniques for getting their focus groups to respond to stimuli in order to help Noxell advertisers "create Cover Girl the
person, for the person, the woman, the consumer, to respond to, relate to, and
to like" and thereby learn how to give the target "a left hook" whenever she
"thinks she knows more about Cover Girl than you do."[51] Likewise, Campbell Soup advertisers are able to manage their efforts to associate their product with warm feelings on the basis of research that allows increasingly refined
analysis of "a household that we can look at, that we can size . . . up from head
to toe and look at what they're doing and who they are."[52] Meanwhile, Pepsi-
Cola continues "to make greater use of data bases that Pepsico units like Pizza Hut, Frito-Lay and Taco Bell [have] developed."[53]

* * *

The corporate marketing revolution has transformed other forms of sales promotion along the same lines as advertising. The marketing practitioners Bud Frankel and H. W. Phillips report that by the mid-1980s, "the vast majority of Fortune 500 companies [had] separate departments designed specifically for nonmedia marketing; and those departments are growing, both in size and in responsibilities."[54] They also report a growing sophistication in the design of a rapidly expanding range of sales channels, including coupons, rebates, refunds, premiums, sweepstakes, games, contests, trade shows, sample distributions, product tie-ins, stamps, trading cards, bonus packs, and point-of-purchase displays. Whereas, in the first days of the big business marketing revolution, firms deployed sales promotions on the basis of a relatively "simple strategy—produce great numbers of displays to show the product and distribute elaborate literature about the product," by the 1980s, sales promotion managers were drawing upon targeting, motivation research, and the rest of the marketing process to make disciplined contributions to the demand management process.[55]

One major nonadvertising element of the typical corporate sales communications effort is public relations. The historian Daniel Pope, for instance, lists public relations among those "tasks that corporations performed informally" before World War II but thereafter formalized and departmentalized.[56] As one case in point, the Campbell Soup Company in 1954 issued a press release announcing its decision to use its newly formalized marketing process to "expand considerably" its "public relations activity." In the press release, Campbell corporate vice chair Oliver G. Willits expounded on the transformation in the relation between Campbell and its public relations: "We once thought that being virtuous was good enough; but I understand that today one must not only be virtuous but also must tell people about it. . . . Advertising sells the product. Public relations sells the Company."[57] In the ensuing years, Campbell turned out a range of public relations releases to help it maintain a hospitable public climate for selling soup. Some aimed to combat government rulings barring Campbell from making claims about its soup's nutritional value. Some countered efforts by groups such as the Center for Science in the Public Interest to document the deceptive nature of Campbell's advertising. Some publicized Campbell's "Labels for Schools" program, through which schools receive free educational equipment in exchange for Campbell Soup labels that they collect and redeem with the firm.

Overall, corporate public relations operations have developed along the same lines as other aspects of salesmanship. First, there has been conscious integration with marketing. As Fred Berger, a top executive at Hill and Knowlton, explains, big business public relations functions within an institutional context where "the marketing manager plans strategy and tactics in such a way that all the communications tools are put to work in a concerted campaign that uses the strength of each to complement the others in the marketing mix."[58] This institutional subordination to marketing gives public relations a familiar tendency toward increasing sophistication of design. As Berger points out, public relations managers make use of the full range of targeting and motivation research in order to create a "carefully targeted message, precisely aimed at a specific audience and using the many means available to reach that audience."[59]

As the marketing race has expanded, big businesses have also funded a growing stable of firms specializing in the detailed documentation and analysis of people's responses to retail environments. One of the best-known of such research agencies is Envirosell, Inc., founded in 1979 by the former urban planner Paco Underhill. With a "Fortune 500 client list [that] includes The Gap, Ann Taylor, CompUSA, Unilever, Gillette, Hewlett Packard, Microsoft, McDonalds, Starbucks, Citibank, and Nationsbank," Underhill notes that "no university, to my knowledge, has ever attempted behavioral research in the retail environment to the degree that we have."[60]

Underhill and Envirosell are unabashedly in the business of bringing Fred Taylor's methods to the retail floor. "A phrase I find myself using over and over with clients," Underhill, echoing Taylor, reports, "is this: The obvious isn't always apparent."[61] Just as Taylor used stopwatches and slide rules to reveal labor-saving potentials concealed in workers' on-the-job practices, so Envirosell uses "patient observation and analysis" to solve retailing "problems that remain hidden in plain view."[62] Likewise, just as Taylor demystified the elements of workplaces for early corporate managers, so Envirosell shows its clients how "an important medium for transmitting messages and closing sales is now the store and the aisle," and how "many purchasing decisions are made, or can be heavily influenced, on the floor of the store itself."[63] "We can tell you," Underhill reports, "how many shoppers in a mall housewares store use shopping baskets (8 percent), and how many of those who actually take baskets actually buy something (75 percent) compared to those who buy without using baskets (34 percent). And then, of course, we draw on all we've learned in the past to suggest ways of increasing the number of shoppers who take baskets."[64]

Envirosell's rise and growth—Underhill brags that "Kodak told us we were the single largest consumer of Super 8 film in the world"—comports with the general logic of the marketing revolution. "As the competition gets heated, there is a need," Underhill writes, "for an edge—a science, if you will. . . . The science of shopping is . . . a highly practical discipline concerned with using research, comparison and analysis. . . . The list of particulars we're capable of studying—what we call deliverables—grows with every new project we take on. At last count, we've measured close to nine hundred different aspects of shopper-store interaction."[65] The pressure to extend such neo-Taylorian digging, Underhill opines, comes from corporate capitalism itself. "If we went into stores only when we needed to buy something, and if once there we bought only what we needed," Underhill observes, "the economy would collapse, boom."[66]

* * *

Since the days of Samuel Johnson, observers and critics have been tempted to announce the completion and perfection of sales communications. Such pronouncements, by focusing attention on the end results of the sales process, rather than on its management, miss the really important point that perfection in sales is not a matter of discovering some universal magic strategy that resolves all mental and physical obstacles to selling. After all, the ever-changing nature of human society, including the patterns created within it by marketing itself, makes this a hopeless fantasy. Perfection in sales communications came instead with the *rationalization* of selling that happened when modern marketing seized it and reoriented it to its real task—the scientific management of people's perceptions of, and contacts with, commodities. As the corporate marketing race has proceeded, corporate sales communications, which had already taken a great leap forward in the first half of the twentieth century, have been transformed from a ragtag, exuberant, adolescent collection of practices into a functionally subordinate part of the overall marketing programs of big business.

The Quantitative Growth of Sales Communications

As every longtime resident of the post–World War II United States ought to know, increasing refinement and rationalization have not been the only effects that the modern corporate marketing race has had on sales communications. Just as the means and modes of targeting, motivation research, and product management have been both thoroughly improved and quantitatively expanded by the marketing revolution, so has the sheer number of sales communications and sales communications "channels" exploded over the past half-century. Advertising, promotions, and direct marketing messages now enter the home in increasing quantities via the mailbox, the telephone, the television, the videocassette recorder, the DVD, the radio, the personal computer, and the window. Advertisements now adorn not just newspaper and magazine pages, breaks between television programs, and billboards, but also the tops of buses, the bottoms of golf holes, the walls of restaurants, the halls of malls, the bathrooms of arenas, the aisles and check stands of supermarkets, and, with the spread of "placement ads" and "integrated marketing," even the backgrounds and foregrounds of movies and television programs themselves.

Sales communications, in short, have penetrated a vast quantity of personal life spaces. This penetration has been fueled by steadily increasing monetary outlays. Between 1890 and 1929, advertising expenditures in U.S. newspapers and magazines—by far the leading ad vehicles of the early corporate era—rose from 0.59 to 1.38 percent of national income.[67] Since 1945, advertising has, in contrast, consistently absorbed something above 2 percent of U.S. gross domestic product. Year-to-year, advertising spending has dropped only a handful of times since the beginning of the marketing revolution.

Advertising spending figures are also less than half the quantitative story. Because other forms of sales communications have in recent decades grown much faster than has advertising, the overall amount of corporate spending on sales communications has grown at a much faster rate than has advertising. As Clancy and Shulman report, "during the last two decades, corporations have been shifting money they spend on advertising to buyer and trade promotion and to sports and event marketing. . . . The ratio, which was roughly two-thirds advertising/one-third promotion, is now three-quarters promotion/one-quarter advertising."[68] Clancy and Shulman concluded that by the early 1990s sales promotion was absorbing about *$420 billion a year* in the United States.[69]

Big Business Marketing, Sales Communications, and American Society

From the point of view of those who make and promulgate them, modern marketing sales communications constitute an attack—it is no accident that advertisers use metaphors of military conquest to conceptualize their work—on the "preference structures," "memory structures," psychological reactions, and mental interpretations that determine whether we buy products. Mental engineering at various levels is the overriding goal of modern sales communications. To name just one representative illustration of this fact, in December of 1983 Campbell Soup marketers circulated an internal confidential memo that assessed the effectiveness of its "Project Goodness" advertising campaign. In the words of the memo, this three-year campaign was "designed in stages to create high levels of awareness, develop attitude change, and increase soup usage" by conditioning targets to associate Campbell's soup with the theme of "nutrition/health/well-being." Its "consumer objectives" were "to create and maintain a significant increase in awareness of the nutritional news about soup" and to "improve consumers' attitudes toward soup in key nutritional areas" by altering "awareness," "recall of nutrition message points," judgments of soup's "salience . . . as a food for meal occasions," "image" of soup in "the primary message area," and "intentions to use."[70]

What are the consequences of the fact that huge business corporations are continually racing to extend and refine their ability to implement such interventionist intentions? On one level, the answer lies in the obvious explosion of such communications into virtually every niche of off-the-job life in the contemporary United States. As ads, junk mail, spam, and billboards come to urinal stalls, golf holes, gas pumps, and shopping carts, a growing percentage of the limited number of symbol perceptions that people are allotted in life are corporate sales pitches. Less directly, as commercial television, music, and movies shove aside other forms of communication, human consciousness and culture become more deeply subordinate to modern marketing and its drive to commodify personal life.

7. Macromarketing and Public Subsidy

Capitalist propaganda continues to imply that *laissez-faire* still holds—that, like the small manufacturers of Adam Smith's era, big businesses still treat their host societies "as an 'uncontrollable' element to which they must adapt."[1] In reality, as we have seen, corporate capitalism fuels a growing marketing race, in which the visible hand of management continually reaches farther and more powerfully into the social determinants of people's off-the-job behavior. Recall the words of the Interpublic advertising agency's founder, Marion Harper Jr.: "The work of marketing is successful exactly to the degree it penetrates and organizes the milieu of the customer in ways favorable to the enterprise."[2]

Reorganizing the milieu of the customer, however, is not all there is to modern corporate marketing. Because people's off-the-job milieux are always importantly influenced and connected by public infrastructures, there is also the issue of manipulating public policy. Corporations, Philip Kotler and Gary Armstrong remind their textbook audience, "operate in a larger macroenvironment of forces that shape opportunities and pose threats to the company. . . . Whenever possible, smart marketing managers will take a *proactive* rather than *reactive* approach to the marketing environment. . . . Rather than simply watching and reacting," these smart marketers "take aggressive actions to affect the publics and forces in their marketing environment." Such actions, Kotler and Armstrong report, include staging "media events to gain favorable press coverage," running "'advertorials' (ads expressing editorial points of view) to shape public opinion," forming "contractual agreements to better control their distribution channels," and hiring "lobbyists to influence legislation."[3]

The marketing term for managing the politics of the macroenvironment is *macromarketing*. As the marketing race has grown, big businesses have expanded and refined their macromarketing efforts, coordinating them increasingly consciously with their targeting, motivation research, product management, and sales communications efforts. By the early 1980s, macromarketing had become important and distinct enough to have its own professional research publication, the *Journal of Macromarketing*.

This relatively late consolidation and rationalization of macromarketing is partly due to the longstanding procorporate character of government in the United States. In his critique of the conventional idea that the Progressive Era of the early twentieth century was devoted to populist "political regulation of the economy," the historian Gabriel Kolko showed that "in virtually every case," leading Progressive Era politicians "chose those solutions to problems advocated by the representatives of concerned business and financial interests."[4] Kolko found that what the Progressive Era actually did was to institutionalize "political capitalism" as the norm in American governance. "Political capitalism," Kolko observed, "is the utilization of political outlets to attain conditions of stability, predictability, and security—to attain rationalization—in the economy," all, of course, defined in terms set by "the major economic interests." Under modern political capitalism, "rationalization," Kolko argued, means "the organization of the economy and the larger political and social spheres in a manner that will allow corporations to function in a predictable and secure environment permitting reasonable profits over the long run."[5]

Nobody, of course, knows the exact nature and full extent of the interplay between macromarketing and office-holding practitioners of political capitalism in the United States. Nevertheless, obtaining particular answers to particular public policy questions has certainly always been of great importance to corporations and their shareholders. Should governments build and maintain transportation infrastructures and provide for their free use? If so, should the favored and encouraged vehicle be the train, the car, the bus, the bicycle, the airplane, or some combination of those? Should governments build and provide subsidized access to housing? If so, how much, and of what quality? Should governments pour money and technology into public broadcasting and media content production, or should it sell the airwaves to private businesses?

Governments' answers to these and other core questions obviously have tremendous impact on the prospects for successful big business marketing. By briefly reviewing some known trends in the U.S. government's activities in these three key areas—public transportation, housing, and media policies—this

chapter encourages readers to begin to grasp just how important macromarketing and political capitalism have been in facilitating the marketing-derived
class advantages of the primary beneficiaries of corporate enterprise.

Cars

Is it mere coincidence that the corporate marketing revolution occurred in
the same decade in which the U.S. federal government passed the Federal-
Aid Highway Act of 1956? This law funded construction of the U.S. Interstate
Highway system, which a historian described in 1997 as "the greatest and the
longest engineered structure ever built" and "among the only human creations that can be seen by astronauts from an orbiting spacecraft" and which
all observers recognize as a decisive event in the turn away from rail transport in America.[6] The serious political work that led to passage of the highway act began in April 1954, when President Dwight D. Eisenhower "told key
members of his administration . . . to devise a 'dramatic plan to get 50 billion dollars worth of self-liquidating highways under construction.'"[7] In 1953,
$50 billion was 13 percent of the U.S. gross domestic product. (In 2000, 13
percent of the U.S. gross domestic product would have been $1.3 *trillion*.[8])

In 1956, after President Eisenhower asked Congress for approval on the
basis that it was "needed for . . . the general prosperity"; after careful shep-
herding by a special Eisenhower administration committee headed by a sci-
on of the billionaire du Pont family, whose main corporation not only manufactured "the explosives so necessary for road construction, but . . . also
owned a substantial portion of General Motors"; and after intense macromarketing efforts by a web of business interests from the construction, concrete, asphalt, rubber, and, of course, automotive and oil industries; the law
passed. The projected sums—and vastly more—got spent, and the interstates,
as well as hundreds of thousands of miles of other publicly provided automobile roads, were built.[9]

The subsequent public spending on automobile roads—which had reached
about $100 billion *per year* by the middle 1990s[10]—has been unmatched by
anything remotely like equal public treatment of the infrastructure of the one
mode of modern transportation renowned in Europe and Japan for its speed,
safety, convenience, energy efficiency, and relative ecological benignity: rail.
"During the [thirty-year] lifetime of Amtrak," the *Washington Post* admitted
in a September 24, 2001, editorial, "the government has put nearly 70 times
more money into highways and aviation than into the train system."[11]

Given that the private automobile system is probably at least 70 times as amenable to corporate profit-making as a comparably subsidized modern rail network would be—to name one relevant example, people who rely on the Paris Metro subway or Japanese bullet trains generally don't need to purchase themselves a new personal rail-car every seven to ten years—who could doubt the dominance of macromarketing and political capitalism over transportation in the United States? This dominance, together with the predictable effects of hundreds of billions of dollars of automobile and oil corporation marketing campaigns, have made public subsidy of automobile infrastructure and public hostility to rail systems more sacrosanct in federal politics than military spending, where Congress is famous for doling out more money than the generals ask for. Nobody debates the pattern. It just happens, because it must, as does a general public "unawareness of even the most conspicuous public obligations to uphold the automobile's sway."[12]

By any sane standard, the results have been a continuing human and ecological holocaust. By the standards of macromarketing and political capitalism, the massively profitable results have been cause for continuing celebration.

Suburbs

Because suburbanization is also vitally important to big businesses, it has also been both aggressively sought by macromarketers and lavishly encouraged by political capitalists throughout the age of marketing.

The business benefits of suburbs are obvious in marketers' eyes. First, suburban housing is often brand new, which means that every element of the house involves a new commodity sale, rather than a mere payment to a former owner of a previously owned home. "Year after year," report the architects Andres Duany, Elizabeth Plater-Zyberk, and Jeff Speck, "homebuilders return to the [National Association of Home Builders] convention in search of those new concepts and appliances that will give their houses *product differentiation,* that will somehow distinguish their output from everyone else's." The materials and appliances they adopt are, of course, largely corporate products.[13] Second, for the most financially well-endowed buyers, suburbanization has long represented an individualized and immediately available—i.e., marketing-friendly— solution to fears of the consequences of economic polarization in a racially segregated society. Third, suburbanization's low population density, greatly increased and convoluted commuting demands, and weakened ethical[14] and community bonds naturally fit corporate interests. Suburbs are ideal settings in which to get people into excellent marketing situations and states. Living far from work, shops, and civic life on a quirky side street, for instance, virtually demands a car. Spending great amounts of time in a house on such a side street is also prone to make one mildly lonely and bored—and thus inclined to flip on the tube or the Internet or to tinker with gadgets.

Just as macromarketing and political capitalism have delivered massive and continual subsidies to automobile marketing, so have they underwritten suburban homeownership. As the corporate marketing revolution was being consolidated, the federal government was funding easy mortgages through the Veterans Administration and the Federal Housing Authority. Under these programs, which facilitated half of all U.S. house sales between 1947 and 1957, the "monthly mortgage payment for a new suburban house," observes the architectural critic James Howard Kunstler, "was commonly less than rent on a city apartment, or the cost of maintaining an older city house"—as this, despite inflation, has remained the case. Likewise, "under [post–World War II] federal income tax rules, mortgage interest became deductible," constituting, in Kunstler's words, "another whopping subsidy for prospective homeowners." Given the tax breaks and free roads, Kunstler notes, "the American Dream of a cottage on its own sacred plot of earth was finally the *only* economically rational choice" for many ordinary Americans.[15]

Corporate macromarketers have aggressively defended this pattern of public policy, which, like automobile roads, is as sacrosanct as anything could be in federal politics. In 1974, for example, the J. Walter Thompson advertising agency planned and promulgated a marketing campaign on behalf of the National Association of Home Builders. "The strategic goal of the current 'Sensible Growth' campaign is to combat the environmentalist moratoriums on building," J. Walter Thompson reported to its client. "The campaign, targeted at key decision-makers in Washington and across the nation, seeks to instill in the community the idea that sensible growth is necessary and beneficial."[16] "Sensible growth," of course, was a marketer's positioning of continued suburbanization, which is, indeed, quite "necessary and beneficial" to corporate capitalism's primary beneficiaries.

Commercial Television

"Television," observes John T. Landry, a long-time Marlboro cigarette marketing executive at the Philip Morris corporation, "is the most omnipresent, intrusive medium in the history of communications." As such, Landry gushes, "when you use television right, it is by far the most effective medium" for conveying marketing stimuli. "You're using all the various appeals to the senses that you can take advantage of with television—just about everything except taste and smell—and, if you're doing it right, your presentation can even influence those senses."[17] What Landry gushes about, of course, is a particular form of television—the federally facilitated commercial television system that dominates personal life in the United States.

The reasons marketers love television are known to many media critics. Television watching is mildly hypnotic and mildly addictive. Televisual storytelling is a particularly effective vehicle for doing the kinds of things corporate marketers need to do—surreptitiously implant psychic threats, flatteries, tropes, and enticements; shift people's mental agendas; manipulate memory banks and information contexts. For these and other reasons, in the age of marketing, corporate capitalism simply could not exist without a pandemic addiction to commercial television watching. And, of course, studies document the existence and progressive growth of precisely such a pandemic.[18]

Beneath this reality, studies also show that, not surprisingly, political capitalism has always ensured the dominance of commercial interests over modern mass media in the United States. As documented by the media historian and critic Robert W. McChesney, ever since capitalists' political defeat of the broadcast reform movement in the mid 1930s, the corporate commercialization of broadcasting in America has been so "entrenched economically, politically, ideologically . . . the topic has been," like automobile infrastructure and suburbs, "decidedly 'off-limits' in public discourse."[19]

The hallmarks of subsidy in this area are the auctioning of airwaves to private purchasers and government's self-imposed severe restrictions on both public broadcasting and public funding for media content production. These policies and restrictions exist to serve corporations' macromarketing needs. Big business marketers are acutely aware of their reliance on sustaining a mass addiction to commercial television and its delicately and expensively crafted web of marketing-governed stimuli. If the public were to impose heavy taxes on private broadcasting and advertising, charge significantly steeper rents for its airwaves, or get seriously into the business of funding truly noncommercial competition with commercial providers of media content, this web would be subject to major attack and decline. Because that prospect is unacceptable to corporate planners and political capitalists, it is kept off the agenda, and the few existing venues of public broadcasting are, in the name of perpetual unexplained budget crises, themselves subjected to creeping commercialization and conformity.

The Marketing Race's Public Basis

But for corporate macromarketing and political capitalism, big business marketing would be far less dominant in Americans' off-the-job lives. Pro-marketing public policies in the areas of transportation, housing, and communications provide big businesses with enormous help. Such policies serve to deliver bodies and eyeballs to corporations in marketing-friendly environments and moods. Stuck in traffic to and from the 'burbs, hooked on commercial television, and dedicated by the intense and growing commodification of our mobile but isolated lives to the work-and-spend rat race, we arrive, soft and vulnerable, at the points where we contact corporate marketing stimuli. We remain uninformed and demobilized about how much of this softness and vulnerability derives from our masters' quiet, businesslike usurpation of our own democratic powers.

8. The Globalization of Marketing

Studying big business marketing's operation in the United States makes sense for two reasons. First, because of U.S. wealth, its early and relatively unrestricted tolerance for corporate capitalism, and its comparatively unscathed emergence from World War II, U.S. corporations have consistently gone first and farthest in marketing. Second, and because many ordinary Americans have both had access to significant labor incomes and remained so vulnerable to being targeted by corporate marketers, the evolution of personal life in America shows the logical consequences of permitting big business marketing to be the prime mover of off-the-job life in a wealthy society. Understanding the fate of ordinary product users in America permits us to assess the real-world consequences of corporate capitalism in the very area its defenders portray as the Promised Land.

Nevertheless, like corporate capitalism, big business marketing is no respecter of national boundaries. While a great many people still believe nationality denotes deep differences between people, big business marketers do not. In fact, as corporate capitalism has expanded and intensified its marketing race, big businesses have increasingly globalized their targeting, motivation research, product management, sales communications, and macromarketing operations. This chapter briefly sketches the logic and meaning of this important aspect of worldwide corporate capitalism.

The Logic of Transnational Marketing

The institutional powers and economic situation that together fuel the big business marketing race have long operated globally. As big businesses have grown increasingly able to incur marketing costs, and as the world economy has continued to make it difficult for corporate planners to find sources of profitable new investment, it has only been natural that big business marketers' endeavors should become increasingly international, as they have.

To corporations, a buyer is a buyer is a buyer, wherever he or she resides. The only question is whether and how he or she may be profitably manipulated into spending money on the firm's wares. Wherever there is a sufficient number of prospective targets, corporate marketing is sure to arrive.

Philip Kotler explains globalization in just this way. "Most companies," writes Kotler, would have preferred "to remain domestic, if their domestic market were large enough." Then, Kotler continues, "managers would not need to learn other languages and laws, deal with volatile currencies, face political and legal uncertainties, or redesign their products to suit different customer needs and expectations. Business would be easier and safer." In reality, though, business competition, the need for "a larger customer base," and the prospect "that some foreign markets present higher profit opportunities than the domestic market," Kotler reports, have been "drawing more and more companies into the international arena."[1]

According to Kotler, taking its marketing operations global presents the individual corporation with an added targeting burden. "The company must . . . decide on the types of countries to consider. Attractiveness is influenced by the product, geography, income and population, political climate, and other factors," advises Kotler.[2] "In creating all elements of the marketing mix," Kotler continues, "firms must be aware of the cultural, social, political, technological, environmental, and legal limitations they face in other countries."[3]

From the data it discovers about its targeted nations, "a company must decide how much to adapt its marketing mix (product, promotion, price, and place) to local conditions. At the two ends of the spectrum are standardized and adapted marketing mixes, with many steps in between."[4] The argument in favor of standardization is cost savings and higher profits. Kotler counsels aspiring corporate marketers that the viability of standardization demands some prior marketing research: "Rather than assuming that its domestic product can be introduced as is in another country," Kotler advises, "the company should review the following adaptation elements and determine which would add more revenue than cost: product features, brand name, labeling, packaging, colors, materials, prices, sales promotion, advertising themes, advertising media, advertising execution."[5]

As one would expect in a world of increasingly scientific marketing and intensifying intercorporate marketing competition, research shows that, by

the 1990s, the vast majority of transnational corporate marketing efforts involved significant degrees of adaptation. One team of researchers estimated
that 80 percent of foreign corporate marketing campaigns involved at least
one major alteration to the marketing mix. Corporations, they also found,
were moving toward marketing strategies "designed from the outset to be
susceptible to extensive modification to suit local conditions while maintaining sufficient common elements to minimize the drain on resources and
management."[6]

Money-saving common elements, meanwhile, are often repackaged tropes
and scripts that have proven to be profitable elsewhere. Peter Troup, the Noxell
Corporation senior marketing vice president, for example, explains how such
replication underlies his firm's Hispanic campaign for Cover Girl makeup.
"What we're doing," Troup relates, "is: We've gone to almost the early roots
of our commercials, which is 'A young girl is discovered and made a cover
girl.'" The marketing idea, says Troup, is "beginning that evolution, because
many of those Hispanics did not bring that core with them. . . . We're developing that aspiration. We're developing the beauty side of the equation."[7]

All in all, as big businesses use their growing demographic and psychographic databases to find ways of spreading such scripts across the globe, the
profit-seeking engineering of off-the-job behaviors has almost certainly become the single most powerful commonality in an otherwise fractious and
disunited world.

Global Effects of Big Business Marketing

Two trends endemic to the globalization of big business marketing strike me
as being especially noteworthy.

Trend 1: Americanization of the Lucky

By 2001 virtually every discussion of corporate capitalism included recognition of the increased importance of transnational business activities. Globalization, as the trend is now known, is actually as old as capitalism and has
always involved Third-Worlders providing cheap resources and labor under
duress to business investors, most of whom reside in the First World countries that house the majority of the most attractive "consumers."

By 2001, of course, globalization included a significant amount of transnational corporate marketing. While nobody knows its exact dimensions,
international marketing expenditures almost certainly mirror the pattern
exhibited by international productive investment. According to the Organi-

zation for Economic Cooperation and Development (OECD), "in the six year period 1993–1999, world [foreign direct investment] flows . . . increased from just over US $200 billion to around $800 billion in 1999, and [were] expected to have passed the US $1 trillion mark in 2000. . . . A distinguishing characteristic of world investment is that the vast majority is amongst OECD countries. More than 90 per cent of [foreign direct investment] world outflows originates in OECD counties, and in recent years the OECD has accounted for around three-quarters of FDI inflows as well."[8]

As global marketing operations have grown, they have increasingly subordinated three distinct populations to the same corporate imperatives that have dominated personal life in the United States for several decades. The first two such populations are ordinary Europeans and ordinary Japanese people. As corporate power and cold war dynamics have eroded these people's sources of democratic political resistance to big business, life in Europe and Japan has become more and more "American." The third group to be similarly subordinated is Third World elites, the small strata of local capitalists, oligarchs, and compradors who grease the rails of corporations' bargain-basement access to their local underlings' labor. Among all three of these groups, commercial television, automobile transportation, fast food, and branded personal products have already gone far toward the global replication of the American pattern of intensively commercialized and commodified lifestyles.

By 2001 there was a sizable literature available on this momentous trend. To the more comfortable writers, it appeared as a mildly bewildering, but essentially happy novelty. "One reason why Melbourne looks ever more like Houston," wrote Pico Iyer, "is that both of them are filling up with Vietnamese pho cafés." To Iyer and other mainstream thinkers, the global homogenization of personal life is simply a by-product of modern technology and travel. "Computer technology," Iyer says, "further encourages us to believe that the remotest point is just a click away. Everywhere is so made up of everywhere else—a polycentric anagram—that I hardly notice I'm sitting in a Parisian café just outside Chinatown (in San Francisco), talking to a Mexican-American friend about biculturalism while a Haitian woman stops off to congratulate him on a piece he's just delivered on TV on St. Patrick's Day. 'I know all about those Irish nuns,' she says, in a thick patois, as we sip our Earl Grey tea near signs that say City of Hong Kong, Empress of China."[9]

Less sanguine observers are more apt to emphasize the corporate sources and political and economic contradictions of the new transnational convergence of "free time" conceptions. "In cities around the globe," writes the Uruguayan journalist Eduardo Galeano, "children of privilege are alike in their habits and beliefs, like shopping malls and airports, which lie outside the realms of time and space. . . . Long before rich kids stop being kids and discover expensive drugs to fool their solitude and shroud their fear, poor kids are sniffing gasoline." This reality, Galeano reports, does not stop Colombian schoolchildren from asking a teacher hit by a car: "'What kind of car was it?' 'Did it have air-conditioning?' 'A sunroof?' 'Did it have fog lights?' 'How big was the motor?'"[10]

For its part, the United Nations Development Program observed that "local and national boundaries are breaking down in the setting of social standards and aspirations. . . . Market research identifies 'global elites' and 'global middle classes' who follow the same consumption styles, showing preferences for 'global brands.' There are the 'global teens'—some 270 million 15- to 18-year-olds in 40 countries—inhabiting a global space, a single pop-culture world, soaking up the same videos and music and providing a huge market for designer running shoes, t-shirts, and jeans."[11]

Trend 2: Dumping on the Poor

According to the United Nations, as of 1998, the richest fifth of the world's people accounted "for 86% of total private consumption expenditures," while the poorest fifth spent "a minuscule 1.3%." Beneath this radical spending disparity, the upper fifth ate "45% of all meat and fish, the poorest fifth 5%." The upper fifth used "58% of total energy, the poorest fifth less than 4%." The upper fifth owned "74% of all telephone lines, the poorest fifth 1.5%." The upper fifth used "84% of all paper, the poorest fifth 1.1%." The upper fifth owned "87% of the world's vehicle fleet, the poorest fifth less than 1%." "In 70 countries with nearly a billion people," says the UN, overall product usage in 1998 was actually lower than it had been in 1973.[12] And, given the high values of the percentages of product usage by the top 20 percent—86, 45, 58, 74, 84, 87—the reality obviously doesn't get very much rosier for the three-fifths of the world's people between these two groups.

Despite this breathtaking inequality, in a few crucial areas the world's poor majority are very important targets of corporate marketing.

CIGARETTES   Cigarettes, conceived as "a meticulously designed device for delivering nicotine" in carefully engineered doses, are extraordinarily important to corporate capitalists.[13] As products that are both very inexpensive to produce and, because of their extremely addictive chemical properties, ideal in marketing terms, cigarettes are truly global, an excellent means of lifting coins from even the smallest pockets.

As First World citizens have started rising up in opposition to the corporate-sponsored smoking holocaust, tobacco conglomerates have diverted more and more of their marketing efforts to more defenseless Third-Worlders. In a horrible irony, according to the Web site of "infact.org," global wealth disparities are actually proving to be the basis for effective corporate tobacco marketing campaigns in poor countries. "Outside the US," InFact reports, cigarette marketers' "central messages are wealth, health, consumption—in short, 'USA.' According to Kenyan physician Paul Wangai, 'Many African children have two hopes. One is to go to heaven, the other to America. US tobacco companies capitalize on this by associating smoking with affluence. It's not uncommon to hear children say they start because of the glamorous life-style associated with smoking.'" Likewise, "in emerging markets from Eastern Europe to Southeast Asia, transnational tobacco giants Philip Morris, RJR Nabisco, and B.A.T. Industries aggressively hawk cigarettes with slogans like; 'L&M: The Way America Tastes,' 'Winston: The Spirit of the USA' and 'Lucky Strikes: An American Original.'" "These themes, and the images that accompany them," InFact concludes, "expand the appeal of this deadly product beyond what has in many countries been an adult male market, to young people and women."[14]

Big businesses achieve these evil results by the same means they use to sell richer people cigarettes and other commodities—through tax-deductible targeting, motivation research, product management, sales communications, and macromarketing efforts.

ENTERTAINMENT   "The last time I checked," writes the social critic and former advertising executive Jerry Mander,

> about 80% of the global population had access to television. . . . In many parts of the world, the TV they see comes from the U.S., with very few local programmes. Even in places where there are no roads—tiny tropical islands, icy tundras of the north, or log cabins—they're sitting, night after night, watching a bunch of people in Dallas driving cars, or standing around swimming pools, or drinking martinis. Life in Texas, California and New York is made to seem the ultimate in life's achievements, while local culture, even where it's still extremely vibrant and alive, is made to seem backward and unworthy. The act of watching TV is quickly replacing other ways of life and other value systems. People everywhere are beginning to carry the same images that we, in the West, are craving: from cars to hairsprays to Barbie dolls. TV is turning everyone into everyone else. It's cloning cultures to be like ours. In *Brave New World*, Aldous Huxley envisioned this cloning process via drugs and genetic engineering. We have those too, but TV does nearly as well, because now life offers few decent alternatives.[15]

The common designs driving the globalization of commercial media, Mander argues, mean, in effect, "that every place on Earth should be more or less like every other place on Earth. Whether it's the U.S. or Europe or once-distant places in Asia or South America, all countries are meant to develop the same way: the same franchise fast food, the same films and music, the same jeans, shoes and cars, the same urban landscapes, the same personal, cultural and spiritual values—monoculture. Such a model serves the marketing needs of the global corporations."[16]

* * *

To fathom what a mistake it would be to ignore poor people's disproportionate suffering within corporate capitalism's increasingly global consumer trap, consider the case of Colombia, a nation-state with one-seventh the population of the United States, but only one-fortieth our gross domestic product.[17] There, the CIA reports that 55 percent of the population of 40 million reside below the official Colombian poverty line, and that the poorest 10 percent of Colombians receive only 1 percent of the money incomes going to Colombians.[18] Despite such startling facts, in 1998, guess which nation saw the highest percentage of advertising expenditures in relation to its gross domestic product. That's right: Colombia.[19]

This astounding factoid suggests at least two things. First, it signals that, in 1998, poor Colombians were probably at least as heavily inundated with cigarette and soda-pop advertising as were relatively fabulously wealthy commoners in the United States, Europe, and Japan. Second, if the UN is correct in observing that corporate marketing means "'Keeping up with the Joneses' has shifted from striving to match the consumption of a next-door neighbor to pursuing the life styles of the rich and famous depicted in movies and television shows," then ordinary Colombians must experience an inordinate amount of pain at the "social exclusion" of being "left out in the cold through lack of income."[20]

The extra costs the world's poor majority pays for its special relationship to corporate marketing are hardly confined to the psyche. Frances Moore-Lappe and Joseph Collins recount a story that conveys a basic pattern undoubtedly replicated in many ways throughout today's Third World: "Fanta Orange [soda pop] is Coca-Cola's biggest seller in Brazil after Coke itself. Despite its name, Fanta Orange contains no orange juice. Yet Brazil is the world's largest exporter of orange juice. Brazil sells almost all of its orange crop to foreigners, mostly to the United States, where Coca-Cola is one of the prime buyers for its . . . Minute Maid . . . brand. Brazilian consumption of oranges is very low and many Brazilians suffer from vitamin C deficiency."[21]

The Need for Global Democracy

Driven by their growing capacities to afford it and by corporate capitalism's effectiveness at creating rising incomes for the wealthy investors who remain its primary beneficiaries, big businesses are rapidly globalizing their marketing operations. In the process, they are increasingly homogenizing and subordinating to the dictates of profit making the personal lives and civil societies of the world's wealthier national working classes. They are also dumping cigarettes, soda pop, and other junk onto the world's poor majority, which is increasingly left to suffer more than its share of anger and sorrow at its exclusion from the more pleasant niches in the global consumer trap. The only thing worse than being targeted is not being targeted, one might say. The costs and dangers of this pattern of socioeconomic development are immense.

It remains to be seen whether the world's working classes can and will begin to respond to their marketing-induced plights by forging new democratic institutions capable of creating a better path to the future. The political, cultural, and technical obstacles to such a development are certainly very great, yet so are the reasons for movement in that direction. To see why this is so, let us now return to an assessment of big business marketing's overall impact on life in its purported Nirvana, the United States of America.

9. The Consumer Trap

How has corporate marketing affected the evolution of personal life in the United States? If we permit it to continue its present trajectory, what further effects will it have? To satiate our corporate overlords, what off-the-job habits have we ordinary Americans adopted, and what new ones will we adopt in the future? What do these coerced habits cost us?

Because such questions strike at the taproot of the claim that private enterprise is the end of history and the ultimate vehicle of human freedom, they have remained unanswered in this, the world's leading business society. Whenever discussion drifts toward these questions, conventional thinkers whip out the conventional defenses: People want and need corporate products. Americans have always been greedy. "Consumers" are free to choose. They bought the stuff, so it must be acceptable. And, anyway, look how trivial marketing campaigns are. How could "Coke Adds Life" be anything worse than a piece of low-brow silliness? Whom does it really hurt? Besides, corporate marketing allows us to enjoy a high-production, wealthy, free-market economy, which, as we all know, guarantees the maximum happiness of the maximum number.

Would it not be remarkable, however, if hundreds of very large, highly organized, rigidly purposeful organizations spending over a trillion dollars a year on behavior-modification projects achieved only minor results?

Of course, if you bother to frame the issues correctly and think things through, you begin to see just how diversionary the conventional excuses are. In reality, for at least several decades now, big business marketing has been a major influence on the ways Americans think, feel, and act. This chapter draws on what we have learned about corporate marketing to explain the mechanisms and implications of this influence.

Class Struggle in Personal Life

Thanks to capitalist propaganda and the timidity of social scientists, we possess little detailed knowledge of big business marketing's overall impact on ordinary Americans' personal lives. Corporate managers and consultants have nothing to gain and much to lose from the development and dissemination of such information. Hence, they have done nothing to promote it. Meanwhile, the stillborn tautologies of "consumer culture" and "consumer society" theory have blocked public-spirited scholars from asking and answering many proper and productive questions about the interactions of marketers and product users.

Nevertheless, there are ways to start drawing intelligent conclusions about this key topic.

First of all, it helps to remind yourself of what many corporate marketers began to take seriously with the marketing revolution of the 1950s: Contrary to capitalist propaganda, people's off-the-job choices are *not* simple products of some primordial realm of pristine, unalterable individual freedom. In the real world, people are social animals whose choices and actions—whether on- or off-the-job—arise as much from *experience* and *learning* within particular environments as from raw intelligence or instinctual, presocial forces. The importance of experience in human development explains, for example, why French people speak French rather than Japanese. The French are not born with innate Frenchness that generates their French-speaking. They speak French because they spend their formative years in France, hearing other people speak French. Likewise, we formulate our off-the-job decisions and actions in large part by reacting to and utilizing the various elements of what the classic marketing theorist Wroe Alderson called "organized behavior systems." The opportunities and cues composing our leisure-time environs will, along with our past experiences and our innate drives and capacities, shape what we do in these places.

As Alderson knew, our off-the-job organized behavior systems, even when not owned by corporations, can include a wide variety of stimuli susceptible to business management.[1] Consequently, even when we are outside formal corporate control, our learning processes are, for big business moguls, "not an uncontrollable, incorrigible force."[2] On the contrary. In the epoch of multitrillion-dollar corporate marketing, honesty requires us to admit that big business planning is one major source of influence over how we conduct our personal lives.

Despite our masters' insistence to the contrary, whenever and wherever a corporate marketer attempts to implant marketing mixes, what happens in

our off-the-job environments is a by-product of a little case of class struggle. On our side of such struggles, within broad limits—for example, we must
eat, drink, and sleep—we have the power to choose what we do with our free
time, and we fight to make that time as fulfilling as possible. Meanwhile, big
businesses have the power to implant objects, images, messages, and material infrastructures in our off-the-job behavior settings, and, thereby, to influence the choices we make in our personal lives. As we have seen, they do
so in order to maximize their shareholders' investment returns. The result
is that, unless you happen to be a wealthy major investor, your personal life
is a field of conflict with the ultra-rich.

* * *

Making sense of the evolution of personal life in the United States thus
requires an honest accounting of the motives and powers big business marketers and commoners bring to their interactions.

As we have seen, corporate marketers enter into relationships with their
targets with an unambiguous goal and clear social-scientific consciousness
of the relationship between human choices and behavior settings. Their goal
is to coax people into habits that maximize profitable consumption—in the
literal, "using-up" sense—of the firm's products. The means to this end is
disguised intervention in off-the-job behavior settings, aimed at unrecognized manipulation—entrapment, that is—of prospective customers' choices
and behaviors.

Despite their frequent public protestations to the contrary, in this endeavor
corporate marketers pay little heed to what a fair-minded observer would
describe as the best interests of their targets. As we have seen, Campbell's Soup
marketers are interested in promulgating marketing stimuli that "trigger soup
usage and accelerate consumption" and "bounce the per capita consumption of soup," regardless of whether eating more salty canned soup is what
prospective Campbell's customers really need.[3] Likewise, Pepsi-Cola marketers are interested in getting children and others to drink their products yet
confide that they "shouldn't."[4] Aiming at "getting the kind of usage we need
to support the brand," Alka-Seltzer marketers do not discourage, but *encourage*, the use of their product as a remedy for "the blahs," a "disease" they know
to be either a code-word for alcoholic hangover or a manifestation of hypo-
chondria. Nike marketers push people to buy $150 athletic shoes, knowing
that only a small proportion of their buyers use the shoes for athletic purposes.[5] Kraft marketers scramble to invent and inculcate new uses for their
products, not out of concern for the impoverished culinary lives of their targets, but in order to resolve their firm's overriding financial concern that, for

instance, their brand of cream cheese would "sit there and people would forget that it's there, and it would get moldy."[6] Cover Girl makeup marketers report with pride that they have taught women "'This is what America's supposed to look like, what you are supposed to look like,'" and also that women who "smeared it on an inch thick" most definitely "did *not* bother" the corporate conscience.[7]

These examples could be multiplied ad infinitum. The point is that corporate marketers put their own firms' profits ahead of the vital requirements and interests of their buyers. In big business marketing, the quality, appropriateness, and costliness of products are the means, not the ends, and only get advanced insofar as they are compatible with profit making.

Of course, corporate marketers do face one very great disadvantage in their relationships with prospective buyers: They do not *own* the right to issue commands to their targets. Employees can be openly bossed and penalized and fired. Prospective customers, however, are punishable only by the little daggers and candies of the mind from which marketers compose their "mixes." Unlike the situation of employees in the corporate workplace, nothing *requires* prospective customers to comply with corporate plans. While the ability to fire workers gives factory and office managers very broad rights to tell their employees what to do and how to think while at work, marketers do not hold the contractual right to compel product users to do or think in particular ways. We targets retain the right to leave or drive past the store, change the channel, hang up the telephone, or otherwise choose a course of action other than the ones desired by corporate marketers.

This right forces big business marketers to camouflage their attempts at behavioral coercion. Prospective buyers fully aware of the types and quantities of planning that go into corporate products, packages, and images would be likely to resist the manipulations and expenses they embody. Indeed, because their efforts are so very vulnerable to reason, in their contacts with their targets marketers are confined to stealthy methods of manipulation.

Fortunately for big business marketers and their primary beneficiaries, there are, as we have seen, many means of stealthily pushing people's buttons. In deploying these means, big businesses enjoy some advantages.

First, big business marketers bring superior knowledge to their relationships with their targets. While ordinary product users usually do not know very much about corporate marketers' methods, corporate marketers know a very great deal about the motives and methods by which their prospective customers compose their off-the-job activities. Recall, for example, that Kraft Foods maintains a computerized database of demographic and psychographic information on 70 million American households. As we have also seen, at any given time, the typical big business is conducting a host of studies, product trials, focus groups, and test markets. Such activities yield rich and detailed information about targeted populations' existing and potential habits.

The second specific advantage corporate marketers hold over product users is one-way communication. While ordinary citizens have virtually no ability to influence the boardrooms, back rooms, executive offices, shareholder meetings, and other venues in which corporate decisions get made, corporate marketers possess wide powers to implant their marketing mixes in households, streets, stores, restaurants, arenas, and practically every other nook and cranny of the venues that condition popular off-the-job choices.

To fathom the meaning of this advantage, try a brief thought experiment: Imagine a world in which corporate planners really were—as capitalist propaganda has it—open-minded public servants and in which ordinary product users could place a broad variety of pointed behavioral stimuli and suggestions before corporate planners, all designed to coax corporate leaders into making and distributing what customers wished them to make and distribute. To make the comparison fair, imagine also that corporate planners had no overriding reason—such as the profit motive—to choose one course of action over another, and that they very often made their production and sales decisions on the basis of a mixture of whim, emotion, and low-involvement learning, rather than on the basis of careful social-scientific study, analysis, and debate of narrow, goal-directed alternatives. In such an inverted, counterfactual world, most of us would probably readily agree that corporate planners would be largely at the mercy of the masses.

In the real world, of course, marketers influence prospective buyers, and prospective buyers—at least to this point in history—merely take it or leave it. Corporate power in personal life enjoys the status of a taken-for-granted force of nature.

* * *

Compared with corporate marketers, we commoners are naive and intellectually diffuse about the architecture of our off-the-job lives. We generally enter our off-the-job behavior settings with the simple intention of living the most enjoyable and fulfilling possible life. In so doing, we typically don't think about the fact that our off-the-job behavior settings bring us into power struggles with various corporate marketers. When we go home from work or out on the town, we don't see ourselves as entering into the class struggle. We just want to live well.

In our efforts to do so, we are more flexible than corporate marketers. While we form definite habits and preferences about the goods, services, and symbols that form our personal environments, we ordinarily don't have nearly as much riding on particular outcomes as do corporate marketers, who are rigidly concerned with profitable results. For us, the issue of whether, how, and why one or another particular routine gets adopted is much less clear and urgent than it is for marketers.

As I noted above, in this endeavor, we ordinary product users do retain the formal right to control many of the off-the-job behavior settings in which we choose and learn particular lifestyle habits. The right to control the distribution of attention and obedience and the material and spatial makeup of private homes, for instance, is usually legally possessed by the home's occupant. Even in stores, customers retain broad formal rights to go where they want and heed what they want.

The second major advantage we commoners have in our relationships with marketers is the power to veto marketing mixes. We can, for instance, block or ignore marketers' messages. There have even been cases of ordinary people combating the very existence of such messages, as in popular calls for cessation of kid-oriented cigarette advertising.

How Marketing Works

If contacts between corporate marketers and the vast majority of product users is a form of class struggle, and if both sides in that struggle wield some power and suffer some disadvantages, how can we begin to estimate the aggregate impact of big business marketing on personal life in the United States?

First of all, simple logic and observation allow us to conclude that there is no such thing as total domination by either marketers or commoners in their struggles over the shape of product-related habits.

On one side, while they may—as I contend below—have consistently held the upper hand in shaping off-the-job behaviors and behavior settings in the post–World War II United States, corporate marketers usually are not *entirely* able to disregard the requirements and interests of their prospective customers. Indeed, while every corporation would love to sell cars that wore out every month, light bulbs that burnt out in an hour, and other such maximally profitable commodities, the truth is that, given the existence of buyers' veto power and of business competition, there are usually certain minimal quality standards that corporate marketers must conform to if they wish to stay in business. This fact alone prevents complete victory for the logic and principles of marketing and commodification.

On the other side—and this side is most mythologized—it is likewise true that, given the nature of modern corporate power, it is patently absurd to contend that ordinary product users exercise complete domination over economic production and distribution in the United States. For one thing, even when a particular corporation faces total failure of its marketing campaigns—when its sales drop, rather than increase—this drives the firm in question back to its, not its customers', drawing board. This is a *capitalist* drawing board, from which it can ordinarily come back swinging, with "new and improved" behavioral stimuli. Moreover, while ordinary product users often ignore, and occasionally combat, marketers' coercions, by what set of presently existing institutions could we even conceivably succeed in formulating and implementing our own, truly autonomous plans for the production and use of goods and services? Lacking such institutions, in a great many areas of personal life, we are relegated to choosing from among corporate offerings.

So, admitting that actual outcomes reflect some kind of balance of power, how often and to what degree are corporate marketers able to succeed in redesigning personal life activities? Given the lack of public-spirited scholarly research on this topic, the best existing way of approaching this issue is to examine marketers' own internal estimates of typical *advertising* campaigns' success rates, and to treat these as a proxy measure of *marketing* campaigns' success rates. The advantage of this view is that, at least when they are talking to themselves, corporate marketers do not have too much incentive to distort the truth. If advertising workers and scholars delude themselves too much about the efficacy of their work, they lose their accounts and positions.

The best publicly accessible estimates of advertising effectiveness come from John Philip Jones, a marketing professor with twenty-seven years' experience as a working advertising executive with the J. Walter Thompson agency. In his book, *When Ads Work,* Jones reports the findings of his study of the reactions of a panel of 2,000 households in various regions of the United States to the different advertising strategies of 142 branded commodities sold in the year 1991.

By using the Nielsen Company's electronic technologies and self-reporting techniques to keep track of what advertisements this panel of households was exposed to every week, then correlating this knowledge with reports of what products they purchased in the same period, Jones was able to draw some solid conclusions about advertising's effectiveness. First, he found that the *advertised* commodities in his sample had higher market shares, had higher rates of penetration into households, and carried higher sales prices than did the *unadvertised* commodities he studied. Such facts strongly suggest advertising does have a significant positive influence on the level and rate of commodification and profit.[8] Jones also found that, for the 78 advertised brands in his study, advertising produced an average increase of 24 percent in short-term sales and an average increase of 6 percent in long-term sales.[9]

When Jones sorted these advertising performances into five quintiles of cases, he discovered that advertising did serious short-term damage—though, it is interesting to note, *not* long-term damage—to sales of the bottom quintile of his cases; produced very sharp short- and long-term sale increases for the top quintile of cases; and served as a long-term reinforcer of specific, corporate-designed buying behaviors for the rest.[10] In other words, about 20 percent of marketing campaigns are major failures in the short run. About 60 percent serve primarily to reinforce existing patterns of commodified behavior. Finally, roughly another 20 percent of advertising campaigns alter buyers' behavior in ways significantly favorable to the corporation.

By extension, these findings suggest corporate marketing as a whole is probably often successful in at least holding established corporation-friendly behaviors in place, and that the old advertiser's quip about half of advertising working is also a solid conservative assessment of the efficacy of marketing in general.

The Piranha Effect: Marketing's Aggregate Influence

If the story of modern corporate marketing ended at the level of the individual campaign, we could concur with the sociologist Michael Schudson that corporate marketing is, on balance, a trivial endeavor and a weak cultural influence. Judged solely case by case, big business marketing is rather unimpressive and unimportant. After all, the marketing campaigns of even the largest corporate conglomerates touch upon only a few areas of our lives. Likewise, even when new corporate products and advertisements truly transform the ways we think, feel, and act, the changes usually alter only small parts of our overall routines. Big business marketing thus seems to involve trivial matters—how we perform this or that little activity—and to shift our established conceptions of such activities only in a minority of cases, and then only by degrees.

Why, then, should we bother to think about big business marketing as a lifestyle teacher at all? A useful device for answering this important question lies in what we know about the behavior of the South American piranha. Zoologists have found that, although the individual piranha has very sharp, flesh-cutting teeth, piranhas *as individuals* do not pose much of a threat to the other organisms that cross their paths. Why, then, are there such spine-tingling legends about the piranha? If they are relatively harmless as individuals, why does their name conjure up images of carnage? The answer is that, while piranhas are quite innocuous as individuals, they can be profoundly potent flesh-devourers *when they act as a group*. When a sick or bleeding animal crosses the path of an individual piranha, not much is likely to occur. However, when a sick or bleeding animal crosses the path of a school of piranhas, only the bones of the unlucky beast are likely to remain.

With this piranha analogy in mind, let us briefly return to what we have learned about big business marketing. First of all, we know that the largest individual corporate marketers have taught themselves to view the off-the-job behavioral routines of prospective customers as raw material that can be managerially reconfigured. Second, we know that in striving to make themselves effective at such reconfiguration, large corporations are constantly inventing and refining powerful techniques of demographic, sociological, and psychological research into the determinants of product-related behavior. Third, we know that the power and coherence of the typical corporation's marketing apparatus has increased greatly over the fifty years since the triumph of the marketing revolution. The scores of large corporations that launched the era of modern marketing with marketing segmentation surveys, depth psychology consultants, 1950s television, and a few shopping malls have entered the new millennium as hundreds of much larger corporations using massive computerized databases, real-time behavioral monitoring, a rainbow of focus groups, studies, and surveys, and the contemporary multimedia to help them manage targets' activities vis-à-vis tidal waves of new products and new roadside, in-mall, in-store, in-school, in-arena, in-theater, in-flight, and in-home retail outlets.

Consider all this now from a holistic, social point of view. What if we were to say, following Jones's figures on advertising's effect on buying behavior, that, in any given year, 20 percent of marketing campaigns are abject failures; another 60 percent are as placeholders of established procorporate behaviors; and that only 20 percent of marketing campaigns are substantially successful at engendering significant new forms of corporation-designed behavior among target populations? What would this suggest about big business marketing at the aggregate, rather than the individual campaign, level?

Before answering, suppose we make the numbers even more conservative by making the further assumption that, of the 20 percent of corporate marketing campaigns that have substantial positive impact on their targets, only one-quarter—or just 5 percent of all campaigns—have really remarkable effects. This would mean that, out of every 100 corporate marketing campaigns, 20 would fail, 60 would merely hold the line, 15 would be mildly successful at behavior modification, and only 5 would be wildly successful.

At first glance, this may seem to confirm Schudson's "dubious effect" thesis. But this is precisely where the piranha analogy becomes indispensable to proper understanding. In the late-twentieth-century United States, product users are not subject to just 100 large corporate marketing campaigns, but to *several* hundred at a time. Even if we assume that only half the 1,000 largest corporations bring marketing campaigns directly to bear on prospective end users of their commodities, this would mean that, at any given time, there are 500 multibillion-dollar corporations inserting managerial stimuli into the spheres of personal life in which ordinary Americans spend their free time. Extending our assumptions, this would also mean that, in a given period, 100 of these campaigns would fail, 300 would be mainly behavior-reinforcers, 75 would be mildly effective engines of new behavioral routines, and 25 would be powerful behavior commodifiers.

If these assumptions are reasonable, two conclusions follow. First, ordinary Americans—even though the market segments they inhabit may not be on the receiving end of more than a small proportion of the full range of existing marketing campaigns—are, at any given point in time, surrounded in their personal milieux by scores of effective reinforcers and boosters of commodified, corporation-prescribed ways of living. Second, as this pattern of exposure to marketing stimuli is renewed over time, its behavioral effects snowball, as personal lives become increasingly inscribed with the effects of present and past exposure to marketing campaigns.

All in all, then, while individual corporate marketing campaigns nibble away at small elements of individual lifestyles, the aggregate effect of corporate marketing on individual lifestyles is much like the aggregate effect of a school of piranhas on a bloody cow wading in the Amazon. From the perspective of the commoner and the cow, the big meaning and traumatic effects reside in the combined action of small mouths, not in the individually trivial fish.

* * *

Looking at big business marketing's piranha effect provides a powerful explanation for many of the major trends in the evolution of personal life in the United States.

First, and perhaps most important, there is the fact that, as corporate marketers have used their behavior-modification methods to pursue their firms' profit goals, the collection of off-the-job behavior settings that encap-

sulate and facilitate personal life in the United States has been radically reconfigured to suit corporate marketers' purposes: Commodity-promoting
shopping malls, roads, resorts, and arenas have progressively supplanted
public spaces such as parks, libraries, train tracks, and wildernesses. To catalog such transformation would require a book all its own, yet consider again
one telling example of the aggregate impact of big business marketing—
commercial television. Commercial television, which exists to deliver pliable
"eyeballs" to corporate advertisers, has been sponsored by hundreds of billions of corporate marketing dollars. Few, if any, other forums for off-the-
job activity have benefited from anything like this kind of funding in the
post–World War II United States. From this perspective, is it any accident
that sitting in front of the set watching commercial television is the leading
leisure activity in the United States?

Corporate marketing's piranha effect has also transformed individual experience and learning. For starters, consider just the case studies at the heart
of this book. Alka-Seltzer marketers struggle to alter and constrain their targets' self-care routines; Campbell Soup marketers struggle to alter and constrain their targets' cooking and eating routines; Cover Girl marketers struggle to alter and constrain their targets' self-care routines; *Glamour* marketers,
on behalf of their corporate advertisers, struggle to alter and constrain a whole
array of their targets' behavioral routines; Kraft marketers struggle to alter and
constrain their targets' cooking and eating routines; Nike marketers struggle
to alter and constrain their targets' dress and footwear routines; and Pepsi
marketers struggle to alter and constrain their targets' cooking, eating, and
drinking routines. Now add to these examples the hundreds of other corporate marketing campaigns reinforcing or boosting the level and intensity of
the commodification of individual Americans' behaviors and behavior settings at any given time. With such realities in mind, the piranha metaphor
barely seems metaphoric. In the aggregate, big business marketing is a gigantic
influence on the structure and composition of American personal life.

To get one's mind around the enormity of the impact, it helps to draw an
analogy between what the wage-earning corporate employee confronts in the
corporate workplace and what ordinary individuals encounter in their off-
the-job living environments. In the corporate workplace, the worker steps
into a setting where the machines, spaces, and job instructions have all been
managerially studied and configured for maximal profit. Because of this, it
is not just the contractual power of the boss, but the various constraints and
enticements placed in the workspace by the industrial engineer that lead
employees to comply with the corporate behavioral agenda. The scientifically
managed design and layout of the machines plays a big part in eliciting what

the bosses want from their hirelings. Likewise, although nobody holds the formal right to boss our leisure-time endeavors, and though we pursue those endeavors in settings beyond the control of any single corporation, the fact that many hundreds of big businesses are constantly trying to use scientific management to more profitably manipulate the objects, events, and infrastructures of our off-the-job lives means that corporate management and profit maximization are nearly as ubiquitous there as they are in a General Motors car plant or the kitchen of your neighborhood McDonald's.

Thus, although corporate capitalism is certainly not a unified, centrally planned collaborative endeavor, in many important respects, the profit motive at its heart makes it operate, from the ordinary individual's perspective, as if it were. When it comes to the design of the environments in which contemporary Americans live out their off-the-job lives, the profit motive seizes hold of virtually everything. Although individual firms produce their behavior-modifying campaigns competitively rather than collaboratively, the logic of these campaigns is consistent, rigid, and clear: This aspect of people's off-the-job life, says each corporate interloper, is a field for marketing, for "meeting needs profitably."

Thus, the piranha effect. As each fish chews its small patch, the cow gets devoured. In the process, over time, the aggregate operation of big business marketing tends to (1) expand the number of personal life behaviors under the sway of marketing; (2) reinforce the growing number of previously commodified behaviors; and (3) continue to make a small but significant number of behaviors more commodified than they previously were. To view this process negatively: Because its individual corporate pursuers are so keenly interested in continuously raising their "share of customers,"[11] in the aggregate, big business marketing tends, over time, to leave fewer and fewer dimensions of personal life uncommodified or, from a business perspective, insufficiently commodified.

Commonsense reflection on history confirms this process. What percentage of meals eaten in the United States were cooked from scratch in 1945? in 2001? How much soda pop and fresh water did Americans drink in 1945 versus 2001? How many kinds of beauty products did American women use in 1945 versus 2001? How many packaged and prepared meals and snacks did people eat in 1945? in 2001? How much money did people spend on a conventional pair of casual shoes in 1945 versus 2001? In each of these areas and hundreds of others, the answer is that personal behavior has both increasingly come under the guiding influence of corporate marketing campaigns and drifted strongly *toward* the more commodified and *away* from the less commodified forms.

While ordinary people certainly did not plan these trends and remain only vaguely aware of their existence, ordinary people certainly bear some degree of responsibility for them. It is, however, a rather egregious case of special pleading to do what mainstream thinkers do if and when they even broach the subject of advancing commercialism and commodification—namely, blame the little folk. Ordinary product users, who, because their purchases can be used to accuse them of choosing what they get, usually take all the transferred blame for capitalists' costly, socially irrational actions.

The main problem with this conventional distraction technique is that it ignores the fact that ordinary product users remain shut out of major economic decisions. Corporations plan, design, and sell goods and services according to their own profit requirements, without providing any means of subjecting basic productive priorities to popular debate and vote. Meanwhile, as stagnant or falling wages and salaries and the rising cost of commodified living compel adults to increase their subjection to the job market, haggard, frenzied commoners find themselves increasingly immersed in and defenseless against big business marketing's embraces. Too tired and underinformed to think it through, people settle into the proffered world of micro-choices, where Ford versus Chevy is a live issue, but cars versus trains is most certainly not.

Ultimately, given what modern marketing is—a powerful, immensely well financed vehicle for implementing the plans of powerful organizations intensely interested in masterminding increasing commercialism and commodification—can there be any doubt where the bulk of the blame and credit belongs? It is basic honesty to observe that the aggregate piranha effect of big business marketing campaigns has been and remains a—and perhaps *the*—primary engine of the evolution of personal life in the United States.

Marketing and the Degradation of Personal Life

In prevailing discourse, the connection between the purchase and use of commodities and the overall quality of modern American life gets treated as a question of "consumer choice." In mainstream circles, the idea is that, as Daniel Boorstin would have it, modern marketing is a simple economic voting booth in which product users cast their autonomously derived ballots.[12] In this interpretive world, every choice of every commodity is by definition both primordially free and an improvement in the purchaser's welfare. In radical circles, meanwhile, the claim is that ordinary people choose to buy and use particular commodities because of the magic, albeit evil, spell of advertising ideology and because of their own selfish egos. One of the many deleterious effects of this alternative consumer culture hypothesis is that it short-circuits consideration of the actual frustrations, dissatisfactions, and costs borne by ordinary product users. Contenting themselves with concocting tales of how the masses became happily brainwashed consumers, would-be radicals have excused themselves from the work of tracking what is really at stake and what has actually happened between big business marketers and commoners in the United States.

* * *

In reality, the ongoing commercialization and commodification of personal life in America has been and is an outcome of the millions of ongoing, conflictual interactions between marketers and product users, with both parties bearing some of the responsibility for achieved results. On one side, big business marketers have intentionally designed and promulgated thousands of sophisticated modern marketing campaigns designed to encourage prospective product users to become users of ever greater amounts of their commodities. On the other side, ordinary people have at least accepted what was offered to them, albeit generally in an unwitting and indirect manner. Hence, realistic and fair explanation and debate of the relative shares of responsibility for commodification and the changing quality of modern American life requires a willingness to ask and answer a complex, two-part question: First, how much relative responsibility for trends does each side in the relationship bear? Second, what practical consequences does each side's pursuit of its logical interests impose on the achieved outcomes?

As I have argued in this chapter, corporations hold several important advantages—including superior financial, political, organizational, and knowledge resources, as well as their near monopoly over the right to make decisions about what to produce and sell. Because of these advantages, big businesses have dominated the evolution of personal life in the post–World War II United States, in which the advancing commercialism and commodification of human activities has been the main trend.

Disagreeing with this assessment does not, however, relieve one of the obligation to admit that big business marketing does have an impact on the real-world evolution of off-the-job activities. Henry Luce was correct in saying that corporate capitalism involves balances of power.[13] The relationships between big businesses and ordinary product users constitute one major variety of such power balances. Nobody honest can deny that both sides in such relationships have some influence and that corporations' interests and actions carry both benefits and costs for the people whom they try to manipulate.

For the reasons enumerated in chapter 1, there has so far been very little serious consideration of these plain institutional facts. What discussion there has been has counted only the claimed benefits of corporate activities, praising corporate products' allegedly ideal facilitation of personal freedom, convenience, amusement, abundance, and so on. Such discussion invariably suffers from an ahistorical frame of reference—many claims about corporate products' convenience, for example, take an exceedingly inconvenient, costly, and frustrating social environment as their ground for comparison—and from a spirit of biased boosterism. Yet I have no desire to quarrel with the proposition that the advance of big business marketing has created many very real lifestyle benefits for ordinary product users. Especially in the areas of abundance and amusement, who could argue with this point? For example, despite its roots in principles of planned obsolescence, who would dare complain about the overall impact of the compact disk player, a relatively affordable commodity that brings many hours of delight at low personal and ecological cost to its users?

Having said this, however, I must also point out that the obverse side of this point has so far gone virtually undiscussed for a half-century: Not only have corporate marketing campaigns brought many benefits to product users, but they have imposed many, and often very dear, costs as well. Although a full treatment of this important topic would require a separate book, I list below some of the major types of human costs that corporate marketing imposes on its targets as a natural, logical, normal part of its continued individual and aggregate-level operation.

1. Clutter

In the age of modern marketing, every possible off-the-job activity becomes a means for inserting a new commodity (including its packaging) into personal life. This causes intractable household messes, collective garbage gluts, traffic jams, waiting in line, and other complications.

2. Junk

Although many goods and services are now quite excellent in quality, there are broad categories in which we tolerate junk. Moreover, as we have seen, modern marketing does *not* use technology and engineering to maximize product quality, meaning that even the best products we now live with could usually be made substantially better under a different set of production and distribution priorities. Indeed, truly maximal quality, since it works against planned obsolescence and repeated purchasing, is understood to be against the interests of corporations. In reality, quality levels are now set in a balance between three factors: (1) what level of crappiness buyers will tolerate without too many returns, (2) marketing principles of planned obsolescence, and (3) the quality levels forced on firms by intercorporate competition.

3. Danger

In several ways modern big business marketing's promulgation of maximally commodified habits is simply hazardous to human health. The prime example is the American transportation system. According the Motor Vehicles Manufacturers Association of the United States, the industry association of car corporations based in the United States, between 1950 and 1989 there were more than 1.7 million people killed in automobile collisions in the United States.[14] This thirty-nine-year total, which does not count those who died as a result of air pollution and ignores the many more millions who have been seriously injured, but not killed, in car crashes, exceeds all U.S. war casualties in American history. These 1.7 million deaths are directly attributable to a socioeconomic system that puts private profits and maximum commodity saturation above all other considerations.

4. Puff and Fluff

Big business marketing promotes "light" attitudes and downright lies. On one hand, by massively subsidizing titillating pastimes that are averse to real controversy and, hence, friendly to the absorption of advertising messages, corporations make shallow frames of reference the dominant moods of life.

Also, though its messages are not as deep and bewitching as some critics believe them to be, as we have seen, advertising works via skillfully conveyed lies of omission and hyped-up nonsense. Given its sheer ubiquitousness, how could this not leave a residue of attitudinal effects? As the economist Robert Heilbroner puts it,

> I do not think we pay sufficient heed to the power of advertising in making cynics of us all: at a business forum I was once brash enough to say that I thought the main cultural effect of television advertising was to teach children that grownups told lies for money. How strong, deep, or sustaining can be the values generated by a civilization that generates a ceaseless flow of half-truths and careful deceptions, in which it is common knowledge that only a fool is taken in by the charades and messages that supposedly tell us "the facts"?[15]

5. Mobile Privatization

Another aggregate effect of modern marketing is to promote lifestyles in which individuals are so surrounded by goods and services that we lose touch with each other. As the late literary critic Raymond Williams explained, the big business drive to commodify life and to insert more commodities into each individual lifestyle, means that people tend to become more surrounded by goods and less surrounded by robust relationships with other people. Williams termed this process "mobile privatization."[16] Sitting at home watching television, driving in enclosed autos, and wandering through malls are all activities that lead to an atomized way of living. Cocooning is the trend. The danger here is this: People must know each other both in order to be sane and in order to make proper use of democratic institutions.

6. Narcissism

Narcissus constantly gazed into his mirror because he was not sure that he really existed. When people lead increasingly atomized lives, they tend to lose robust contacts with other people, meaning that they lose the human responses that help us all define and validate who we are as unique rational and ethical beings. When the quality and quantity of such contacts erodes, people affix self-concepts to shallow, commodifiable symbols.[17] The spread of vanity license plates is a good example of this psychic cost of commodification.

7. Personal Deskilling

As marketers find ways of turning our personal habits into more and more commodified products, they sell what used to be our own personal skills back to us in the form of processed things and ideas. Restaurant meals and heat-and-serve foods save work but also keep us from practicing cooking. As buying devours doing, we tend to forget how to do the things required to make and use products.

    The philosopher Cheryl Mendelson discusses the example of the creeping impoverishment of home life in the United States. "American housekeeping and home life are in a state of decline," Mendelson argues. "Comfort and engagement at home have diminished to the point that even simple cleanliness and decent meals—let alone any deeper satisfactions—are no longer taken for granted. . . . [A]lthough a large, enthusiastic minority of home cooks grow more and more sophisticated, the majority become ever-more deskilled. Dirt, dust, and disorder are more common . . . than they used to be." Mendelson traces much of this trend to "an unfortunate cycle" in which "As people turn more and more to outside institutions to have their needs met (for food, comfort, clean laundry, relaxation, society, entertainment, rest), domestic skills and expectations further diminish, in turn decreasing the chance that people's homes can satisfy their needs. The result is far too many people who long for home even though they seem to have one." More television, processed foods, and spray-bottle cleaning products with extravagant chemical claims, Mendelson observes, mean not just less home sociability, cooking, and cleaning work, but also, over time, less *knowledge about how and why to socialize, cook, and clean.* "It is not in goods that the contemporary household is poor," Mendelson writes, "but in comfort and care."[18]

Personal deskilling takes effect at a mental level, too: For example, researchers are discovering that television, which in the United States is 99 percent a marketing machine and is governed by its larger purpose of delivering pliable audiences to advertisers, destroys our ability to form our own mental pictures.[19]

While this is not the place for a deep survey of personal deskilling, and while it is important to recognize that corporate marketers do, of necessity, teach us some new skills as they strip away old ones,[20] consider their role in the trends recounted in this report from a 1995 edition of the *New York Times:*

> A science skillfully practiced by the ancient Egyptians is slowly becoming a dying art at home. . . .
>
> Today, many people think the term "baking by scratch" means opening a box of mix. And because of consumer impatience and a lack of baking skills, manufacturers are making the mixes even easier to use. . . . Pillsbury introduced one-step, just-add-water . . . mixes, and they have been popular. . . . For those intimidated by every aspect of baking, some new mixes from Duncan Hines don't even require greasing a pan. . . .
>
> Joy Taylor, the senior food editor at *Better Homes and Gardens* magazine, said that her 7.6 million readers had less knowledge about baking than preceding generations had. "It's a shame," she said, "because techniques and recipes are not being passed down through the generations. People's heritages are being lost."
>
> The skills are not being taught outside of the home, either. "Few take home economics or 4-H classes anymore," said Sharon Maasdam, home economist for *The Oregonian* newspaper in Portland. Ms. Maasdam, who has run the paper's food help line since 1980, said people had scant knowledge about food in general and baking in particular. "When they do call with a baking question, it is usually about a simple technique," she said.
>
> The lack of technical proficiency was recorded by Land O'Lakes Holiday Bakeline, which received a record-breaking 40,000 calls from November 1 to December 24 last year. (More baking is done between Thanksgiving and Christmas than at any other time of the year.) The most common question was how to prevent cookies from spreading when baked on a cookie sheet.
>
> The only real growth in the home baking industry seems to be in bread-baking machines, which do everything but butter the bread. . . . Bread from these

machines often has a gummy texture, and few people, besides the manufacturers, would claim that the results taste as good as bread made from scratch.[21]

Evidence also suggests that advancing commercialism and commodification are crowding out and weakening citizenship skills. The sociologist Robert
D. Putnam reports that "the fraction of sixth-graders with a television set in
their bedroom grew from 6 percent in 1970 to 77 percent in 1999."[22] Such
trends reflect the deepening hold of commercialism on successive American
generations. Not only is television watching increasingly crowding out reading and newspaper subscription, but, Putnam also reports, even within the
realm of television watching, "interest in the news per se . . . is declining
generationally. . . . While the average age of the audience for all prime-time
[television] programs was forty-two, the average age of the audience for
nightly newscasts was fifty-seven."[23] Robust democracy requires strong lit-
eracy—the stronger, the better, in fact.[24] That reading is, for a host of reasons,
far superior to television as a means of acquiring information for successful
citizenship is beyond doubt to anybody who considers the issue seriously.
Because reading is a highly conscious, hard-to-control activity, it also makes
a marketing platform distinctly inferior to the mildly addictive, trance-
inducing, subliminal suggestion–friendly medium of television.[25] In sum,
more big business marketing means less reading, more television, and weaker
citizens.

On top of this, evidence suggests that the sheer saturation of life with the
half-truths, shallow flattery, and low-quality discourse that big business marketing relies upon to create effective behavior-modifying carrots and sticks
has a serious degrading effect on our learned capacities. As our experience
becomes increasingly saturated with marketing talk, marketing vocabulary,
marketing attitudes, and marketing environments, such basic human skills
as courtesy, civility, critical thought, and articulate speech are crowded out of
our personal behavioral repertoires.[26]

8. Personal Dependence

As we lose personal skills within each generation—and especially between
them—we as individuals become more dependent on buying and using processed corporate products that leave little room for the practices of cooking,
making, fixing, and figuring that have sustained human beings for tens of
thousands of years. One effect of this is that, to continue enjoying the fruits
of cooking, making, fixing, and figuring, each new, less-skilled generation
becomes more dependent on the big businesses that have sucked up, commodified, and sold back to us so many of the capabilities that our ancestors

have handed down to us. In a country that still prides itself on commonsense know-how and individual inventiveness, the irony of this trend is hard to overstate.

9. Time and Energy Drain

Big business marketing causes a mammoth waste of human energy. First, just the act of operating and managing the many products that suffuse our lives often creates a time crunch. Second, the increasing commodification of personal activity means that everything we do requires money, and, hence, more hours of paid work. We end up having to "work off" the very corporate marketing expenditures that invade our lives and entrap our thoughts and deeds. The economist Juliet Schor calls this work-and-spend cycle the squirrel cage effect.[27] Finally, the sheer number of hours Americans spend watching television advertisements that they would rather not see, opening and discarding junk mail, answering telemarketing calls, deleting spam, sitting in traffic, calming, restraining, and negotiating with marketing-addled children, and so forth, is a major deduction from the limited energy supplies all people have to spend during their earthly days.

Our energy supplies are more finite than we realize. As the social psychologist Mihalyi Csikszentmihalyi explains, "it is possible to process at most 126 bits of information per second, or 7,560 per minute, or almost half a million per hour. Over a lifetime of seventy years, and counting sixteen hours of waking time each day, this amounts to about 185 billion bits of information."[28] This, Csikszentmihalyi notes, "seems like a huge amount, but in reality it does not go that far." The reason is the energy intensity of human consciousness. In order "to understand what another person is saying," Csikszentmihalyi observes, "we must process 40 bits of information each second. If we assume the upper limit of our capacity to be 126 bits per second, it follows that to understand what three people are saying simultaneously is theoretically possible, but only by managing to keep out of consciousness every other thought or sensation."[29]

Because everything we do as human beings derives from our ability to consciously direct our energy expenditures, the quality of our lives is always a product of the quality of our available options and the degree of individual skill, self-awareness, and autonomy we attain. As Csikszentmihalyi puts it, "It is out of [our finite] total of [expendable mental energy] that everything in our life must come—every thought, memory, feeling, or action."[30]

Human life energy is finite—so how much do we really want to spend on the things we now do? This should be hotly debated. Aren't forces that unnecessarily waste or warp our options, abilities, or freedoms good candidates for reform or elimination?

10. Bloat

Big business marketing promotes sedentary modes of personal life. This is because profitable shopping, both intended and unintended (aka looking at ads), requires the maintenance of mental states conducive to what experts call low-involvement learning. Creation and preservation of such states is the common foundation of the design of shopping malls, television programming, and commercial movies. Hard work, intense physical exertion, and active, critical thought are all anathema to optimal marketing stimulation.

At another level, big business marketing both encourages the overconsumption of food and drink and relies on fat, salt, sugar, and chemicals to maximize the appeal and marketability of foodstuffs.

Finally, commodification's "squirrel cage" effect makes it hard to find time to eat right and exercise. Going to the gym for a run and some weightlifting takes a couple of hours. Those holding down jobs, performing family obligations amid traffic jams, and watching television avidly are highly unlikely to find these hours.

Big business marketing, in other words, is fattening. More of it means more obesity.

11. Frustration

As people become less connected to others and to viable, friendly community life, and as they lose personal skills and suffer the other ill effects of marketing, they get frustrated with life and with one another. Living a normal life means needing to work more. Working more means less free time and more need for convenience. Being rushed and burned out means greater vulnerability to fast food and television. Fast food and American television are crappy and personally costly, especially when taken in large doses.

12. Salt on Poverty's Wounds/Envy

Many of these forms of degradation are suffered more intensely as one moves down the income ladder. To be poor in the United States is to suffer doubly by living amid a marketing juggernaut that gives you only its worst aspects while constantly exposing you to its "ideal" lifestyle prescriptions. Also, remember that unemployed people watch more television and that there is a direct correlation between one's chances of being poor (one's class situation), one's chances of being poorly educated, and one's vulnerability to advertising's schemes.

13. Market Totalitarianism

Totalitarianism is the thorough and detailed domination of all major spheres of life—state, economy, and personal life—by a ruling elite.[31] Since this concept has so far been developed by critics of state forms of totalitarianism—Nazi Germany and the Soviet Union being the prime examples—nobody has yet bothered to notice that the contemporary United States displays many of the markings of totalitarianism. In the words of the conservative "end of history" theorist Francis Fukuyama, totalitarian societies are distinguished by socioeconomic systems ruled by elites that advance "a comprehensive view of human life"; operate in ways that tend "to destroy [autonomous development in] civil society in its totality"; and tend to generate "a society whose members [are] reduced to 'atoms,' unconnected to any 'mediating institutions.'"[32]

While Fukuyama does not imagine that these core totalitarian tendencies might arise from the realm of economic life rather than from the state, consider their applicability to the contemporary United States and its dominant business class. While U.S. business moguls do not concern themselves with running society as a whole, does their central credo—that people are born "consumers," behavior settings are platforms for selling, and money is the measure of all things—not constitute "a comprehensive view of human life" that has powerful practical effects on the underlying population? Have the aggregate and inexorable workings of modern big business marketing not seized hold of civil society in its totality and radically undermined the autonomy of its development? Have ordinary Americans, under big business marketing's constantly expanding piranha effect, not been atomized and severed from autonomous mediating institutions? Indeed, substitute *private corporations* for *the state* and *commodification* for *ideology* or *politics*, and one can read the whole conservative literature on totalitarianism as a very helpful and enlightening discussion of contemporary American society.

All in all, big business marketing is a phenomenon that leads, in the aggregate, to the rigid, precise, overriding, and undemocratic domination of personal life on behalf of a small class of profit-seeking investors whose innermost interests compel them to strive to commodify every possible aspect of everyday living. The inexorable advance of big business marketing leads to a society in which both sides of civil society—the economy and personal life—as well as public policy come under the smothering universal dominance of profit maximization for the primary benefit of super-rich shareholders. Though the resulting tendency to *market totalitarianism* advances differently and less harshly than did state totalitarianism, it nonetheless leads to all the classic symptoms of state-based totalitarianism: atomization, political apathy and irrationality, the hollowing and banalization of purportedly democratic political processes, mounting popular frustration, and so forth.

14. *The Degradation of Personal Life*

Contrary to prevailing dogma, big business marketing is *not* a force that uniformly and continuously improves the fit between human desires and the available supply of goods and services. In many areas, modern marketing leads to an *absolute degradation* of this fit—the creation of worse standards than had been previously obtained. For instance, witness the marketing-imposed costs just enumerated. If we keep history in mind, we can see the more important point that modern marketing also causes serious *relative degradation* in the usefulness and enjoyability of products. That is, if we had had a mechanism to exert some democratic control over major investment decisions, all the wealth that has flowed through the United States probably could have created a much healthier, happier, and less wasteful off-the-job environment.

While we have been taught to assess lifestyle costs and benefits and the quality of life on the basis of the best standards that one can expect from a society in which the priorities of the business community come first, it is well to recall that, for all the material wealth we now possess, modern capitalist society has systematically prevented us from making concern for human welfare the top priority of our economic activity. As the anthropologist Marvin Harris has said, "In our era of industrial mass production and mass marketing, quality is a constant problem because the intimate sentimental and personal bonds which once made us responsible to each other and to our products have withered away and been replaced by money relationships."[33]

10. Escaping the Consumer Trap

Old-school leftists used to contend that, for the human race, the choice was "socialism or barbarism." By the end of the twentieth century, however, the criminality and ineptitude of Stalinism, socialism's first actually existing wave, as well as the comprehensive, militant, and often military antisocialism of corporate capitalist elites had stifled debate of alternative human futures. In this concluding chapter, I argue that, for two reasons, the big business marketing race compels us *at least to discuss* the idea of finally using public enterprise to displace private business interests from the commanding heights of modern socioeconomic power.

Reason 1: Marketing and the Accumulating Costs of Corporate Capitalism

Behind the scenes, big business marketers know that their trade contradicts the core assumptions of the capitalist "end of history" thesis. If you doubt this, consider the fact that, in 1999, Gregory S. Carpenter and Rashi Glazer, both professors at elite business schools and active corporate consultants, received the American Marketing Association's William F. O'Dell Award, given annually to the *Journal of Marketing Research* article that proves, five years after its publication, to have "made the most significant long-term contribution to the marketing discipline."[1] The 1999 O'Dell award honored Carpenter and Glazer's 1994 *JMR* article, "*Meaningful* Brands from Meaningless Differentiation: The Dependence on Irrelevant Attributes," in which the authors used social science experiments to disentangle the psychological mechanism by which marketers' false product claims "can produce a meaningfully differentiated brand."[2]

Carpenter and Glazer's experiments confirmed that emphasizing a product "attribute that implies greater benefit [than alternatives], sometimes on a key function, but in reality does not provide the implied benefit" can be an effective marketing tool "in a surprising number of situations."[3] The authors found that skilled manipulation of a product's "attribute structure" and the "information available" about it often succeeds in prompting prospective buyers into "inferring that the irrelevant but distinguishing attribute is valuable. . . . especially if the differentiating attribute is difficult to evaluate."[4] Properly managed false product differentiation, Carpenter and Glazer reported, "can bias decisions systematically."[5] By implying phony "relevance [and] prompting positive associations," marketers are often able to trigger prospective buyers into making "causal inferences about [the irrelevant attribute's] impact on product performance," allowing their firms to "garner the advantages" of genuine product superiority without actually providing it.[6]

After offering their professional audience extended advice about how to understand "the conditions under which meaningless differentiation could be successful," Carpenter and Glazer admit "Our results are somewhat disquieting."[7] "Contrary to the model of rational choice," which portrays product users' choices as "fixed, exogenous [to sellers' spheres of control], and revealed by choice," in reality, many determinants of people's "preferences are context dependent" and quite "endogenous" to sellers' spheres of control.[8] Because of its heavy reliance on "meaningless differentiation," modern, marketing-centered corporate enterprise, the authors observe, is actually not "a race to meet customer needs best at the lowest price," but rather a "battle over the structure of consumer preferences." In this battle, "competitive advantage is possible through differentiation that, rather than meeting customer needs better than competitors, provides no *meaningful* value to the customer." Corporate marketing is thus something other than "catering to consumer preferences," and the relationship between what gets sold and what has the most "objective value" is very far from pure.[9]

Carpenter and Glazer, of course, do not enumerate the reasons for disquiet over their findings. Nevertheless, their article provides an excellent introduction to these reasons, which reside in the direct and indirect costs of big business marketing.

For example, is it not true that, from the perspective of the ordinary product user, the entire corporate marketing process is a *system for manufacturing meaningless product differentiation?* As Philip Kotler explains to his students and clients, any would-be commodity seller is, in the final analysis, in the business of providing customers a "fundamental service," to which the product to be sold is merely a means. "A hotel guest is buying 'rest and sleep,'" Kotler reminds his readers. "The purchaser of a drill is buying 'holes.'"[10] And, because marketing is "meeting needs profitably," big business marketers are, of course, in the business of meeting such needs—but *only when they can do so at a high enough profit.*

Consider again what this last qualification means when judged against the yardsticks of functional benefit and fundamental service. In these ultimate terms, buyers of automobiles are really buying transportation. Given the technical possibilities of modern manufacturing, how do automobiles rate as a means of attaining that functional benefit? Is it easier to get from Point A to Point B in either Tokyo or Paris than in Denver or Los Angeles? What is the list of other human activities that a person might undertake while being transported on the Paris Metro subway? Between cities on the Japanese Shinkansen bullet train? Riding in a Ford Expedition on a Los Angeles freeway or an interstate highway? What are the relative risks of being hurt or killed in all those modes of transportation? Since its inception in 1968, nobody—not one single person—has died in a Shinkansen train accident. What are the relative economic and ecological costs of trains versus cars? Aren't the incessant multibillion-dollar marketing campaigns of the car corporations, in large part, efforts to fix our attention on product attributes that are either trivial or meaningless as compared with the functional benefits of modern rail, bus, and bicycle transportation? Given the automobile's astounding economic and ecological inefficiencies and the stresses, dangers, and bodily and mental limitations car driving imposes, are not the auto marketers' efforts to emphasize the car's one true benefit—namely, its usefulness as a vanity statement to passersby—and to define automotive safety only in terms of one's relative chances in auto-versus-auto collisions classic examples of making "meaningful brands from meaningless differentiation?"

In transportation, as in other areas, the meaningful consideration for ordinary product users is how they can get the best possible products at the lowest possible cost. Authentic analysis and genuine free choice on this topic require access to good information about the technological possibilities and relative costs and benefits of possible transportation vehicles and infrastructures. Car marketing is entirely hostile to such information, analysis, and choice. Choose your color, style, and odds of surviving a crash, car sellers insist. Such are the limits of your options.

Of course, the direct costs of such planned product differentiation are but half the story. Because it provides corporate investors with their main avenue of escape from the economic contradictions of their own excessive power, big business marketing also deserves a large share of the blame for capitalism's other costs as well. There are at least four major categories of such costs.

First, there is the problem of economic polarization. Because its constituent business firms both extend themselves into every promising area for accumulating wealth and aggressively limit labor costs and incomes while increasing property and management incomes, the capitalist world economy is a powerful engine for the creation of both mass poverty and elite megawealth. As the anthropologist Marvin Harris explains,

> Throughout much of the world, class identity continues to be sharp and unambiguous. Among most contemporary nations, differences in class-linked lifestyles show little prospect of diminishing or disappearing. . . . Indeed, given the increase in luxury goods and services available to contemporary elites, contrasts in lifestyles between the rich and powerful and the people of peasant villages or urban shantytowns may be reaching an all-time high. During the recent epochs of industrial advance, governing classes throughout the world have gone from palanquins to Mercedes to private jets, while their subordinates find themselves without even a donkey or a pair of oxen. The elites now have their medical needs taken care of at the world's best medical centers, while vast numbers of less fortunate people have never even heard of the germ theory of disease and will never be treated by modern medical techniques. Elites attend the best universities, while half of the people in the world remain illiterate.[11]

Despite business boosters' continuing promises of a trickle down effect that will someday create prosperity for all, there is little prospect that a big business world either can or will do anything to reverse the alarming trend toward increasing economic disparity.[12] Moreover, as corporate capitalism continues to chip away at labor incomes in its core areas of selling, economic stagnation, financial disorder, unemployment, underemployment, and "junk jobs" plunge wider areas of First World societies into Third World conditions.[13]

Second, there is the problem of ecological destruction. As the ecologist and political economist John Bellamy Foster explains, in their endless pursuit of rising investment returns, private investors treat natural resources as free gifts to capitalists and regard the ecosystem as a sink or toilet into which pollutants can be dumped without cost. This ecological insanity creates a catch-22: On one hand, as Foster argues, given its reliance on environmental disregard, significant easing of its environmental burdens would require equally significant downsizing of corporate business activities. On the other hand, by its very nature, "capitalism cannot exist without constantly expanding the scale of production: any interruption in this process will take the form of an economic crisis." Foster concludes that "the kind of rapid economic growth that the system has demanded in order to sustain its very existence is no longer ecologically sustainable."[14] While it may turn out that one, several, or most of the mounting ecological problems presently emanating from modern business society—for example, global warming, ozone layer destruction, atmospheric pollution, soil erosion, garbage gluts, resource depletion, rapid population growth, the spread of toxic substances, and so on—will prove to be less catastrophic than they presently appear, a monumental ecological crisis is virtually certain, if basic social priorities do not change.

Third, there is the problem of the ongoing degradation of personal life by big business marketing. If one projects the corporate drive to commercialize and commodify human lifestyles into the future, it seems almost certain that the amount of clutter, junk, danger, puff and fluff, mobile privatization, narcissism, personal deskilling, personal dependence, time drain, bloat, psychological frustration, envy, and market totalitarianism that citizens would be subjected to will greatly increase over their already high state. Moreover, even if only a few of these trends make further advances on the human mind and body, their impact on democracy and general well-being seems sure to be ugly. Already, the United Nations Development Program has reported that "poor nations and rich are afflicted by growing human distress—weakening social fabrics, rising crime rates, increasing threats to personal security, spreading narcotic drugs and a growing sense of individual isolation."[15] While big business marketing's piranha effect is not the only cause of such trends, it is certainly responsible for a large share of them.

Finally, and perhaps most dangerously, there is the connection between big business marketing and war. We know that corporate capitalism requires maximal commodification of off-the-job habits. This, in turn, means that First World nations require disproportionate access to Third World resources, both natural and human. In the area of personal transportation, for example, corporate capitalism's need for new markets creates very strong corporate promotion of personal automobile ownership and use. This requires generous supplies of cheap oil. Consequently, as recent history shows, corporate capitalists have felt compelled to maneuver to ensure such supplies, with brutal, extremely dangerous side effects. Generally speaking, corporate capitalism's geopolitical requirements—and especially its intolerance of democracy in the Third World—have been and remain a major cause of complex, violent conflicts, including retaliatory blowback, around the world.[16] In the new millennium, the prospect of such consequences spiraling out of control seems all too real and immediate, as does our elites' hostility to fair, humane, and democratic solutions to the immense dangers their system has created.

Taken together, the four crises endemic to modern corporate capitalism—economic polarization, ecological destructiveness, cultural degradation, and war—leave little hope that a bright human future will arise from within business society.[17] Will worsening mass poverty and eroding labor incomes bring too much population growth, huge famines, horrible resource wars, and economic depression? Perhaps yes, perhaps no. Will unrelenting ecological dumping, burning, looting, and carelessness cause a catastrophic environmental collapse that severely damages or destroys the basis for human camaraderie and democracy? Perhaps yes, perhaps no. Will a further expanding big business marketing race so trivialize, atomize, and frustrate popular majorities that the capacity for active, autonomous citizenship evaporates in the heat and fury of the commodified society? Perhaps yes, perhaps no. Will our elite's aversion to democracy in the Third World and its sponsorship of Third World despots lead to nuclear or chemical wars? Perhaps yes, perhaps no. If we follow our present course of big business–led social development, will at least *one* of these massive calamities befall us in the next century? The answer is almost certainly yes.

* * *

This, then, is the situation that now faces humanity. Because of the tremendous size and reach of the business corporations that increasingly dominate the world's economies, the main practical challenge that vexes their managerial efforts to make greater profits—the crisis of "consumer behavior" caused by the ironic aggregate economic effects of corporate success itself—causes them to devote increasing energy to the task of inserting commodities into the daily lives of money holders. As the scale, scope, and intensity of this marketing drive increase, the structure and composition of personal life in the core countries asymptotically approaches complete commodification. As powerful institutions' aggregate promotion of commodity-friendly activities increases and their aggregate tolerance of commodity-unfriendly ones decreases, more and more ordinary routines fall under the relentless and rigidly narrow logic of private profit, without anybody ever really noticing. As the human costs of this pattern of social development grow larger and more ominous, citizens become couch potatoes—Ronald K. L. Collins and Michael F. Jacobson aptly note that, among opinion leaders in the United States, "The very idea of *citizen* has become synonymous with *consumer*"[18]—and events march us toward a future that seems bleak and inescapable.

Reason 2: Big Business Marketing's Ironic Contribution to Socialism

Public enterprise and public administration deliver Americans' mail, pave their streets, teach their children, and train and arm their soldiers. According to capitalist dogma, however, public enterprise would suddenly become horribly unworkable the moment it contacted production and distribution of goods and services that compete with big businesses. Only capitalism, capitalists and their champions claim, can provide us with high-quality transportation and toothpaste. Even democratically controlled public enterprise, we are told, would inevitably lead us back to the Soviet Union and its lines for gristly sausages.

Consider, however, what happened at the one moment in U.S. history when there was some serious political consideration of using public authority to organize and operate industrial production of goods and services that would compete with corporate wares. This moment came in 1934, at the bottom of the Great Depression, when the Roosevelt administration was thinking of expanding the small "production-for-use" programs it had sponsored as part of the New Deal. If corporate capitalists truly believed public industry is inherently doomed to fail, would capitalists of the time not have laughed at such pitiful, hopeless folly? In actuality, their attacks on the "production-for-use" idea were the most vehement part of their intense, unrelenting opposition to New Deal employment programs.[19] And the vehemence of their attack was not a product of concern for saving public tax dollars, but a manifestation of corporate fears of the *threat of a good example*. As *Business Week* reported in its July 28, 1934, issue, for capitalists the very idea of public production-for-use created "the uncomfortable thought that government manufacture might be expanded widely and might become permanent."[20] If public industry is so inherently doomed, why the discomfort?

Of course, nobody should forget the intervening horrible record of public enterprise in the Soviet Union and other Stalinist societies. Some of that record was probably a result of the fact that Russia, China, Cuba, Vietnam, and North Korea were not exactly swimming in capital and technology when the Stalinists took over. Nevertheless, it seems undeniable that the lack of democracy, both within economic institutions and in the wider society, was the factor that doomed the Soviet command economy to its infamous crimes and woes. Able to churn out AK-47s and dachas for the commissars, Stalinism proved fatally unable to produce more than strange, haphazard batches of white elephant goods and maddening trickles of venally inadequate services.

Notwithstanding these systemic woes of first-wave socialism, just for a moment, let us indulge in a thought experiment. Suppose that we were to decide to try to create a social order in which democracy would be the predominant regulating force in all three spheres of modern life—in the state, in the economy, and in personal life. Judged in relation to big business society, at least on paper, the great advantage of such a social order would be that, by breaking the rigid fixation of economic planners on profit and bringing economic priorities into closer alignment with robustly debated democratic interests, it would promise to increase greatly both the flexibility and the democratic nature of economic life, hence freeing humanity to preempt the mounting costs of corporate capitalism. Socialism, which should always have been understood primarily as a major advance in democracy, after all means a system in which *social* rather than *money and property* priorities could and would come first.

The main prerequisite for the creation of a universally democratic society would be the creation of a strong, coherent, and democratic mass movement of those whose interests are not greatly and directly tied to profit making in the present society. Such a movement would have to make the extension of democracy into and over economic life its main political demand, although it would inevitably need to make questions of basic social decency, tolerance, equality, and fairness also a fundamental part of its program. This economic demand would be aimed at replacing—probably over time and in stages—the arbitrary prerogatives and rights of the major owners of big businesses with popular prerogatives and rights while simultaneously greatly increasing the power of hired workers within workplaces and at the collective bargaining table. It would also have to concern itself with developing procedures for proposing, debating, voting on, and implementing broad economic plans that would direct major areas of economic production in accordance with the autonomous priorities of the majority of citizens. In such an order, "citizen" would be the predominant category of identity, as open political decision making and popular sovereignty would extend not just to matters of state but to matters of economy as well.

The main practical problems that would inhere in the admittedly difficult political process that would be set in motion by such a movement would be ethical and technical, as conservative assailants against the idea of socialism have long maintained. First, it is open to question whether people would be constitutionally or culturally able to create and sustain a mass movement for universal democracy and the sustenance of the social order that such a movement, through its political victory and subsequent dominance, might create. On one hand, since democratic socialism has never been seriously tried on a large scale, we do not know the answer to the constitutional question. On the other hand, given the deep alterations in human character that the modern business world has engendered, it is also open to question whether our constitutions have been too encrusted with pettiness, narcissism, greed, and isolated passivity to permit the creation and maintenance of universal democracy. In other words, either human nature or capitalist history's effect upon it—or both—may prevent democratic socialism from emerging and thriving.

The second major roadblock to the creation and maintenance of a universally democratic society lies in the sphere of economic decision making. Here, the problem is twofold. Capitalism has been able to survive because of the curious rigidity and intensity of the profit drive at its heart, a drive that makes the task of selecting and evaluating alternative courses of investment and managerial action relatively simple, if not easy, for business planners. In a democratic socialist society, however, economic decisions would be both more open to a variety of priorities and intensely debated and voted on by the population at large. As a result, democratic socialism would tend to throw into a new, less certain, and one-dimensional orbit both the large, momentous investment decisions that shape the infrastructure of social and economic life and the smaller, more technical questions of how to organize work and deliver well-made and popularly desired products to end users.

Now, to continue our thought experiment: Suppose that a mass movement has indeed decided to try to build a democratic socialist society that would replace big business capitalism. Suppose further that such a movement has managed to win enough electoral power to begin to implement the social and economic reforms needed to bring about such a transition. What would such a social movement then have to do in order to consolidate the new order of universal democracy?

The first answer is that such a movement would want to pass laws that made it both a standard right and normal political practice to hold frequent and regular national, regional, and local referenda on major questions of economic policy. Do the citizens want to continue to build and live with the infrastructure and products that now make the automobile king of the road, or do they want to greatly increase, modernize, and perhaps even make luxurious the infrastructure and products that might bring modern public transit to the fore? Do the citizens want to spend 5 percent of gross domestic product on military institutions and less than 1 percent on foreign aid, or do they want to devote 5 percent of yearly production to helping end world poverty and less than 1 percent to the military? Do the citizens want to raise the minimum wage and create a guaranteed citizen's income, to assure that nobody goes without modern life's necessities? Such questions and many others would be subject to both formal and substantial political democracy in a democratic socialist society.

This, of course, raises the great question of how to make such a political economy actually work satisfactorily at the level of real-world investment, management, production, and distribution. After all, it is one thing to debate and vote on a fine-sounding economic plan; how to bring such big economic decisions into reality at the detailed level of actual life is another matter.

Now, at first glance, this is just where the case against democratic socialism would seem immovable. After all, even though the former Soviet Union provided no mechanisms for political democracy and never opened up the question of major economic priorities to popular debate and choice, it nevertheless did try to create and implement economic plans not based on capitalist market criteria. And, of course, nobody sane would claim that the Soviet economy ever came remotely close to providing Soviet citizens with supplies of high-quality and democratically desired goods and services. On the contrary, while the Soviet army had world-class guns, airplanes, tanks, and missiles, ordinary people could hardly get a decent cucumber or piece of meat, let alone the many other necessities and niceties they might have desired. Finally, while the Soviet elites' corruption and self-interest definitely greatly distorted economic planning and decision making, at least some of the blame for the poor economic performance of the Soviet economy was attributable to one fact that conservative critics of the idea of socialism have long contended would inevitably be the case in all modern planned collectivist economies: The Soviet implementers of the investment, production, and distribution decisions that any economy with modern production techniques requires did not know what product availability, features, and designs end users genuinely wanted.

How would our hypothetical social movement for universal democracy get around this seemingly intractable dilemma? How would they take the larger economic plans developed in the political sphere and turn them into detailed blueprints for successfully allocating and organizing the people, things, spaces, and labor processes required for carrying them out? Obviously, the whole population neither could nor should be involved in making every detailed choice of individual and organizational activity. How, then, would a universally democratic society, where commanding economic power rested in the citizenry as a whole, solve the problem of successfully making the little economic decisions?

The answer lies in a very ironic place: big business marketing. In our example, the social movement for economic democracy would, if it were wise, recognize that, while business society's academic ideological defenders continue to presume that pure price competition and market signals tell capitalist planners which products to make in what quantities, the giant business corporations that dominate today's economy rely on their marketing research procedures, rather than on oblique price trends in markets, for formulating the bulk of their investment, production, and distribution decisions. While economists still presume that both the designs and prices of commodities are dictated by general business conditions beyond the control of individual firms—that is, by markets—in general, the truth is that, when they want to know how to design and price their products, big business planners rush out and do focus groups, demographic research, and other nonmarket kinds of studies. The obvious conclusion is that, although we do not now recognize the fact, we already have an example of an economic system whose constituent units use complex research and planning, rather than simple competitive reaction, to turn large priorities—in this case, maximum profit—into small economic decisions about the details of investment, production, and distribution processes. Corporate capitalism, then, offers a source of many answers about whether it is possible to run a complex economy without allowing market signals to dominate small economic decisions.

This suggests that the real final irony of big business marketing is that, if separated from the capitalist context that makes them manipulative of, rather than genuinely responsive to, popular small-scale economic wishes, needs, and desires, many of modern corporate marketers' already highly developed methods and principles could rather easily be brought to bear on solving the productive and distribution problems of a universally democratic socialist society. After political and economic priorities have been set in the sphere of debate and voting, economic planners—themselves elected and fired by either workers or citizens, in accordance with the level of decision making involved—could deploy armies of public-minded, democratically charged researchers to go into the field and do surveys, studies, and scientifically sampled but genuinely democratic and open focus groups, all aimed at successfully and dutifully connecting the large-scale priorities of truly sovereign citizens with their small-scale wishes and requirements.

Thus, without anybody seeming to realize it, the marketing methods that corporations have developed, if removed from their present profit-über-alles institutional context and used for democratic ends, could go a long way toward resolving the great technical problem that any society that extended democracy over modern economic institutions would face—namely, the problem of how to use economic resources in the manner in which people want them to be used. In fact, while conservative thinkers never tire of asserting that such a society would be doomed to failure because of the curtailment of free market pricing that it would require, the truth is that today's large business corporations themselves no longer rely on market signals in the classic sense in making their production decisions. Instead of checking prices and rushing into production, big businesses now go out and conduct extensive marketing surveys, focus groups, panel studies, demographic research, and so forth, and then come back and set the prices and physical details of the commodities they plan to produce. Why, then, could a publicly charged and accountable economic organization not use many of the same sophisticated techniques and technologies that big business marketers have devised? Why could public enterprises not mimic the performance of ideal free markets while also taking into central account the genuine, truly autonomously debated and generated economic wishes of the people at large? The answer to this question seems to me to be that there is no *technical* reason why such an undertaking would be doomed to fail. If corporations now compete on a nonprice basis and make their decisions by analyzing marketing studies, why could a chain of cooperative productive facilities that had their largest priorities and policies set by open democratic political debate and popular political voting not do exactly the same thing?

Indeed, none other than Philip Kotler once admitted that "public sector services are generally poor in quantity and quality" because of biased politics, not technical or organizational impossibility. "Nonprofit organizations," Kotler wrote, in fact "have a great opportunity to improve their services by adopting the same marketing orientation that has worked so effectively in the commercial sector."[21] Though Kotler never pursued this point, his recognition of the feasibility of the not-for-profit use of modern marketing tools belies longstanding capitalist legend. Careful practical attention to prospective users' mundane realities does not, as prevailing ideology has it, require putting profit first.

Conclusion: Reclaiming Our Macro Choices

Seen in historical perspective against the long history of class domination and democracy, modern corporate marketing is, in the final analysis, *an instrument for preventing the democratic governance of large-scale economic institutions and the big decisions that they make.* Indeed, while marketing is not an intentionally political set of practices, as a tool for perpetuating the successful dominance of an ascendant class of major business investors who are unwilling to even contemplate the extension of democracy into modern economic life, it effectively functions to keep the process of choosing basic economic priorities safely isolated from popular debate and decision. This is so because, as long as big corporations can use modern marketing to find still more ways to sell new batches of commodities, capitalism and its arbitrary, profit-fixated command of the largest economic priorities will continue to suppress all other methods and criteria for setting the course of social and economic development. Moreover, as the piranha effect and the universal market progressively frustrate and degrade personal life, the likelihood that people will come to recognize this important fact may be decreasing over time.

The enormous irony is that corporate marketing and private, exploitative, antidemocratic control of society's commanding economic heights are in ascendance just as the social ramifications of the big decisions made by large corporations are more profoundly significant than ever. Because of their very ability to use modern marketing methods, big businesses have been able to penetrate into and reorganize the finest details of human activity across the whole spectrum of personal life. In effect, big businesses in the age of modern marketing function as unrecognized, but quite real and powerful, social engineering agencies. Consequently, the irony is that the age-old claim of the business owner that "My business is private," while still true as a description of existing property rights, is now decidedly and blatantly false as a claim about the human impact of the ordinary operation of the giant corporations that dominate the contemporary economy. We live in a world that is at least formally democratic in several areas yet hides its overriding and radically undemocratic logic within the black box of the private enterprise system that is relentlessly leading us to disaster.

Meanwhile, if the marketing methods of present-day corporate capitalism's largest corporations ironically demonstrate the technical feasibility of democratic socialism and universal democracy, then all hope for a better human future is not necessarily lost. If it is technically possible to use modern marketing methods to overcome the informational problems that arise when major economic institutions are run without subjection to capitalism's rigid profit-maximizing imperatives, then we can at least conclude that humanity now faces a potential choice between *four,* rather than just three, possible future courses of social development: If democratic socialism is technically possible, then the list includes fascism, Stalinism, corporate capitalist democracy, and universal (or democratic socialist) democracy. Moreover, if the last type of social order is technically possible, then history offers humanity a way of constructively transcending both the harsh evils of fascism and Stalinism and the softer but no less real evils of corporate capitalism and its consumer trap. In a universally democratic society, people would at least imaginably be able to retain and expand their ability to make free public and personal choices while also averting the crises of economic polarization, ecological destruction, cultural degradation, and war that are endemic to modern capitalist democracy. In short, a new epoch of hope and humanity could emerge with the creation of a universally democratic socialist world.

What, then, are the prospects that the sort of massive, powerful, and democratic social movement that would be needed to create and maintain universal democracy will actually come into existence and succeed in moving the human race beyond the Consumer Trap in which it now resides? That is, in the final analysis, what are the chances of forming a politics of progressive resistance to big business marketing?

Certainly, there are powerful forces and factors that would, and now do, militate against the formation and success of such a movement.

First, there is the simple fact that the main beneficiaries of the workings of the big business institutions that generate the Consumer Trap—that is, the world's few hundred thousand families of extremely wealthy investors—are not just a ruling social class, but history's richest and most managerially sophisticated ruling class. As a result, any social movement for democratic socialism would have to expect to meet fierce, sophisticated, and constant resistance to its efforts.

Second, there is the problem of political organizing itself. In order to build a successful social movement for universal democracy, members of such a movement would have to find a way to unite a wide, and sometimes bitterly divided, set of popular constituencies. The difficulties here would be many: If the movement focused on the problems of marketing and personal life to the exclusion of labor organizing and politics, or vice versa, the anticapitalist and prodemocracy unity needed to advance plausible arguments for creating a different social order would evaporate. If the movement did not devote energies to redressing existing economic, racial, and sexual divides and inequalities, such unity would be impossible. If the leaders of such a movement did not ensure that they and their followers were strictly accountable to democratic control from below, the movement would fail to be an effective vehicle for the advance of universal democracy. The list of such political challenges is very long.

Finally, there is the question of ideology and the creation of a liberating understanding of present dilemmas. While radical social critics have hitherto presumed that the whole point of big business marketing campaigns has been to implant conservative ideology into popular minds, the truth is that, when its comes to marketing and the relations of modern personal life, the real problem of ideology lies outside marketing campaigns themselves—in the very way that even radicals think and talk. When debating issues of paid work, would we ever agree that it is proper to conceive of ourselves primarily as employees rather than workers? Obviously not, since we immediately recognize that the former term presupposes the very relations of power, subordination, and conflict that currently make our existence as workers problematic. Why, then, do we think and talk so readily of ourselves as consumers rather than product users and citizens? The answer is that, when it comes to the area of personal life and product choice and usage, established business biases remain virtually unexamined, not to mention undented. The problem here is that it is extremely doubtful whether a movement for universal democracy and democratic socialism could either arise or succeed if it failed to transcend the present imprisonment of thought and language within vocabulary promoted by the architects and cheerleaders of the Consumer Trap.

* * *

Having said all this, however, it is important to note that there are also very powerful and important forces and factors that militate *in favor of* the transcendence of the Consumer Trap.

One important reason that a movement for democratic transcendence of the Consumer Trap might arise and succeed is the fact that big business marketers' domination of popular psychological and bodily habits is a mile wide but only an inch deep. Indeed, while it is impossible to understand modern corporate marketing without recognizing that it is a direct extension of the 5,000-year history of ruling classes' elitist methods of converting the people, things, symbols, and spaces that make up popular personal life environments into behavior-altering threats and enticements, it is nevertheless true that many of the carrots and sticks that corporate marketers wield are, despite their tremendous aggregate impact on people's lives, of the weakest possible variety. Of course, it is also vital to bear in mind that (1) there are still many very harsh elite threats built into the structure of capitalist life—in most American cities, for example, not owning a car means not being able to hold a job; and (2) even though many marketing threats and enticements are merely mild psychological tricks, the overall lifestyle impact of living amid a sea of such tricks carries with it enormous costs, as I have argued. Unlike the chains, whips, guns, beatings, and religious mysteries that served as exploitative threats and enticements in earlier and more arbitrary class societies, and also unlike the firings, harsh commands, and paychecks that serve as exploitative carrots and sticks in the engineering of corporate capitalism's paid workplaces, the little guilt trips, untruths, diversions, flatteries, amusements, and suggestions that modern marketers use to nudge contemporary personal life activities in prescribed directions often become ineffectual—

or even backfire—when their perceivers perceive them analytically and actively, rather than subconsciously (in motivation researchers' terms, "where the fish swim") and passively.

Indeed, while big business marketing is one of the primary vehicles for the spread of market totalitarianism, it is crucial to note that *market* totalitarianism is not the same as *state* totalitarianism. Where state-based totalitarian rulers have been necessarily concerned with harshly repressing independent political organizing and dissident thought, at least when it comes to capitalism's core countries, today's corporation-based rulers are ordinarily more interested in selling commodities and outdoing their rival firms in the race for profits than they are in promulgating the sorts of political regimentation that characterized the Soviet Union or Nazi Germany. Hence, in many important respects, countries such as the United States continue to permit a wide degree of political freedom to exist within the underlying population. Consequently, while virtually the whole of American society has been thrown open to the corporate drive to strategically and profitably place marketing stimuli before targets, the truth is that, for all their sophistication and power to alter perceptions and actions, most of corporate marketers' carrots and sticks are, at least individually, softer and weaker than were the prison camps and rifle barrels that conditioned the personal lives of residents of Hitler's and Stalin's lands.

A second factor militating in favor of the formation of organized democratic resistance to the Consumer Trap lies in the fact that, despite people's apparent marketing-induced apathy, loss of personal skills, and fascination with commodified images and objects, there is *already* a deep and simmering, if still incoherent, cauldron of popular resentment of the costs imposed by the Consumer Trap. Indeed, while it is relatively easy and commonplace to catalog the many ways in which Americans, for instance, are mesmerized by the niceties and diversions of the commodified life—in the 1980s, for example, more than 90 percent of U.S. teenage girls reported that shopping was their favorite activity[22]—we often forget that Americans also derive recurrent feelings of irritation, helplessness, alienation, and disgust from their ordinary confrontations with marketing stimuli. In 1990, for instance, a *Business Week* magazine article reported that marketing executives were increasingly "afraid that consumers—fed up with being bombarded by up to 3,000 marketing messages a day—are becoming less receptive to the blandishments of Madison Avenue."[23] "Consumers are like roaches—you spray them and spray them and they get immune after a while," laments David Lubars, an advertising executive with the Omnicom Group.[24]

Generally speaking, it seems certain that, if as much energy were ever devoted to studying these and the countless other manifestations of popular frustration with, and spontaneous resistance to, big business marketing campaigns as has been poured (mainly by putative radicals) into ruminations on the ways that people are charmed and diverted by advertising, we would rapidly have to abandon the idea that product users are anywhere near as fully integrated into modern business society and its Consumer Trap as most mainstream and radical opinion leaders would have us believe. In fact, this already large pool of public resentment of the costs of a commodified society would almost certainly become politically explosive if a major social movement for universal democracy were ever to succeed in helping a mass audience understand and politicize the basic nature and logic of big business marketing.

Indeed, if we stop to think about it, the history of our own century reveals that not only is frustration with, and commonsense resistance to, the corporate engineering of personal life a constant reality for individuals, but that, in the United States alone, such frustration and resistance has already fueled three major episodes of political organization and movement against it. The first wave of such activism came in the first decade of the twentieth century, when muckraking journalists and writers, such as Ida Tarbell and Upton Sinclair, who were concerned with the negative social implications of the consolidation of huge business corporations, exposed the problem of corporations' promulgation of unsafe food and drugs and thereby "ignited public outrage."[25] The second wave of popular political mobilization around issues of corporations' impact on personal life occurred in the 1920s, as a response to the increasing levels of disinformation being injected into personal life by the rise of modern advertising. It was in this era that the group Consumers Union, the publisher of the magazine that became *Consumer Reports,* was founded. Finally, in the 1960s, the phenomenon of the modern consumer movement came into existence under the leadership and inspiration of figures such as Vance Packard, John Kenneth Galbraith, Rachel Carson, and Ralph Nader. The core of the resulting political movement has been a circle of membership organizations, community networks, and political lobbying groups that have aimed both to give product users a regular voice in U.S. political processes and to plan and organize defensive responses to the worst depredations and costs of big business marketing.[26]

The history of consumer politics is loaded with implications and lessons relevant to assessing the prospects of a potential social movement for universal democracy. While this is not the place for a full digression on this topic, it is important to note two basic facts about it.

First, one of the great shortcomings of efforts to create a consumer movement has been that even its most ardent and thoughtful leaders have failed to appreciate fully the magnitude or the nature of the problem they faced. While the normal logic of the big business system of class domination and economic surplus extraction generates an expanding marketing race that inherently imposes market totalitarianism and enormous personal costs on underlying populations, leaders of the consumer movement continue to limit their work to attacks on the worst excesses of the corporate order and the most egregious ill effects of the Consumer Trap. They never quite get around to assailing the corporate capitalist institutional order of which these excesses and ill effects are a necessary and logical part. This attitude comes across in a book produced by leading figures from the Center for the Study of Commercialism. The book, by Michael F. Jacobson and Laurie Ann Mazur, is loaded with insightful analysis and criticism of corporate marketing. Nonetheless, as even its title—*Marketing Madness: A Survival Guide for a Consumer Society*—conveys, the underlying message of the authors' criticisms is that (1) marketing is somehow a form of madness and excess rather than a normal and necessary part of modern capitalism, and (2) resistance to marketing should take the form of a politics of survival and minor reform within such a social order.[27]

Second, despite this and other major habitual flaws in the modern consumer movement—which include its uncritical use of the word *consumer*—there is the larger point that the very existence and popularity of this kind of movement amidst a thoroughly hostile, procapitalist political climate suggests that there is energy available for the creation of a democratic movement to escape the Consumer Trap and transcend the system of class domination of which it is a central and increasingly important part. As corporate marketers are all too aware, in our isolated, unorganized ways, we have already developed rather keen personal "marketing radar," as a natural expression of what the media critic Douglas Rushkoff calls "our instinctual capacity to sense what we want." If we decided to organize ourselves, might we not come to see that, as Rushkoff puts it, "even when the coercer has vanished into the machinery, we still have the ability to recognize when we are being influenced," and to take democratic action "to lessen the effect of these techniques"?[28]

Hence, in the final analysis, it turns out that not only is there reason to believe that the creation of a universally democratic society is likely to be technically feasible, but that there are several major reasons to believe that the required mass movement from below may arise. In effect, this means that the only remaining reason to rule out the possibility of this course of popular action is the charge that people lack the ethical capacity or psychological disposition to forge a democratic socialist society. Even here, however, the prospects are not as dim as they might seem at first glance. As Albert Einstein, in an essay entitled "Why Socialism?" once said,

> The priests, in control of education, made the class division of society into a permanent institution and created a system of values by which people were thenceforth, to a large extent unconsciously, guided in their social behavior. But historic tradition is, so to speak, of yesterday; nowhere have we really overcome what Thorstein Veblen called "the predatory phase" of human development. The observable economic facts belong to that phase. . . .
>
> [Yet] modern anthropology has taught us, through comparative investigation of so-called primitive cultures, that the social behavior of human beings may differ greatly, depending upon prevailing cultural patterns and the types of organization which predominate in society. It is on this that those who are striving to improve the lot of man may ground their hopes: human beings are not condemned, because of their biological constitution, to annihilate each other or to be at the mercy of a cruel, self-inflicted fate.[29]

In an ironic but important way, reality may be forcing us to look again at the questions of popular sovereignty and our capacities for collective history making.

Seen in proper historical perspective, the conscious struggle for democracy—a word that literally means "rule by the people"—has always been a practical popular response to the reality of class domination and the economic exploitation and manipulative management on which it always rests. For the vast majority of the 5,000-year history of the class domination of human societies, democracy was mostly unconscious, inchoate, and only sporadically manifest in events such as bread riots and other early forms of popular self-defense. However, once capitalism's business classes began to push aside their noble predecessors, they often found themselves compelled to at least tolerate—and sometimes even advance—the notion that inherent human dignity bestows on all people the right to equality before, and equal say over, the law. As this principle consequently took firm root among popular constituencies, the question of democracy was both formalized and permanently placed on the human agenda.

In principle, the ideal of democracy is founded on the implicit understanding that all people are both biologically able and ethically entitled to exert control over their own lives, as long as it does not cause serious harm to others' chances to do the same. One famous expression of this basic premise was, of course, Thomas Jefferson's Declaration of Independence, which proclaimed the notion that it was "self-evident, that all Men are created equal, that they are endowed by their Creator with certain unalienable Rights, that among these are Life, Liberty, and the Pursuit of Happiness . . . , [and] that whenever any Form of Government becomes destructive of these Ends, it is the Right of the People to alter or abolish it."[30]

In the terminology of modern psychology, we might translate and extend this fundamental statement of democracy as follows: People are born with the capacity to understand and consciously alter the world they live in. They are also able to understand the different consequences in pleasure, pain, and human meaning that different lifestyles and lifestyle regimes tend to embody. Moreover, ordinary people tend to prefer fulfilling and pleasurable, rather than unfulfilling and unpleasurable, lives. Finally, because entrenched elites— aka ruling classes—are always inherently inclined to impinge on other people's lives in basic and harmful ways, democracy, or the egalitarian popular governance of the collective conditions that make particular lifestyle outcomes possible, is always the best possible way to organize and conduct the necessary cooperative endeavors that underlie all human lives and societies.

In this light, what has business society achieved as a form of democracy? The answer is that it has permitted and even encouraged the development of many important means and principles of democratic decision making, *while at the same time almost completely isolating major economic decisions from the influence of these procedures.* Indeed, the ultimate truth is that, at least in its core areas, modern business society can tolerate *capitalist democracy*— that is, the reign of popular sovereignty everywhere but in the sphere of economic decisions—but not *universal democracy*—which would be a system of popular sovereignty that made no distinction between economic and political decisions, and that therefore subjected both to popular governance.[31] The reason for this intolerance is obvious: If people in general were able to set the guidelines for major economic decisions, they would very often impose economic priorities and rules on economic planners that would conflict with the drive to generate maximum profits and rising property incomes for investors. At the very least, if democracy were to conquer the economic sphere of life, it would place severe limitations on the private priorities that presently drive it. The people might then enjoy not just a wide array of micro choices—which deodorant, toothpaste, car, or magazine to buy—but also an unprecedented degree of control over macro choices, including the option of putting people before profits.

Notes

Chapter 1: Thinking the Unthinkable

1. According to corporate consultants Kevin J. Clancy and Robert S. Shulman, "American business spent perhaps $1 trillion on all forms of marketing" in 1992 (Clancy and Shulman, "Marketing with Blinders On," *Across the Board,* Oct. 1993, 38). It is also vital to note that aggregate corporate marketing expenditures almost always grow faster than the overall economy. Likewise, foreign multinationals probably spend at least as much marketing to Americans as U.S.-based corporations do marketing to foreigners. Hence, corporate marketing expenditure in the United States very probably now exceeds *two* trillion dollars a year.

2. According to the OECD's "Education at a Glance 2001" statistics, in 1998 total public and private primary, secondary, postsecondary, and tertiary educational spending in the United States was 6.03 percent of 1998 U.S. GDP, or roughly $525 billion. "Indicator B2" figures, downloaded Mar. 1, 2002, from <http://www.oecd.org>.

3. World Bank Group, *World Development Report 2000–2001,* 275, downloaded Mar. 1, 2002, from <http://www.worldbank.org/poverty/wdrpoverty/report/tab1.pdf>.

4. Alfred D. Chandler Jr., *The Visible Hand: The Managerial Revolution in American Business* (Cambridge, Mass.: Belknap Press of Harvard University Press, 1977), 492.

5. Lecture by David Satcher, M.D., surgeon general of the United States, U.S. Department of Agriculture symposium Childhood Obesity: Causes and Prevention, Washington, D.C., Oct. 27, 1998. News report downloaded Sept. 20, 2001, from <http://www.niddk.nih.gov/health/nutrit/winnotes/winter99/artcl7. htm>.

6. Neil Postman, *The Disappearance of Childhood* (New York: Random House, 1982), 4.

7. Leslie Savan, *The Sponsored Life: Ads, TV, and American Culture* (Philadelphia: Temple University Press, 1994), 4.

8. See Raymond Williams, *Keywords: A Vocabulary of Culture and Society,* rev. ed. (New York: Oxford University Press, 1983), 78–79.

9. Karl Marx and Friedrich Engels, *The German Ideology,* pt. 1 (New York: International Publishers, 1988), 64 (emphasis in original).

10. "The unmentionable five-letter word" is Noam Chomsky's phrase. See Noam Chomsky and David Barsamian, *Keeping the Rabble in Line: Noam Chomsky Interviews with David Barsamian* (Monroe, Maine: Common Courage Press, 1994), 103.

11. Alex Carey, *Taking the Risk Out of Democracy: Corporate Propaganda versus Freedom and Liberty* (Urbana: University of Illinois Press, 1997), 18.

12. Gordon Webber, "P&G—Thursday, March 8, 1968: Presentation before Al Harris' Group—Bonus, Cheer, Dash, Ivory Snow Liquid," business meeting presentation to Procter and Gamble executives, B&B box 6, D'Arcy Masius Benton & Bowles Collection, John W. Hartman Center for Sales, Advertising, & Marketing History, Duke University, Durham, North Carolina.

13. Philip Kotler, *Marketing Management: Analysis, Planning, and Control,* 3d ed. (Englewood Cliffs, N.J.: Prentice Hall, 1976), 17.

14. Henry R. Luce, "The Reformation of the World's Economies," *Fortune,* Feb. 1950, 62.

15. W. W. Rostow, *The Stages of Economic Growth: A Non-Communist Manifesto,* 3d ed. (Cambridge: Cambridge University Press, 1990), 11, 10.

16. Daniel J. Boorstin, *The Americans: The Democratic Experience* (New York: Vintage Books, 1974), 148.

17. Daniel Bell, *The Cultural Contradictions of Capitalism* (New York: Basic Books, 1976), 77 (emphasis added).

18. Ibid., 37. Of note, like most later cultural critics, Bell, the purportedly eminent sociologist, reduces culture to personal life. "Culture," Bell says, is "a conception of self, and a style of life which exhibits those conceptions in the objects that adorn one's home and oneself" (ibid., 36).

19. Ibid., 77.

20. Chandler, *Visible Hand,* 1.

21. Francis Fukuyama, *The End of History and the Last Man* (New York: Free Press, 1992), 93, xi.

22. Herbert Marcuse, *One-Dimensional Man: Studies in the Ideology of Advanced Industrial Society* (Boston: Beacon Press, 1964), 11–12.

23. Stuart Ewen, *Captains of Consciousness: Advertising and the Social Roots of the Consumer Culture* (New York: McGraw-Hill, 1976), 14, 19.

24. Jean Baudrillard, *The Society of Consumption,* translated and quoted in Douglas Kellner, *Jean Baudrillard: From Marxism to Postmodernism and Beyond* (Stanford: Stanford University Press, 1989), 15–16.

25. William Leach, *Land of Desire: Merchants, Power, and the Rise of a New American Culture* (New York: Pantheon Books, 1993), 5.

26. John C. Ryan and Alan Thein Durning, *Stuff: The Secret Lives of Everyday Things* (Seattle: Northwest Environment Watch, 1997).

27. C. Wright Mills, Introduction to the Mentor Edition of Thorstein Veblen, *Theory of the Leisure Class* (New York: Mentor Books, 1953), vi.

28. Vance Packard, *The Hidden Persuaders* (New York: David McKay, 1957); John Kenneth Galbraith, "The Dependence Effect," pp. 152–60 in Galbraith, *The Affluent Society* (Cambridge, Mass.: Riverside Press, 1958); Paul A. Baran and Paul M. Sweezy, "The Sales Effort," pp. 112–41 in Baran and Sweezy, *Monopoly Capital: An Essay on the American Economic and Social Order* (New York: Monthly Review Press, 1966).

29. Thorstein Veblen, *The Theory of the Leisure Class* (1899; rpt., New York: Mentor Books, 1953).

30. Thorstein Veblen, *The Instinct of Workmanship and the State of the Industrial Arts* (1918; rpt., New York: Augustus M. Kelley, 1964), 185.

31. Ibid., 183 (emphasis added).

32. Ibid., 185.

33. Ibid., 159, 187, 354.

34. Ibid., 312.

35. Thorstein Veblen, *The Theory of Business Enterprise* (1904; rpt., New York: Charles Scribner's Sons, 1932), 56–57n.

36. Thorstein Veblen, *Absentee Ownership and Business Enterprise in Recent Times: The Case of America* (1923; rpt., New York: Augustus M. Kelley, 1964), 309–10.

37. Ibid., 307n.

38. Ibid., 288.

39. Ibid., 312.

40. Ibid., 303.

41. Ibid.

42. Ibid., 300.

43. Ibid., 306.

44. Ibid., 307.

45. Ibid., 314.

46. Ibid., 393–94.

47. Ibid., 395.

48. Veblen, *Instinct of Workmanship*, 315.

Chapter 2: The Marketing Race

1. Daniel A. Wren and Robert D. Hay, "Management Historians and Business Historians: Differing Perceptions of Pioneer Contributors," *Academy of Management Journal* 20.3 (September 1977): 470–75.

2. Frederick Winslow Taylor, "Why Manufacturers Dislike College Students," quoted in Robert Kanigel, *The One Best Way: Frederick Winslow Taylor and the Enigma of Efficiency* (New York: Viking Penguin, 1997), 144; Taylor, "Shop Management" in Taylor, *The Principles of Scientific Management* (1911; rpt., New York: Harper, 1947), 143.

3. Taylor, *Scientific Management*, 8, 119.

4. Harlow S. Person, "Shaping Your Management to Meet Developing Industrial Conditions," *Bulletin of the Taylor Society* 8.6 (Dec. 1922): 213, 215.

5. Ibid., 213–14.

6. Ibid.

7. Ibid., 215–16.

8. Ibid., 214.

9. Eric Foner, *Reconstruction: America's Unfinished Revolution, 1863–1877* (New York: Harper and Row, 1988), 477.

10. Richard Hofstadter, *The Age of Reform: From Bryan to F.D.R.* (New York: Vintage Books, 1960), 136.

11. Louis Galambos, "The U.S. Corporate Economy in the Twentieth Century," in *The Cambridge Economic History of the United States,* vol. 3, ed. Stanley L. Engerman and Robert E. Gallman (Cambridge: Cambridge University Press, 2000), 932.

12. See Arthur H. Dean, *William Nelson Cromwell, 1854–1948: An American Pioneer in Corporation, Comparative, and International Law* (New York: Ad Press, 1957).

13. Richard B. DuBoff, *Accumulation and Power: An Economic History of the United States* (Armonk, N.Y.: M. E. Sharpe, 1988), 57–58.

14. Herbert Stein and Murray Foss, *The Illustrated Guide to the American Economy,* 3d ed. (Washington, D.C.: AEI Press, 1999), 151.

15. John Bellamy Foster, *The Theory of Monopoly Capitalism: An Elaboration of Marxian Political Economy* (New York: Monthly Review Press, 1986), 70–71.

16. Baran and Sweezy, *Monopoly Capital,* 47.

17. Adam Smith, *Wealth of Nations* (1776; rpt., Oxford, U.K.: Clarendon Press, 1976).

18. "Mr. Edison Is Satisfied," *New York Times,* Feb. 21, 1892, 2.

19. Joseph Schumpeter, *Capitalism, Socialism, and Democracy* (New York: Harper and Row, 1942), 90n.

20. Robert J. Dolan and Hermann Simon, *Power Pricing: How Managing Price Transforms the Bottom Line* (New York: Free Press, 1996), 10, 8–9.

21. Akshay R. Rao, Mark E. Bergen, and Scott Davis, "How to Fight a Price War," *Harvard Business Review* 78.2 (Mar.–Apr. 2000): 109.

22. Rob Grunewald, "Consumer Price Index (Estimate) 1800–2000," on "Woodrow," World Wide Web site of the Federal Reserve Bank of Minneapolis, downloaded Apr. 12, 2001, from <http://www.minneapolisfed.org/economy/calc/hist1800.html>.

23. Robert E. Gallman, "Economic Growth and Structural Change in the Long Nineteenth Century," in *The Cambridge Economic History of the United States,* vol. 2, ed. Stanley L. Engerman and Robert E. Gallman (Cambridge: Cambridge University Press, 2000), 6.

24. U.S. Bureau of Labor Statistics, "Inflation Calculator," downloaded Mar. 22, 2001, from <http://www.stats.bls.gov>.

25. Chandler, *Visible Hand.*

26. Ibid., 464–67.

27. Oral history interview with A. G. (Jeff) Wade II, by Dolores C. Cogan, Oct. 2 and 29, 1980, series 5C, box 16, p. 22, Alka-Seltzer Oral History and Documentation Project, collection #184, compiled by Stacy Flaherty and Mona Morris, revised by Mimi Minnick, Center for Advertising History, Archives Center, National Museum of American History, Smithsonian Institution, Washington, D.C. [hereafter Alka-Seltzer Collection].

28. Ibid., pp. 22, 12.

29. Robert Kanigel, *The One Best Way: Frederick Winslow Taylor and the Enigma of Efficiency* (New York: Viking, 1997), 229.

30. Ibid., 304.

31. Ibid., 323.

32. Ibid., 7.

33. Peter F. Drucker, *Management: Tasks, Responsibilities, Practices* (New York: Harper and Row, 1974), 200.

34. Baran and Sweezy, *Monopoly Capital,* 71.

35. Based on U.S. Bureau of Economic Analysis figures, using 1996 dollars. See <http://www.bea.doc.gov>.

36. Arthur B. Kennickell, "An Examination of Changes in the Distribution of Wealth from 1989 to 1998: Evidence from the Survey of Consumer Finances," downloaded Mar. 29, 2001, from <http://www.federalreserve.gov/pubs/oss/oss2/scfindex.html>. Data cited are from ibid., table 6d, p. 18.

37. "Parasites and Politics: An Interview with Kevin Phillips," *Multinational Monitor,* Dec. 1994, 21.

38. U.S. Department of Commerce, Bureau of Economic Analysis, "National Income and Product Accounts Tables," June 27, 2002 revision, Table 2.1, downloaded July 24, 2002, from <http://www.bea.doc.gov/>.

39. The 2000 census found 106 million households in the United States. See Table DP-1, "Profile of General Demographic Characteristics: 2000," <http://www.factfinder.census.gov/>.

40. Doug Henwood, "Wall Street: Class Racket," downloaded Mar. 4, 2002, from <http://www.panix.com/dhenwood/WS_Brecht.html>. Not all of the $880,000 per elite household was actual cash income. Personal dividend and interest statistics include imputed sums and funds retained by certain nonprofit organizations. It is entirely reasonable, though, to assume that our elite winds up benefiting disproportionately from such imputations and organizations, as well, in the end.

41. Kennickell, "Examination of Changes," table 6d, 18.

42. Arthur B. Kennickell, Martha Starr-McCluer, and Brian J. Surette, "Recent Changes in U.S. Family Finances: Results from the 1998 Survey of Consumer Finances," *Federal Reserve Bulletin,* Jan. 2000, table 5b, 11.

43. Edward N. Wolff, "Recent Trends in Wealth Ownership, 1983–1998," Working Paper No. 300, Jerome Levy Economics Institute of Bard College, downloaded July 24, 2002, from <http://www.levy.org/>.

44. Floyd Norris, "Market Watch," *New York Times,* Aug. 30, 1992, sec. 3, 1.

45. Philip Mattera, *Prosperity Lost* (Reading, Mass.: Addison-Wesley, 1990), 18.

46. David M. Gordon, *Fat and Mean: The Corporate Squeeze of Working Americans* (New York: Free Press, 1996), 19.

47. Author's calculations from U.S. Department of Commerce/Bureau of Economic Analysis, "National Income and Product Accounts Tables," Tables 2.1 and 7.1. Downloaded July 24, 2002, from <http://www.bea.doc.gov/>.

48. John Kenneth Galbraith, *American Capitalism: The Concept of Countervailing Power* (Boston: Houghton Mifflin, 1952), 5.

49. Oral history interview with Richard B. White, by Barbara Griffith, Mar. 17, 1989, at Stamford, Conn., interview #6, series 3, subseries B, box 10 [hereafter White interview], Campbell Soup "Red & White" Advertising Oral History and Documentation Project, c. 1904–1990, collection #397, compiled by Mimi Minnick, Center for Advertising History, Archives Center, National Museum of American History, Smithsonian Institution, Washington, D.C. [hereafter Campbell Soup Collection]; oral history interview with Tom Dillon, by Scott Ellsworth, May 23, 1984, n.p., interview #00, series 2, box 13, folder 6 [hereafter Dillon interview], "Pepsi Generation" Oral History and Documentation Project, 1938–1986, collection #111, compiled by Carol L. Dreyfus, revised by Mimi Minnick, Center for Advertising History, Archives Center, National Museum of American History, Smithsonian Institution, Washington, D.C. [hereafter Pepsi Collection]. Procter and Gamble CEO Durk Jager quoted in Jack Neff, "'Emerging Markets' Wreak Havoc on Package Goods," *Advertising Age,* Mar. 5, 2002 [QwikFIND ID No. AAN25V, <http://www.adage.com/>].

50. Regis McKenna, *Total Access: Giving Customers What They Want in an Anytime, Anywhere World* (Boston: Harvard Business School Press, 2002), 2.

51. Robert J. Keith, "The Marketing Revolution," in *Marketing Classics: A Selection of Influential Articles,* ed. Ben M. Enis and Keith K. Cox (Boston: Allyn and Bacon, 1969), 83, 86.

52. Richard Ott, *Creating Demand: Powerful Tips and Tactics for Marketing Your Product or Service* (Burr Ridge, Ill.: Irwin, 1992), viii.

53. Wroe Alderson, "The Analytical Framework for Marketing," in *Marketing Classics: A Selection of Influential Articles,* ed. Ben M. Enis and Keith K. Cox (Boston: Allyn and Bacon, 1969), 8, 12, 15.

54. Marion Harper Jr., "Transcendental Marketing: A Perspective on Managing Growth in the Large Private Enterprise, 1975–1995," undated manuscript, Marion Harper Papers, Archives Center Collection #394, series 2, subseries 1, box 4, "Unpublished Manuscripts: Business and Marketing," 71, National Museum of American History, Smithsonian Institution, Washington, D.C.

Chapter 3: The Targeting Race

1. The Housemartins, "Get Up off Our Knees," track 2 of *Hull 4, London 0* (New York: Electra/Asylum Records, 1986).

2. Kevin J. Clancy and Robert S. Shulman, *Marketing Myths That Are Killing Business: The Cure for Death Wish Marketing* (New York: McGraw-Hill, 1994), 99.

3. Thomas C. Kinnear and Kenneth L. Bernhardt, *Principles of Marketing,* 2d ed. (Glenview, Ill.: Scott, Foresman, 1986), 106.

4. Clancy and Shulman, *Marketing Myths,* 99.

5. Alexander Hiam and Charles D. Schewe, *The Portable MBA in Marketing* (New York: John Wiley and Sons, 1992), 151.

6. Theodore Levitt, *The Marketing Imagination,* exp. ed. (New York: Free Press, 1986), 141.

7. Philip Kotler, *Marketing Management,* millennium ed. (Englewood Cliffs, N.J.: Prentice Hall, 2000), 2.

8. Oral history interview with R. Gordon McGovern, by Barbara Griffith, Sept. 6, 1989, at Camden, N.J., interview #17, series 3, subseries B, box 9, Campbell Soup Collection [hereafter McGovern interview].

9. E. Jerome McCarthy and William D. Perrault, *Essentials of Marketing,* 5th ed. (Homewood, Ill.: Irwin, 1991), 56.

10. Drucker, *Management,* 67; McCarthy and Perrault, *Essentials of Marketing,* 56.

11. Hiam and Schewe, *Portable MBA,* 136 (emphasis in original).

12. Kotler, *Marketing Management,* 3d ed., 139–40, 138.

13. Peter Francese and Rebecca Piirto, *Capturing Customers: How to Target the Hottest Markets of the '90s* (Ithaca, N.Y.: American Demographics Press, 1990), 38.

14. Thomas C. Kinnear and James R. Taylor, *Marketing Research: An Applied Approach,* 5th ed. (New York: McGraw-Hill, 1996), 31.

15. Richard Polenberg, *One Nation Divisible: Class, Race, and Ethnicity in the United States since 1938* (Harmondsworth, U.K.: Penguin, 1980), 63–64.

16. Gabriel Kolko, *Maincurrents in Modern American History* (New York: Pantheon Books, 1984), 317.

17. Paul D. Converse and Robert V. Mitchell, *The Elements of Marketing,* 5th ed. (New York: Prentice Hall, 1952), 20.

18. "Another County Heard From," *Business Week,* Apr. 8, 1950, 74.

19. "Science Can Find Their Market," *Business Week,* Oct. 27, 1956, 47.

20. Ibid., 48, 50.

21. Kolko, *Maincurrents,* 317.

22. Harold G. Vatter, *The U.S. Economy in the 1950s* (Chicago: University of Chicago Press), 106.

23. Wendell R. Smith, "Product Differentiation and Market Segmentation As Alternative Marketing Strategies," in *Marketing Classics: A Selection of Influential Articles,* ed. Ben M. Enis and Keith K. Cox (Boston: Allyn and Bacon, 1969), 382, 381.

24. Ibid., 377.

25. Ibid., 380.

26. Ibid., 378, 382 (emphasis added).

27. Ibid., 379, 382, 380–81.

28. Ibid., 382.

29. See Werner J. Severin and James W. Tankard Jr., *Communication Theories: Origins, Methods, and Uses in the Mass Media* (New York: Longman, 2001); and Severin and Tankard, eds., *Measurement and Prediction,* vol. 4 of *Studies in Social Psychology in World War II,* Samuel A. Stouffer, Louis Guttman, Edward A. Suchman, Paul F. Lazarsfeld, Shirley A. Star, and John A. Clausen, general editors (Princeton, N.J.: Princeton University Press, 1949).

30. Allan J. Magrath, *The Six Imperatives of Marketing: Lessons from the World's Best Companies* (New York: AMACOM Books, 1992), 15.

31. "Glamour in Fact" report, Estelle Ellis Collection, series 3, box 3.5, folder 4, Center for Advertising History, Archives Center, National Museum of American History, Smithsonian Institution, Washington, D.C.

32. "Canned Soup Perceptual Mapping Study," July 28, 1971, series 1, box 3, folder 22, Campbell Soup Collection.

33. Smith, "Product Differentiation," 383–84.

34. Michael J. Weiss, *The Clustering of America* (New York: Harper and Row, 1988), 10.

35. Ibid., 11–12.

36. Eric Clark, *The Want Makers: Inside the World of Advertising* (New York: Viking Penguin, 1988), 163.

37. Weiss, *Clustering of America,* 14; Erik Larson, *The Naked Consumer: How Our Private Lives Become Public Commodities* (New York: Henry Holt, 1992), 43.

38. See Weiss, *Clustering of America.*

39. R. Gordon McGovern, "Remarks to Institute of Food Technologists," speech delivered on June 20, 1988, in New Orleans, La., series 1, box 2, Campbell Soup Collection.

40. Howard Schlossberg, "Marketing's 'Stepchild' Gets Respect," *Marketing News,* Mar. 15, 1993, 1.

41. Larson, *Naked Consumer,* 152.

42. Ibid., 8.

43. Polk Market Analysis Group advertisement, *American Demographics,* Oct. 1992, 20.

44. Jack Honomichl, "'Hypertargeting Scenario Not As Farfetched As It Seems," *Marketing News,* Nov. 9, 1992, 11–12.

45. Elizabeth Kolbert, "TV Viewing and Selling, by Race," *New York Times,* Apr. 5, 1993, C7.

46. "Company News: AT&T to Begin Sale of New Communicator," *New York Times,* Apr. 17, 1993, 17.

47. Ronald Grover and Laura Zinn, "Big Brother Is Grocery Shopping with You," *Business Week,* Mar. 29, 1993, 60.

48. These descriptions of the Clinton administration come from Susan B. Garland, Richard S. Dunham, and Laura Zinn, "Polling for Policy," *Business Week,* Feb. 22, 1993, 35, and from James Grant, editor of *Grant's Interest Rate Observer,* quoted in Floyd Norris, "Bond Traders Love Clinton and Vice Versa," *New York Times,* Mar. 14, 1993, sec. 3, 1.

49. Philip Elmer-Dewitth and David S. Jackson, "Take a Trip into the Future," *Time,* Apr. 12, 1993, 54.

50. Ibid., 55.

51. Regis McKenna, *Relationship Marketing: Successful Strategies for the Age of the Customer* (Reading, Mass.: Addison-Wesley, 1991), 18.

52. Jonathan Berry and John Verity, "Database Marketing," *Business Week,* Sept. 5, 1994, 56–57, 58.

53. Gary Saarenvirta, "Operation Data Mining," downloaded July 30, 2002, from <http://www.db2mag.com/db_area/archives/2001/q2/saarenvirta.shtml >.

54. "Claritas History," downloaded Oct. 19, 2001, from <http://www.claritas.com/5_company_info/sub/history.htm>.

55. Symmetrical Research, "Press Release," downloaded Oct. 19, 2001, from <http://www.symmetrical.com>.

56. See Larson, *Naked Consumer.*

57. Quoted from <http://www.claritas.com/>, July 30, 2002.

58. Ibid., 15.

59. Quoted in Berry and Verity, "Database Marketing," 58.

60. Larson, *Naked Consumer,* 9.

Chapter 4: The Motivation Research Race

1. Harper, "Transcendental Marketing," 72.

2. Alderson, "Analytical Framework for Marketing," 8.

3. Norbert Elias, *The Society of Individuals* (London: Basil Blackwell, 1991), 184.

4. Douglas S. Massey, "A Brief History of Human Society: The Origin and Role of Emotion in Social Life," *American Sociological Review* 67, no. 1 (Feb. 2002): 2 (emphasis in original).

5. Philip Kotler and Gary Armstrong, *Principles of Marketing,* 5th ed. (Englewood Cliffs, N.J.: Prentice Hall, 1991), xx.

6. Ibid., 9. Note that Kotler and Armstrong remove their historical explanation of marketing by their 8th edition, to which I also refer in later pages.

7. Ibid., 10.

8. Ibid., 7.

9. Ibid., 10.

10. Ibid., 5–6.

11. Ibid., 146.

12. Ibid., 147–58.

13. Kotler and Armstrong, *Principles of Marketing,* 5th ed., 120.

14. Ibid., 119.

15. See Kerry W. Buckley, *Mechanical Man: John Broadus Watson and the Beginnings of Behaviorism* (New York: Guilford Press, 1989).

16. From the text of a 1922 speech cited in ibid., 137.

17. Corporate marketers also study and utilize the insights of cognitive psychology. For a good overview of the eclectic, all-inclusive, and pragmatic attitude to studying and interpreting the human psyche in modern marketing practice, see Foxall and Goldsmith, *Consumer Psychology,* chap. 4.

18. Rebecca Piirto, *Beyond Mind Games: The Marketing Power of Psychographics* (Ithaca, N.Y.: American Demographics Books, 1991), 127.

19. Ibid.

20. Kotler and Armstrong, *Principles of Marketing,* 5th ed., 119.

21. Ibid.

22. See White interview; oral history interview with Jean Rindlaub, by Barbara Griffith, Mar. 17, 1989, at Stamford, Conn., interview #7, series 3, subseries B, box 10, Campbell Soup Collection [hereafter Rindlaub interview]; oral history interview with Betty Cronin, by Barbara Griffith, Sept. 19, 1989, at Camden, N.J., interview #21, series 3, subseries B, box 8, Campbell Soup Collection [hereafter Cronin interview]; oral history interview with Joseph A. Prior, by Barbara Griffith, Mar. 13, 1989, at New York, N.Y., interview #5, series 3, subseries B, box 10, Campbell Soup Collection [hereafter Prior interview]; oral history interview with Richard J. Mercer, by Barbara Griffith, June 16, 1989, at New York, N.Y., interview #13, series 3, subseries B, box 9, Campbell Soup Collection [hereafter Mercer interview]; and McGovern interview.

23. Dillon interview; oral history interview with Treva Van Solingen, by Barbara Griffith, Oct. 22, 1986, at Elkhart, Indiana, interview #3, series 3, subseries B, box 2, Alka-Seltzer Collection [hereafter Van Solingen interview].

24. R. Dale Wilson and Noreen K. Moore, "The Role of Sexually-Oriented Stimuli in Advertising: Theory and Literature Review," in *Advances in Consumer Research,* vol. 6, ed. William L. Wilkie (Ann Arbor, Mich.: Association for Consumer Research, 1979), 55–61; James T. Strong and Khalid M. Dubas, "The Processing of Marketing Threat Stimuli: A Comprehensive Framework," in *Research in Marketing,* vol. 11, ed. Jagdish M. Sheth (Greenwich, Conn.: JAI Press, 1992), 221–63.

25. Wilson and Moore, "Role of Sexually-Oriented Stimuli," 55; Strong and Dubas, "Processing of Marketing Threat," 255.

26. Revson quoted in Michael Hiestand, *Marketing Made Easy* (Los Angeles: Price Stern Sloan, 1990), 16.

27. Dillon interview.

28. Oral history interview with George Weissman, by Scott Ellsworth, Apr. 27, 1987, at New York, N.Y., interview #59, series 3, subseries B, box 5 [hereafter Weissman interview],

Marlboro Oral History and Documentation Project, c. 1940–1986, collection #198, compiled by Stacy Flaherty and Mona Morris, revised by Allison Lee, Center for Advertising History, Archives Center, National Museum of American History, Smithsonian Institution, Washington, D.C. [hereafter Marlboro Collection]; oral history interview with John Benson, by Scott Ellsworth, Apr. 14, 1986, at Chicago, Ill., interview #4, series 3, subseries B, box 1, Marlboro Collection [hereafter Benson interview]

29. Weissman interview.

30. R. Gordon McGovern, "Campbell's Strategy Shifts with Lifestyles," *Progressive Grocer,* June 1982, 61.

31. Aradhna Krishna, Imran S. Currim, and Robert W. Shoemaker, "Consumer Perceptions of Promotional Activity," *Journal of Marketing* 55.2 (Apr. 1991): 4–5.

32. Harper W. Boyd, "The Role of Marketing Research in Marketing Management," in *Handbook of Modern Marketing,* 2d ed., ed. Victor P. Buell (New York: McGraw-Hill, 1986), 33–11.

33. Arch Shaw, "Some Problems in Marketing Distribution," *Quarterly Journal of Economics* 32 (Aug. 1912): 703.

34. Piirto, *Beyond Mind Games,* 10–11.

35. Dik W. Twedt, ed., *1973 Survey of Marketing Research* (Chicago: American Marketing Association, 1973), 21.

36. Boyd, "Role of Marketing Research," 33–5.

37. Ibid.

38. Piirto, *Beyond Mind Games,* 11.

39. Douglas McGregor, "'Motives' As a Tool of Market Research," *Harvard Business Review* 52.1 (Autumn 1940): 42–43.

40. Ibid.

41. Boyd, "Role of Marketing Research," 33–5.

42. Thomas C. Kinnear and James R. Taylor, *Marketing Research: An Applied Approach,* 3d ed. (New York: McGraw-Hill, 1983), 27.

43. Compare Twedt, *1973 Survey of Marketing Research,* and Twedt, ed., *1978 Survey of Marketing Research* (Chicago: American Marketing Association, 1978).

44. David J. Luck, Hugh G. Wales, Donald A. Taylor, and Ronald S. Rubin, *Marketing Research,* 5th ed. (Englewood Cliffs, N.J.: Prentice Hall, 1978), 14.

45. Boyd, "Role of Marketing Research," 33–6.

46. Thomas C. Kinnear and Ann R. Root, eds., *1988 Survey of Marketing Research* (New York: McGraw-Hill, 1989), 43–44.

47. Ibid., 43.

48. Steuart Henderson Britt, "The Strategy of Consumer Motivation," *Journal of Marketing* 14.5 (Apr. 1950): 666, 669, 668.

49. Ibid., 672.

50. Piirto, *Beyond Mind Games,* 15.

51. Ibid., 15–16.

52. Packard, *Hidden Persuaders,* 142–43.

53. "Coffee Saga Continues," *Wall Street Journal,* Jan. 6, 1993, B8 (eastern ed.); "Nescafe Commercial for Instant Coffee Inspires U.K. Novel, *Wall Street Journal,* Feb. 8, 1993, B6 (eastern ed.).

54. "Alka-Seltzer: Its Users, Their Personalities, and Attitudes," series 5, subseries A, box 2, folder 2, pp. 46–49, Alka-Seltzer Collection.

55. Ibid., 64.

56. Van Solingen interview.

57. Piirto, *Beyond Mind Games,* 124.

58. Ibid., 17.

59. Leon G. Schiffman and Leslie Lazar Kanuk, *Consumer Behavior,* 4th ed. (Englewood Cliffs, N.J.: Prentice Hall, 1991), 11.

60. Ibid.

61. Stevens, "Consumer Behavior Research," 144.

62. Daniel Yankelovich, "New Criteria for Market Segmentation," *Harvard Business Review* 42.2 (Mar.–Apr. 1964): 84.

63. Ibid., 89.

64. Ibid.

65. Daniel Pope, *The Making of Modern Advertising* (New York: Basic Books, 1983), 288–90.

66. Kinnear and Taylor, *Marketing Research,* 5th ed., 28.

67. See Piirto, *Beyond Mind Games,* 229–31.

68. See Stan Rapp and Tom Collins, *The Great Marketing Turnaround: The Age of the Individual and How to Profit from It* (Englewood Cliffs, N.J.: Prentice Hall, 1990), 136–43.

69. James U. McNeal, "Growing Up in the Market," *American Demographics,* Oct. 1992, 46–51.

70. "With Brickstream, You See It All," promotional brochure downloaded Aug. 2, 2002, from <http://www.brickstream.com/>, pp. 4, 3, 2.

71. C. Wright Mills, "Situated Actions and Vocabularies of Motives," in *Symbolic Interaction: A Reader in Social Psychology,* ed. Jerome G. Manis and Bernard N. Meltzer (Boston: Allyn and Bacon, 1972), 394, 398, 396.

72. Jonathan Bond and Richard Kirshenbaum, *Under the Radar: Talking to Today's Cynical Consumer* (New York: John Wiley and Sons, 1998), 1, 30, 212, 213.

73. Simson Garfinkel, *Database Nation: The Death of Privacy in the 21st Century* (Cambridge, Mass.: O'Reilly and Associates, 2001), p. 3.

74. For overviews of these real procedures, see, respectively, Jan Larson, "A Segment of One," *American Demographics,* Dec. 1991, 16–17; Laura Zinn and Jonathan Berry, "Teens: Here Comes the Biggest Wave Yet," *Business Week,* Apr. 11, 1994, 76–86; Laura Zinn and Christopher Power, "Move Over, Boomers," *Business Week,* Dec. 14, 1992, 74–82; and Geoffrey Smith and Ron Stodghill II, "Are Good Causes Good Marketing?" *Business Week,* Mar. 21, 1994, 64–66.

Chapter 5: The Product Management Race

1. Oral history interview with Richard Courtice, by Tom Wiener, May 14, 1992, at Orlando, Fla., interview #9, series 2, subseries B, boxes 5–8 [hereafter Courtice interview], Kraft Television Theater Oral History and Documentation Project, collection #464, compiled by Mimi Minnick, Center for Advertising History, Archives Center, National Museum of American History, Smithsonian Institution, Washington, D.C. [hereafter Kraft Collection].

2. Susan Strasser, *Satisfaction Guaranteed* (New York: Pantheon Books, 1989), 4–5.

3. Strasser, despite her documentation of P&G's reasons for introducing Crisco, mistakenly treats it as the first example of a product that was based on full-fledged marketing planning. Despite the otherwise excellent nature of her work on marketing history, Strasser seems to fall into this trap because she fails to escape completely the mass consumption critics' habit of reading conclusions from products themselves, rather than from the managerial and other human relationships behind them (ibid., 14).

4. Alfred P. Sloan, *My Years with General Motors* (Garden City, N.Y.: Doubleday, 1964), 64.

5. James J. Flink, *The Automobile Age* (Cambridge, Mass.: MIT Press, 1988), 234.

6. Ibid.

7. David A. Aaker, *Managing Brand Equity: Capitalizing on the Value of a Brand Name* (New York: Free Press, 1991), 5.

8. Social scientists treat "Fordism" (assembly-line production in supposedly high-wage factories) as a central organizing principle of corporate capitalism. Yet, as Flink suggests in *Automobile Age,* chap. 12, "Sloanism" (marketing-driven product manipulation) is the better label for the central managerial principle in big business.

9. Richard B. Countess and Mearritt A. Williamson, "New Product Development," *Encyclopedia of Management,* 3d ed., ed. Carl Heyel (New York: Van Nostrand Reinhold, 1982), 733.

10. Arthur J. Kuhn, *GM Passes Ford, 1918–1938: Designing the General Motors Performance-Control System* (University Park: Pennsylvania State University Press, 1986), 89.

11. Keith, "Marketing Revolution," 84–86.

12. Quoted in Kinnear and Bernhardt, *Principles of Marketing,* 14.

13. David L. Wilemon, "Product and Market Managers," in *Handbook of Modern Marketing,* ed. Buell, 52–1.

14. J. S. Bayliss, *Marketing for Engineers* (London: Peter Peregrinus, 1985), 1, 11, xvi.

15. Richard S. Latham, "The Role of the Industrial Designer in Product and Package Development," in *Handbook of Modern Marketing,* ed. Buell, 21–1.

16. See, for example, Philip Kotler and Gary Armstrong, *Principles of Marketing,* 8th ed. (Englewood Cliffs, N.J.: Prentice Hall, 1999), chap. 8.

17. Kotler, *Marketing Management,* millennium ed., 344, 347.

18. Ibid., 420.

19. Ibid., 340.

20. Ibid., 421.

21. Levitt, *Marketing Imagination,* 84.

22. Dillon interview.

23. Oral history interview with Sheri Colonel, by Scott Ellsworth, Feb. 28, 1990, at New York, N.Y., interview #12, series 3, subseries B, box 9 [hereafter Colonel interview], Cover Girl Make-up Advertising History Collection, 1959–1990, Oral History and Documentation Project, collection #374, compiled by Mimi Minnick, Center for Advertising History, Archives Center, National Museum of American History, Smithsonian Institution, Washington, D.C. [hereafter Cover Girl Collection].

24. Clark, *Want Makers,* 24.

25. "Account Summary," July 18, 1974, Box 6, J. Walter Thompson Review Board Records,

John W. Hartman Center for Sales, Advertising, & Marketing History, Duke University, Durham, North Carolina.

26. Memorandum, September 26, 1957, Box 30, J. Walter Thompson Review Board Records, John W. Hartman Center for Sales, Advertising, & Marketing History, Duke University, Durham, North Carolina.

27. "Account Summary," June 26, 1974, Box 26, J. Walter Thompson Review Board Records, John W. Hartman Center for Sales, Advertising, & Marketing History, Duke University, Durham, North Carolina.

28. "Account Summary," January 30, 1963, Box 9, J. Walter Thompson Review Board Records, John W. Hartman Center for Sales, Advertising, & Marketing History, Duke University, Durham, North Carolina.

29. "L&M New Products Presentation Outline," February 1969, Box 20, J. Walter Thompson Review Board Records, John W. Hartman Center for Sales, Advertising, & Marketing History, Duke University, Durham, North Carolina.

30. Al Ries and Jack Trout, *Positioning: The Battle for Your Mind* (New York: Warner Books, 1981), 8.

31. Ibid., 2.

32. Ibid.

33. Stephen Fox, *The Mirror Makers: A History of American Advertising* (London: Heinemann, 1985), 324.

34. Aaker, *Managing Brand Equity*, 7.

35. Ibid., 46.

36. Ibid., 16–18.

37. Naomi Klein, *No Logo: Taking Aim at the Brand Bullies* (New York: Picador USA, 2000), 17.

38. Kotler and Armstrong, *Principles of Marketing*, 5th ed., 258.

39. Aaker, *Managing Brand Equity*, 19.

40. Ibid., 85.

41. Clark, *Want Makers*, 26.

42. Dillon interview.

43. Veblen, *Absentee Ownership*, 278, 108.

44. Oral history interview with John Bergin, by Scott Ellsworth, Feb. 15, 1990, at New York, N.Y., interview #8, series 3, subseries B, box 9, Cover Girl Collection [hereafter Bergin interview].

45. Allan Kozinn, "On Remembered Joys of the LP Recording," *New York Times*, July 12, 1993, B3.

46. Kotler and Armstrong, *Principles of Marketing*, 5th ed., 520.

47. Fox, *Mirror Makers*, 173.

48. See inter-department correspondence between H. M. Stevens and J. A. McGlinn, series 1, box 2, file 2, Campbell Soup Collection.

49. Thomas Hine, *The Total Package: The Evolution and Secret Meanings of Boxes, Bottles, Cans, and Tubes* (Boston: Little, Brown, 1995), 215.

50. Ibid., 212.

51. Levitt, *Marketing Imagination*, 190.

52. Oral history interview with Peter Moore, by Scott Ellsworth, Nov. 21, 1990, at Port-

land, Ore., interview #11, series 3, subseries B, box 10, Nike Advertising Oral History and Documentation Project, c. 1976–1992, collection #448, compiled by Mimi Minnick, Center for Advertising History, Archives Center, National Museum of American History, Smithsonian Institution, Washington, D.C. [hereafter Moore interview].

53. Barry L. Bayus, "Accelerating the Durable Replacement Cycle with Product Marketing Mix Variables," *Journal of Product Innovation Management* 5 (1988): 219, 223.

54. Kotler and Armstrong, *Principles of Marketing,* 5th ed., 267–68.

55. Dillon interview.

56. Samuel C. Johnson and Conrad Jones, "How to Organize for New Products," *Harvard Business Review* 35.3 (May–June 1957): 49.

57. Oral history interview with Anthony Adams, by Barbara Griffith, Feb. 22, 1989, at Camden, N.J., interview #3, series 3, subseries B, box 10, Campbell Soup Collection [hereafter Adams interview]; Sharon Sexton, "Who Wants to Feed Us?" *Horizon* 8.12 (Dec. 1987): 38–42; Judy Rice, "Frozen, Microwavable Soup and Sandwich Combos," *Food Processing,* Dec. 1987, 66–67; Daniel Best, "The Restructuring of R&D," *Prepared Foods,* Jan. 1988, 10–12.

58. McGovern interview.

59. Alfred P. Sloan, "Message to Shareholders," in GM's 1924 Annual Report. See corporate history page at <http://www.gm.com/>.

60. Oral history interview with William D. Hunt, by Scott Ellsworth, Apr. 4, 1990, at Lutherville, Md., interview #15, series 3, subseries B, box 9, Cover Girl collection.

61. Oral history interview with Peter Troup, by Scott Ellsworth, Jan. 15, 1990, at Hunt Valley, Md., interview #1, series 3, subseries B, box 10, Cover Girl Collection [hereafter Troup interview].

62. Moore interview.

63. Ibid.

64. *Business Week,* Mar. 15, 1993, 53–54.

65. Harvey Levenstein, *Paradox of Plenty: A Social History of Eating in Modern America* (New York: Oxford University Press, 1993), 101.

66. Quoted in B. C. Forbes, ed., *The Forbes Scrapbook of Thoughts on the Business of Life* (Chicago: Triumph Books, 1992), 489.

Chapter 6: The Sales Communications Race

1. Savan, *Sponsored Life,* 10.

2. Clark, *Want Makers,* 14, 13.

3. Pope, *Making of Modern Advertising,* 10.

4. Ewen, *Captains of Consciousness,* 89.

5. Dillon interview.

6. T. J. Jackson Lears, *Fables of Abundance: A Cultural History of Advertising in America* (New York: Basic Books, 1994), 380, 12, 17.

7. Max Sutherland, *Advertising and the Mind of the Consumer: What Works, What Doesn't, and Why* (St. Leonards, Australia: Allen & Unwin, 1993), 6.

8. Ibid., 12.

9. McGovern interview.

10. "Account Summaries," July 5 and 8, 1960, Association of Playing Card Manufacturers, Box 5, J. Walter Thompson Review Board Records, John W. Hartman Center for Sales, Advertising, & Marketing History, Duke University, Durham, North Carolina.

11. Oral history interview with Ed Vorkapich, by Scott Ellsworth, Nov. 23, 1984, at New York, N.Y., interview #00, series 2, box 13, folder 27, Pepsi Collection [hereafter Vorkapich interview].

12. Prior interview.

13. Ibid.

14. Colonel interview (emphasis added).

15. These basic themes, or, in the language of marketing, "core equities," are described, respectively, in the following sources: Dillon interview; Colonel interview; oral history interview with Fran Harrison, by Scott Ellsworth, Feb. 19, 1990, at Sarasota, Fla., interview #7, series 3, subseries B, box 9, Cover Girl Collection [hereafter Harrison interview]; Moore interview; Van Solingen interview; "Glamour in Fact" booklet; Adams interview; and White interview.

16. Alan Resnik and Bruce L. Stern, "An Analysis of Information Content in Television Advertising," *Journal of Marketing* 41 (Jan. 1977): 50–53.

17. For major instances of this argument, see Fox, *Mirror Makers*; and Roland Marchand, *Advertising the American Dream: Making Way for Modernity* (Berkeley: University of California Press, 1985).

18. Michael Schudson, *Advertising, the Uneasy Persuasion: Its Dubious Impact on American Society* (New York: Basic Books, 1984), ix.

19. Ibid., xv, xiv.

20. See, for example, John Philip Jones, *When Ads Work: New Proof That Advertising Triggers Sales* (New York: Lexington Books, 1995); and Ed Papazian, ed., *TV Dimensions '93* (New York: Media Dynamics, 1993), 406, 419–20.

21. Carl E. Bartecci, Thomas D. MacKenzie, and Robert W. Schrier, "The Global Tobacco Epidemic," *Scientific American,* May 1995, 47, 51.

22. Schudson, *Advertising,* 179–80.

23. Ed Papazian, *Medium Rare: The Evolution, Workings, and Impact of Commercial Television* (New York: Media Dynamics, 1991), i.

24. Kotler and Armstrong, *Principles of Marketing,* 5th ed., 457.

25. Clancy and Shulman, *Marketing Myths,* 171, 172.

26. Kotler and Armstrong, *Principles of Marketing,* 5th ed., 675.

27. Hiam and Schewe, *Portable MBA,* 374.

28. Kotler and Armstrong, *Principles of Marketing,* 5th ed., 359.

29. Ibid., 360.

30. Stan Luxenberg, *Roadside Empires: How the Chains Franchised America* (New York: Penguin Books, 1985), 8.

31. Ibid., 22.

32. Kotler, *Marketing Management,* millennium ed., 527.

33. Clancy and Shulman, *Marketing Myths,* 221.

34. Ibid.

35. Kotler and Armstrong, *Principles of Marketing,* 5th ed., 676–77.

36. On the subject of the commodification of everyday life, Harry Braverman makes

the important, if neglected, point that, despite all the progress in this area over the first few centuries of capitalism, the real breakthrough came with the rise of monopoly capital: "During the last hundred years industrial capital has thrust itself between farm and household, . . . thus extending the commodity form to food in its semi-prepared or even fully prepared forms. For example, . . . the proportion of flour used by commercial bakeries climbed rapidly from only one-seventh in 1899 to more than two-fifths by 1939. And during this same period, the per capita consumption of canned vegetables multiplied fivefold, and of canned fruits twelve times over. As with food, so with clothing, shelter, household articles of all sorts: the range of commodity production extended itself rapidly" (Harry Braverman, *Labor and Monopoly Capital: The Degradation of Work in the Twentieth Century* (New York: Monthly Review Press, 1974), 274–75).

37. Samuel Johnson, quoted in *The Columbia World of Quotations*, ed. Robert Andrews, Mary Biggs, and Michael Seidel, downloaded Aug. 7, 2002, from <http://www.bartleby.com/66/>.

38. Fox, *Mirror Makers*, 40.

39. On the history of these trends, see Leach, *Land of Desire*; and Kolko, *Maincurrents*, 284.

40. Klein, *No Logo*, 6.

41. Pope, *Making of Modern Advertising*, 291.

42. Fox, *Mirror Makers*, 176.

43. Ibid.

44. Oral history interview with Jim Blocki, by Tom Wiener, Feb. 4, 1992, at Arlington Heights, Ill., interview #1, series 2, subseries B, boxes 5–8, Kraft Collection.

45. Van Solingen interview.

46. J. P. Jannuzzo, "The Advertising Program," in *Handbook of Modern Marketing*, ed. Buell, 80–82.

47. David A. Aaker and John G. Myers, *Advertising Management*, 2d ed. (Englewood Cliffs, N.J.: Prentice Hall, 1982), 34–35.

48. Keith L. Reinhard, "The Role of the Advertising Agency," in *Handbook of Modern Marketing*, ed. Buell, 81–82.

49. Aaker and Myers, *Advertising Management*, 17.

50. Clark, *Want Makers*, 63–64 (emphasis added).

51. Colonel interview.

52. Adams interview.

53. Stuart Elliott, "The Media Business," *New York Times*, Dec. 15, 1993, C23.

54. Bud Frankel and H. W. Phillips, *Your Advertising's Great . . . How's Business?* (Homewood, Ill.: Dow Jones–Irwin, 1986), vi.

55. Ibid., 10.

56. Pope, *Making of Modern Advertising*, 255.

57. Anonymous memo, "With Public Ownership—Broadened Public Relations," series 1, box 2, folder 4, Campbell Soup Collection.

58. Fred Berger, "Public Relations Aspects of Marketing," in *Handbook of Modern Marketing*, ed. Buell, 86–3 to 86–4.

59. Ibid., 86–12.

60. "Envirosell: Our History," downloaded Mar. 2, 2002, from <http://www.envirosell.com/ history.html>; Underhill, *Why We Buy,* 21.

61. Underhill, *Why We Buy,* 19.

62. Ibid., 18, 26.

63. Ibid., 32.

64. Ibid., 17.

65. Ibid., 31, 17.

66. Ibid., 31.

67. Paul A. Baran and Paul M. Sweezy, "Theses on Advertising," in *The Longer View,* ed. Paul A. Baran (New York: Monthly Review Press, 1969), 225.

68. Clancy and Shulman, *Marketing Myths,* 171.

69. Ibid., 7.

70. Memo "Inter-Dept. Correspondence—General Office," from W. P. Bill and E. D. Russell to J. W. Dodd, Marketing Director, series 1, box 3, folder 24, Campbell Soup Collection.

Chapter 7: Macromarketing and Public Subsidy

1. Kotler and Armstrong, *Principles of Marketing,* 8th ed., 86.

2. Harper, "Transcendental Marketing," 71.

3. Kotler and Armstrong, *Principles of Marketing,* 8th ed., 86.

4. Gabriel Kolko, *The Triumph of Conservatism: A Reinterpretation of American History, 1900–1916* (New York: Free Press, 1963), 2.

5. Ibid., 3.

6. Tom Lewis, *Divided Highways: Building the Interstate Highways, Transforming American Life* (New York: Viking, 1997), ix.

7. Quoted in ibid., 99.

8. U.S. Department of Commerce GDP numbers downloaded Oct. 28, 2001, from <http:// www.bea.doc.gov/bea/dn1.htm>.

9. Lewis, *Divided Highways,* 119, 99, 110.

10. Jane Holtz Kay, *Asphalt Nation: How the Automobile Took Over America and How We Can Take It Back* (New York: Crown, 1997), 118.

11. "Keep the Trains Running," *Washington Post,* Sept. 24, 2001, A20.

12. Kay, *Asphalt Nation,* 118.

13. Andres Duany, Elizabeth Plater-Zyberk, and Jeff Speck, *Suburban Nation: The Rise of Sprawl and the Decline of the American Dream* (New York: North Point Press, 2000), 112.

14. "Moral minimalism," reports the sociologist M. P. Baumgartner, "dominates the suburbs. On a day-by-day basis, life is filled with efforts to deny, minimize, contain, and avoid conflict." Suburbia, Baumgartner finds, "is a kind of limited anarchy" where people "move in and out of relationships frequently and live their lives under conditions of privacy, individuation, [and] material independence" (Baumgartner, *The Moral Order of a Suburb* [New York: Oxford University Press, 1988], 127–28).

15. James Howard Kunstler, *The Geography of Nowhere: The Rise and Decline of America's Man-made Landscape* (New York: Simon and Schuster, 1993), 104–5.

16. "Account Summary," National Association of Home Builders, September 16, 1974,

Box 21, J. Walter Thompson Review Board Records, John W. Hartman Center for Sales, Advertising, & Marketing History, Duke University, Durham, North Carolina.

17. Oral history interview with John T. Landry, by Scott Ellsworth, Mar. 12, 1986, at New York, N.Y., interview #1, series 3, subseries B, box 3, Marlboro Collection.

18. See, for example, Robert D. Putnam, *Bowling Alone: The Collapse and Revival of American Community* (New York: Simon and Schuster, 2000), esp. chap. 13; and John P. Robinson and Geoffrey Godbey, *Time for Life: The Surprising Ways Americans Use Their Time* (University Park: Penn State University Press, 1997), esp. chap. 9.

19. Robert W. McChesney, *Telecommunications, Mass Media, and Democracy: The Battle for the Control of U.S. Broadcasting, 1928–1935* (Oxford, U.K.: Oxford University Press, 1993), 3.

Chapter 8: The Globalization of Marketing

1. Kotler, *Marketing Management,* millennium ed., 367.

2. Ibid., 370.

3. Ibid., 388.

4. Ibid.

5. Ibid., 380–81.

6. David M. Szymanski, Sundar G. Bharadwaj, and P. Rajan Varadarjan, "Standardization versus Adaptation of International Marketing Strategy: An Empirical Investigation," *Journal of Marketing* 57.4 (Oct. 1993): 1–17.

7. Troup interview.

8. Organization for Economic Cooperation and Development, "Foreign Direct Investment and Sustainable Development," downloaded June 12, 2001, from <http://www.oecd.org/daf/investment/fdi/fmt79trends.pdf>.

9. Pico Iyer, *The Global Soul: Jet Lag, Shopping Malls, and the Search for Home* (New York: Vintage, 2001), 11.

10. Eduardo Galeano, *Upside Down: A Primer for the Looking-glass World* (New York: Metropolitan Books, 1998), 12–13.

11. United Nations Development Program, "Human Development Report 1998: Overview," downloaded Oct. 25, 2001, from <http://www.undp.org/hdro/e98over.htm>.

12. Ibid.

13. See Bruce Livesey, "The Cigarette Papers," downloaded Aug. 29, 2001, from <http://www.eye.net/eye/issue/issue_12.16.99/news/cigarettes.html >.

14. See "Tobacco Marketing to Young People," downloaded Oct. 25, 2001, from <http://www.infact.org/youth.html>.

15. Jerry Mander, "Who Benefits Most?" downloaded Oct. 3, 2001, from <http://www.gn.apc.org/resurgence/issues/mander208.htm>.

16. Ibid.

17. See <http://www.cnn.com/WORLD/global.rankings/>, consulted Oct. 26, 2001.

18. CIA, *World Fact Book,* consulted Oct. 25, 2001, at <http://www.cia.gov/cia/publications/factbook/geos/co.html#Econ>.

19. United Nations Development Program, "Human Development Report 1998."

20. Ibid.

21. Frances Moore-Lappe and Joseph Collins, *Food First: Beyond the Myth of Scarcity* (New York: Ballantine Books, 1977), 332.

Chapter 9: The Consumer Trap

1. Alderson, "Analytical Framework for Marketing," 8.
2. Ott, *Creating Demand,* viii.
3. White interview.
4. Dillon interview.
5. Moore interview.
6. Courtice interview.
7. Bergin interview.
8. Jones, *When Ads Work,* 32.
9. Ibid., 23.
10. Ibid.
11. Don Peppers and Martha Rogers, *The One to One Future* (New York: Currency/ Doubleday, 1997), 5.
12. Boorstin, *The Americans,* 148.
13. Luce, "Reformation of the World's Economies," 62.
14. Motor Vehicles Manufacturers Association, *MVMA Facts and Figures* (Detroit: MVMA, 1990), 90.
15. Robert Heilbroner, *Business Civilization in Decline* (New York: W. W. Norton, 1976), 114.
16. See Raymond Williams, *Resources of Hope* (London: Verso, 1989), 171.
17. See Christopher Lasch, *The Culture of Narcissism: American Life in an Age of Diminishing Expectations* (New York: W. W. Norton, 1979); and David Riesman, *The Lonely Crowd* (New Haven, Conn.: Yale University Press, 1950).
18. Cheryl Mendelson, *Home Comforts: The Art and Science of Keeping House* (New York: Scribner, 1999), 7–8.
19. See Barry Sanders, *A Is for Ox: Violence, Electronic Media, and the Silencing of the Written Word* (New York: Pantheon Books, 1994).
20. Sociologist Anthony Giddens has rightly pointed out that the effect of what he calls abstract systems—that is, the capitalist money economy—on human skills "is not only a one-way process" (Giddens, *Modernity and Self-Identity: Self and Society in the Late Modern Age* [Stanford: Stanford University Press, 1991], 22). Indeed, by definition, *deskilling* always involves the learning of new, lower-quality, less empowering, skills to replace the old, better-quality, more empowering, ones that get lost in the process, just as, when it occurs, *upskilling* requires that better skills supplant lesser ones. This is so because human beings without skills of any kind would very shortly die.
21. Tanya Wenman Steel, "Who Can Find Time to Bake a Cake When Buying One Is As Easy As Pie?" *New York Times* (national ed.), Feb. 8, 1995, B1, B4.
22. Putnam, *Bowling Alone,* 223.
23. Ibid., 219, 221.
24. On this topic, see Postman, *Disappearance of Childhood*; and Jürgen Habermas, *The*

Structural Transformation of the Public Sphere: An Inquiry into a Category of Bourgeois Society (Cambridge, Mass.: MIT Press, 1991).

25. For a good explanation of the basis of these characteristics of television, see Robert Kubey and Mihaly Csikszentmihalyi, "Television Addiction Is No Mere Metaphor," *Scientific American,* Feb. 2002, 74–81.

26. On the decline of courtesy and civility and its connection to marketing, see James Lincoln Collier, *The Rise of Selfishness in America* (New York: Oxford University Press, 1991). On the decline of mental and verbal articulateness and its connection to marketing, see Tom Shachtman, *The Inarticulate Society: Eloquence and Culture in America* (New York: Free Press, 1995).

27. Juliet B. Schor, *The Overworked American* (New York: Basic Books, 1993).

28. Mihalyi Csikszentmihalyi, *Flow: The Psychology of Optimal Experience* (New York: Harper and Row, 1990), 29.

29. Ibid.

30. Ibid.

31. The standard definition of the concept is in Carl J. Friedrich and Zbigniew Brzezinski, *Totalitarian Dictatorship and Autocracy,* 2d ed. (Cambridge, Mass.: Harvard University Press, 1965).

32. Fukuyama, *End of History,* 24.

33. Marvin Harris, *Why Nothing Works: The Anthropology of Daily Life* (New York: Simon and Schuster, 1981), 23.

Chapter 10: Escaping the Consumer Trap

1. Award description downloaded Oct. 20, 2001, from <http://www.ama.org/pubs/jmr/awards/index.asp>.

2. Gregory S. Carpenter and Rashi Glazer, "*Meaningful* Brands from Meaningless Differentiation: The Dependence on Irrelevant Attributes," *Journal of Marketing Research* 31.3 (Aug. 1994): 339–51 (1–20 in pdf format). Downloaded Oct. 20, 2001, from EBSCOhost Academic Search Elite.

3. Ibid., 3, 2.

4. Ibid., 13, 2.

5. Ibid., 13.

6. Ibid., 15, 14.

7. Ibid., 2, 13.

8. Ibid., 13.

9. Ibid., 14, 2.

10. Kotler, *Marketing Management,* millennium ed., 394–95.

11. Marvin Harris, *Culture, People, Nature: An Introduction to General Anthropology* (New York: Harper Collins, 1988), 408.

12. Evidence suggests that most aid programs and loans nominally devoted to Third World development are actually more geared to the preservation and extension of good business conditions for global corporations and local elites than to genuine concern with raising the standard of living of their nominal beneficiaries. See, for example, Cheryl Payer, *Lent and Lost: Foreign Credit and Third World Development* (London: Zed Books, 1991).

13. According to the CIA, there is "30 percent combined unemployment and underemployment in many non-industrialized countries" (<http://www./cia.gov/cia/publications/factbook/fields/unemployment_rate.html>). Although we have learned to treat unemployment as somehow natural, it is well to recall that capitalism is the only social system in world history to make it a structural and normal feature of social life.

14. John Bellamy Foster, *The Vulnerable Planet: A Short Economic History of the Environment* (New York: Monthly Review Press, 1994), 124.

15. United Nations Development Program, *Human Development Report 1994* (Oxford, U.K.: Oxford University Press, 1994), 2.

16. See Chalmers Johnson, *Blowback: The Costs and Consequences of American Empire* (New York: Metropolitan Books, 2000).

17. The threat of a Third World War between rival trading blocs of great capitalist nation-states, while presently not strong, cannot be ruled out either. If such a war were to occur, Einstein's observation that, although he was not sure what weapons would be used in World War III, he was quite certain that World War IV would be fought with sticks and stones, is probably a good assumption about the consequences.

18. Ronald K. L. Collins and Michael F. Jacobson, "Commercialism vs. Culture," in *Buying America Back,* ed. Jonathan Greenberg and William Kistler (Tulsa, Okla.: Council Oak Books, 1992), 313.

19. See Nancy E. Rose, *Put to Work: Relief Programs in the Great Depression* (New York: Monthly Review Press, 1994).

20. "FERA Factories," *Business Week,* July 28, 1934, 22.

21. Kotler, *Marketing Management,* 3d ed., 496.

22. See Myron Magnet, "The Money Society," *Fortune,* July 6, 1987, 26.

23. M. Landler and W. Kovad, "Consumers Are Getting Mad, Mad, Mad, Mad at Mad Ave," *Business Week,* Apr. 30, 1990, 70.

24. Klein, *No Logo,* 9.

25. Robert N. Mayer, *The Consumer Movement: Guardians of the Marketplace* (Boston: Twayne, 1989), 18.

26. See ibid., 25–58.

27. Michael F. Jacobson and Laurie Ann Mazur, *Marketing Madness: A Survival Guide for a Consumer Society* (Boulder, Colo.: Westview Press, 1995).

28. Douglas Rushkoff, *Coercion: Why We Listen to What "They" Say* (New York: Riverhead Books, 1999), 15.

29. Albert Einstein, "Why Socialism?" *Monthly Review* 1.1 (May 1949): 9, 12.

30. "A Declaration by the Representatives of the United States of America, in General Congress Assembled," July 4, 1776.

31. For a discussion of the concept of capitalist democracy, see Ralph Miliband, *Socialism for a Sceptical Age* (London: Verso, 1994).

Index

Aaker, David A., 84–85, 110
Absentee ownership. *See* Capitalism, corporate
A. C. Nielsen Company: passive TV meter, 47
Adams, Anthony, 72. *See also* Campbell Soup
Advertising: agencies, number of, in United States, 110; antirealism of, 100–101; effects, scale of, 99–101; goals of, 99; myths about, 98–106; repetition and, 99; spending on, in United States, 115; subordination of, to marketing, 4, 98, 104; and teeter-totter analogy, 99; transformation of, after marketing revolution, 109–10; Veblen on, 13, 97
Agres, Stuart, 82
Alderson, Wroe, 34, 54, 133
Alka-Seltzer: motivational strategies for, 60, 68–69; product definition, 77; quality of, 88
American Demographics, 72
Americanization of Europe and Japan, 127
Amtrak, 119
Armstrong, Gary, 86, 91, 117. *See also* Kotler, Philip
Arousal, sexual, 60
Aspirations, marketing uses of, 61–62, 100–101
Assets, financial, distribution of, in United States, 30–31
Association of Playing Card Manufacturers, 99–100
Automobiles: costs and benefits of, 2, 147,

157; planned obsolescence of, 88, 90; public subsidy of, 119–20; styling of, 90

Baran, Paul A., 11, 21, 28
Baudrillard, Jean, 10
Behavior, off-the-job: analogous to workers' on-the-job movements, 54; commodification of, 94; degradation of, 154; evolution of, in United States, 144–54; power and, 74, 96, 133–37; psychological determinants of, 56; as raw material to marketers, 54, 56, 57–58
Behaviorism, 58–59
Behavior settings, 76, 117, 133, 134
Bell, Daniel, 8–9
Benson, John, 62. *See also* Marlboro cigarettes
Berger, Fred, 113
Bergin, John, 88–89. *See also* Johnson and Johnson; McCann-Erickson advertising agency
Big business marketing. *See* Marketing
Blocki, Jim, 109. *See also* Kraft–General Foods
Blowback, risk of, 159–60
Boorstin, Daniel, 8, 144
Boyd, Harper, 65
Brand management. *See* Product management
Brands: advantages of, 84–85; definition of, 84; marketing and, 81–85; Naomi Klein on, 85

Watson, John Broadus: advertising work of, 58; consumer-frog analogy, 58
Webber, Gordon, 7
Weiss, Michael J., 45
Weissman, George, 62. *See also* Marlboro cigarettes
Williams, Raymond, 148

Willits, Oliver G., 112
Wolff, Edward N., 31
World War II: economic effects of, 38; exhaustion of economic effects of, 40–41
Wren, Daniel, 16

Yankelovich, Daniel, 70

MICHAEL DAWSON is a part-time lecturer in the Department of Sociology at Portland State University and also works as a paralegal.

The History of Communication

The University of Illinois Press
is a founding member of the
Association of American University Presses.

Composed in 10.5/13 Adobe Minion
with Minion display
by Celia Shapland
for the University of Illinois Press
Designed by Dennis Roberts
Manufactured by Thomson-Shore, Inc.

University of Illinois Press
1325 South Oak Street
Champaign, IL 61820-6903
www.press.uillinois.edu